THE BLOCKAGE

Rethinking Organizational Principles for the 21st Century

Eva Kras

American Literary Press
Five Star Special Edition
Baltimore, Maryland

The Blockage:
Rethinking Organizational Principles for the 21st Century

Library of Congress
Cataloging-in-Publication Data
ISBN-13: 978-1-56167-981-2

Library of Congress Card Catalog Number:
2007905043

Published by

American Literary Press
Five Star Special Edition

8019 Belair Road, Suite 10
Baltimore, Maryland 21236

Manufactured in the United States of America

TABLE OF CONTENTS

Preface

The Need For This Book

Since the Industrial/Scientific Revolution, our societies, particularly in the Western world, have established a number of principles or assumptions that we believe in as truths. These are based on values and principles that we have adopted, lived with for many generations, and which have governed human activity in these regions of the world.

These principles and their underlying values have also formed the basis for all our institutions, governments, business sector, and civil society in general. This whole "package" of values and principles we usually refer to as the essence of our accepted "conventional thinking."

In recent years we have begun to experience some worrisome, destructive ecological, social and economic consequences related to the practices and policies emanating from our conventional thinking and values.

As a society we have attempted to deal with these destructive consequences in a number of ways. These attempts include:

1) Changing some policies and practices to reflect concerns for ecological and social issues, but without questioning or changing our underlying conventional thinking and values base on which these policies are seated. This has meant superimposing "sustainable" sounding policies and practices on top of conventional principles and values. The outcomes of these attempts have proven disappointing and mostly ineffective. (This point forms an important focus of the book.)

2) A few small-scale diverse models of new "sustainable thinking" are emerging (models that involve ways to alleviate our ecological and social destruction) in many regions. These are usually associated closely with the culture of the region, or a particular discipline or sector of society in which they are being developed. As a result we have seen a few examples of positive outcomes in some areas, but when attempting to move these models into a broader transcultural environment, or into another discipline or sector of society, many misunderstandings and controversies have resulted.

In light of these attempts, it appears that *something else* is needed to bridge the gap between often good intentions on the one side and unfavorable outcomes on the other. In this process we need to search for the roots of our misunderstandings and misinterpretations in organizations, both national and international, as well as across cultures, disciplines and societal sectors.

We are in the middle of a dilemma:

We desperately need to find a viable solution to the worrisome, growing destruction of our ecological and social systems. We do not have the luxury of time, as the breakdowns are becoming very serious in some regions, and we are already in "overshoot" conditions, based on some studies by specialists in the field.

What can we do?

It appears that we need to search much deeper into the roots of our destructive behavior. We need to find principles and values that all organizations, disciplines, sectors and cultures can relate to and agree upon in this interconnected world.

This book is an attempt to search for a common viable values foundation, especially related to organizations and transcultural situations. It argues that we need to delve deeply into the human mind to find the source of our dilemma, that is, to locate our deep positive human values, which many visionaries have identified as the source of positive human development. These have been described by specialists as deeply held values that we all possess, but through time have often been disregarded or forgotten within our "conventional system" and values. In essence, in this search we are bringing into a new light the very "nature of man," one which many experts in the field believe to contain a number of "universal" positive values that are common to all cultures, but which have been mostly suppressed or undervalued for a long time. These seem to also be the values that form the foundation of the few emerging examples we have of activities and behaviors that have had positive outcomes.

In this study, therefore, the author argues that once we can identify and reconnect with these deeply felt, commonly held universal values, we will be able to develop: a) a way of dealing positively with our dilemma locally, and b) be able to agree on a deeply seated set of universal values, common to all cultures, disciplines and societal sectors. In this way, different cultures, sectors and disciples will firstly agree upon a common set of universal values, and then identify an additional set of values on top of the universal ones that are specific to their particular culture or discipline, and do not clash with universal values. As a result, cultural diversity and tastes related to different areas are also honored, and respected at the same time.

To provide credibility for this approach, the author has drawn on the thinking and wisdom of a number of internationally respected visionaries. Based on the wisdom shown by these visionaries, it appears that a genuine solution to our dilemma requires a fundamental "change in thinking" (values).

Therefore this visionary wisdom, related to universally held values, is considered key in our search for a viable long-term solution to our dilemma.

In summary, it appears we need to delve deeply into our human consciousness—the source of our deeply held positive universal values. These values then form a solid foundation for policies and practices to solve our ecological, social and economic problems in all cultures, disciplines and societal sectors.

The Search: Personal Background

Following over twenty-five years of living and working in mostly developing countries, I have now returned to Canada. The major part of this time was spent in Latin America (mostly Mexico), with a few years in Europe.

These experiences have had a profound impact on how I have come to interpret the culture and values of both the developing countries of Latin America (and others) as well as the highly industrialized developed countries of the Western world. As I am now floating on the bridge between two major cultures and "ways of thinking," it seems to me that somehow we have to learn to accept the important contribution of each in formulating a solid sustainable world. It certainly appears that the highly industrialized countries have an obviously well-developed superiority in different areas of technology and organizational capacities, while the developing countries have some superiority in the depth of development in human values and relationships that we need if we are going to genuinely move toward sustainability. The acceptance of this situation is sometimes proving a real challenge, as some highly industrialized rich countries find the concept difficult, in accepting that poorer countries (economically) actually possess something important to contribute in our common search for sustainablility. At the same time, the developing countries are often concerned about "speaking up," so to speak, as they are usually being advised that their future depends on adopting values that place emphasis on money, power and consumerism. In fact, many of the wealthy elite (including both business and government sectors) in many developing countries already embrace these values as within their best interests in a globalized marketplace.

My background is in the business world, and more specifically in business management. Much of my work and studies during my years abroad have been focused on transcultural management and organizational development areas. This has brought me face to face with the realities of very different cultures and values, mainly working with Anglo-Saxon (US) and Latin American (Mexico) business managements. The differences between the two cultures are enormous, both in how they manage organizations and in the values underpinning their different management styles.

Throughout many years I have struggled with these management differences, and finally have come to the point of being able to identify some of the most important differences that affect management of organizations, leading to an initial step in helping them to communicate with each other in a cooperative, positive atmosphere.

During these years, the whole question of values, cultures and the different "realities" that exist has become a constant challenge and focus of my research. This has finally led to the realization that somehow we had to find some commonalities among these cultures to actually communicate on an "even playing field."

Throughout this period of questioning and study, I had the privilege of meeting and knowing Willis Harman, an incredibly wise and insightful visionary. This man helped me "put the pieces together," and I consider him my mentor.

These years have produced several books, published (and

rewritten) for both English and Spanish-speaking readers. This has also resulted in university teaching in Latin America (in Spanish), as well as in US and Canada. Combined with this, a wide variety of business consultancies have developed. This combination of academic work and business "hands on" experience has also led to numerous presentations to groups in business, universities, government, and nonprofit organizations throughout North and South America, as well as other international locations.

These challenges and other related ones involving the interconnection between values and nature and the cosmos (to form a complete picture) have finally brought me to the present book project. When I started on this project, I felt I understood how the general theme would unfold. How wrong I was. It has certainly been a lesson in humility, and an incredibly rich experience. It has indeed confirmed my discomfort related to how little we really understand about this whole subject, as it has been so broken up into so many different disciplines, and many of these have difficulty communicating with each other. However, this is gradually changing, and we can look forward to an exciting and fulfilling time ahead as we come to learn more about how different disciplines and different cultures can all contribute to sustainability.

Now the challenge is becoming more real, as the breakdowns around us are more apparent. It appears we will need a transformation in our way of thinking (underlying values) about our problems. The search for positive, commonly held values seems key to being able to form a solid foundation for long-term sustainability.

This search appears necessary across the spectrum from the business sector to governments at all levels to universities, among others, and it appears that we especially need to focus on youth. Their future is at stake, and most still have open minds that can more easily absorb what is really happening around us. We need to try to understand how they perceive our present reality in order to take appropriate steps with this group in the transformation process.

This book is an initial attempt to provide some insights into some of the most personal and complex aspects of our individual way of thinking about transformation and the values that control us. Hopefully it will provide some meaningful food for thought to a wide spectrum of disciplines and readers, as well as a starting point for a new path toward sustainable thinking and actions.

Book Organization

The organization of this book hopefully allows the reader to gain insight into the different interpretations of the concept of values and the key role values play in every aspect of life, work, communities, governments, and society as a whole. This includes the identification of a number of commonly held "universal" values as the foundation for sustainability. It then develops some principles based on these values, followed by an extensive case study, which provides insights into the challenges involved in a cross-cultural business management environment.

The initial two chapters provide some background to remind us of the magnitude of this change in thinking we are confronting based on some profound insights from a number of highly respected international visionaries from different backgrounds and disciplines.

This is followed by Chapter III, which provides a discussion on a number of interpretations of "values" from different levels and disciplines. It also includes some insights from scholars focused on the concept of "universal" values as ones that are common to all, and that require the development of our minds in sometimes different ways than we are accustomed to; that is, the need to balance and develop both the objective conscious mind as well as the unconscious mind, where a wealth of knowledge and wisdom is stored (usually referred to as higher consciousness). It is considered in this study that this balance in development between our conscious and unconscious minds is essential to fully understand the values that underpin genuine sustainability.

Chapter IV outlines a number of important universal values, as identified by a number of international studies in the field. These values are presented in three major groups: values related to the self; values related to family, work and community; values related to nature and the cosmos.

This section is followed by Chapter V, which "translates" these universal values into principles that can become useful in implementation of values, and forms a central role in policy development for business sectors, governments, and universities, as well as a whole spectrum of NGOs and civil society organizations.

Chapter VI involves an e-mail "conversation" between two business executives with two different views of their realities; that is, two different sets of values that underpin their views on work and life. They have had work experience in different countries and business operations, and the "conversation" is meant to provide readers with food for thought about how businesses operate differently and how their managers think.

Chapter VII consists of my real life working experience in transcultural organizations. It is a case study that spans about twenty years, and reveals some interesting realities that exist in the ongoing challenge to find common ground in values so we can begin to build a strong, viable foundation for sustainability across cultures.

Finally, Chapter VIII provides some brief conclusions arising from the book.

GLOSSARY

This study contains terminology well known to most readers, but some concepts can have a diversity of interpretations or meanings. In order to clarify the interpretations used for this particular study, the author offers some explanations of the most important concepts used throughout the book. It may be useful to review these before reading the book, so they are offered at the beginning of the study.

1. VALUES/BELIEFS: The concept of values and beliefs are used interchangeably in the book. Values refer to a number of deeply held beliefs about the nature of human beings and how they relate to each other; beliefs about the realities of nature and how humans relate to nature; and beliefs about the cosmos or outer space and how humans view the cosmos.

2. CONVENTIONAL "SYSTEM" THINKING OR VALUES: These terms all refer to what most people believe to be the realities of the modern world for many generations. These includes what most people believe to be the basic nature of human beings, how people relate to each other, how we view the role of nature in society, and how we relate to outer space. A group of conventional values underpins the whole conventional "system" and affects all conventional thinking, including attitudes, behaviors, way of working and decision making.

3. EMERGING "SYSTEM" THINKING OR VALUES: This refers to a new evolving way of thinking, new values and resulting new behaviors. This involves the evolution of emerging new and rediscovered values that create a new view of the realities of the world, including a new view of human nature, a new view of nature and our relationship with nature, plus a new view related to work, organizations and decision making.

4. UNIVERSAL VALUES: These values are ones that are deeply seated in the human mind, and access to them requires the development of both the conscious and unconscious aspects of the human mind. They are believed to be an important part of emerging values. Universal values surpass all cultures, countries and ethnic groups, and are considered common to all humans.

5. CONSCIOUS AND UNCONSCIOUS MIND OR THINK-ING: "Conscious" thinking is associated with the objective mind. This includes all rational, objective and logical thought. It is considered associated directly with human intellectual capacities that we use every day.

"Unconscious" thinking is associated with the deep unconscious mind (also referred to as consciousness). It includes deep sensitivities, intuition, deep feelings of purpose and meaning in life, deep contemplation, deep creativity, and spirituality in its broadest sense. In this study it is associated with natural human capacities for "higher consciousness," and plays a vital role in the full comprehension of universal values, and the concept of sustainability in general.

Many scholars in this field believe that we can draw "thinking" from our unconscious to our conscious minds, and then to utilize the full potential of this "thinking" to develop new ways of perceiving in our conscious world. That is a premise in this study in relation to the process of transformation in thinking.

6. PRINCIPLES / ASSUMPTIONS / TRUTHS: These three terms are used interchangeably. They refer to what we believe as the realities of our world, associated with the nature of humans, how we naturally relate to each other, the realities of nature and how we relate to it, and the realities of outer space and how it works. Principles are seated on a group of values and form the cornerstones or foundation for organizational policies and practices.

7. INDIVIDUALISM AND PERSONAL RESPONSIBILITY: The term individualism in this study usually refers to individualistic thinking as associated with conventional thinking, and refers to "survival of the fittest" assumptions related to today's society. On the other hand, the term personal responsibility refers to our innate responsibility for our actions and consequences of these actions, and refers to people who have embraced universally held emerging values in life and work.

8. SPIRITUALITY, HIGHER CONSCIOUSNESS, RELI-GION: Higher consciousness is a capacity or power of the mind that humans are believed to possess. It is located in the deep unconscious mind, and is believed to also be the source of human capacities for deep sensitivities, intuition and spirituality. Many scholars view

higher consciousness as the place where humans can relate to a deep, incomprehensible universal spirit, or power. This concept is usually referred to as spirituality and is believed to provide "the centre" for experiencing deep inner peace and tranquility, as well as expanded human capacity to fully comprehend universal values.

Religion refers to different cultural forms of interpreting spirituality. It includes different rituals and dogmas that are most suited to particular groups in different regions of the world. Spirituality in general is believed to provide fulfillment and meaning in human lives and positive human behaviors.

9. SUSTAINABILITY: This term has its origin in the concept of sustainable development, associated with the "Bruntland Report," 1987, under the auspices of the United Nations, and published as "Our Common Future." According to this highly respected report, the term sustainable development refers to:

"Humanity has the ability to make development sustainable, to ensure that it meets the needs of the present without compromising the ability of future generations to meet their own needs."

The key to this statement is consideration for future generations. This naturally restricts our behaviors to act within the limits of nature to regenerate itself and to provide social opportunities for people to have a decent living. Consequently, sustainability and all the terms associated with the word, such as sustainable development, sustainable organizations, sustainable activities, sustainable thinking, sustainable policies and values, among others, refers to human behaviors and actions that place priority on our responsibilities to live within the limitations of nature, to have a lifestyle that permits equity for humans in the access to and use of natural resources, and to provide economic activities that respect both of these factors.

Sustainability relates directly to long-term thinking, in harmony with long-term ecological time spans.

Acknowledgments

This book spans research and important learning experiences over a period of over twenty-five years. As a result there are many people from many countries to whom I am grateful for helping me learn, and making this book project possible.

I would like to recognize a few individuals who have had a particular impact over the years on my understanding of this complex subject, as well as some individuals who have been most involved and helpful during my attempt at writing this book.

Firstly, I would like to especially show my appreciation for Willis Harman, who was the person who was so instrumental in helping me "put the pieces together." Throughout several years I was able to draw on his wisdom and insights while I was trying to understand the complexities of the main theme.

I am also very grateful to the many thoughtful business leaders and academics who have helped provide me with valuable insights through their own work and studies. This group of scholars and business leaders I believe in many ways has made it possible for me to dare to attempt this often controversial and complex adventure.

During the actual writing process I have benefited immensely from the insight and thoughtful critiques of a number of key people. I would especially like to recognize the valuable input of Peter Soderbaum as an European voice, Victor Toledo as a Latin American voice, as well as Mathis Wachernagel as a valuable international thinker.

Naturally, the project would not have been possible without the support and encouragement of my family. This has meant so much to me every day, as the project has become long and at times very difficult.

Finally, I would like to show my appreciation for my publisher, and for the patience and supportive efforts of the whole team in bringing this book to publication. This has meant a great deal to me.

Chapter I

A. Our Dilemma

Most of us believe in a "sustainable" approach to life and work, where the goal is advancing the well-being of both people and the world's ecosystems. We are accustomed to hearing and reading about many well-publicized policies, both from governments and business, which express their commitment to "sustainable development" in support of human and ecological well-being.

But a dilemma exists:

Why do we see so few concrete actions implemented in spite of all these expressed good intentions?

The reason is certainly not that the need is starting to vanish. Rather, environmental and social challenges are on the rise. We seem to increase global overshoot[1] (exceeding nature's capacity to regenerate) while the gap between the wealthiest one billion and the other 5.5 billion people seems to be increasing to an extent where increasing populations are struggling to make ends meet, and many regions are sinking into extreme poverty.[2]

Why is there so little progress?

In other words: WHERE IS THE BLOCKAGE?

Are we trying to implement policies that are seated on principles and values that are not compatible? Are we trying to mix oil and water?

Do we have policies and values that are in conflict . . . that is, values that will not permit the implementation of policies that are considered positive for human development and ecologically sustainable for the long term?

Does a blockage exist at a deeper level, our core foundation of values, which restricts policy implementation as intended?

B. The Blockage

It certainly appears that we have been attempting for many years to develop "sustainable" policies and practices without questioning their compatibility with our deeper core values that underpin them—in other words, without disturbing our deeply held beliefs or values we have held most of our lives. These values have obviously been influencing our way of thinking—our practices, attitudes and behaviors at all levels. Our "business as usual" values have prevailed as unquestioned truths.

This is the area we need to examine in order to gain insight into which deeply held core values produce positive sustainable outcomes, and which values produce negative outcomes, resulting in the present intractable human and ecological problems we face.

Here lies the challenge in dealing with our dilemma.

Many visionaries and researchers have been studying this dilemma for many years, with some encouraging results. These appear to identify the deep source of the blockage is in our thinking. The insights of a number of these researchers are found throughout this book but a few examples are included here in order to begin to visualize the depths to which we need to penetrate in our thinking to locate the source of our blockage.

To benefit fully from these insights, we need to briefly outline what is meant by some terms that are commonly used by these visionaries, such as the terms objective and subjective thinking. Further insights into the meaning of these terms are more fully developed later in this chapter, but a brief definition is essential at this point.

Objective thinking or mind: In this study this refers to our conscious thinking, our everyday logical and objective view of our reality. Objective thinking is key to fully understanding our present-day scientific-based logical reality. It is based on quantitative thinking.

Subjective thinking or mind: In this study this refers to a part of the mind usually considered unconscious (or subconscious), our higher consciousness. Here resides our intuition, our feelings "of the heart," our deep creativity, our sense of purpose and fulfillment in life, and our spirituality in its broadest sense.

Our values are associated with the way we think, and therefore are closely related to how our mind works and develops. From the foundation of our values we develop certain assumptions about the "truths" in which we believe, and these assumptions basically control our everyday attitudes and behaviors.

The following visionaries use these terms to provide us with some insights into what they believe to be the source of our present-day problems and blockage.

a. Willis Harman[3]

Willis Harman was a scientist and visionary. Much of his work is closely related to the study of the human mind as the source of the core values that are associated with positive, sustainable thinking and behaviors. This brought him to study the origins of scientific objective thinking, and the value of both the objective and subjective aspects of the mind, which have provided valuable insight into our present blockage. He was convinced that we need to search into these deep levels of our thinking and values to find the source of our problems.

Some of his insights include:

"The Western neglect of the realm of subjective experience has had serious consequences in our confusion about values. For it is ultimately in this realm of the subjective, the transcendent, and the spiritual that all societies have found the basis for their deepest values, commitments and sense of meaning."

Harman also talks about "assumptions," which are the assumed "truths" that flow out of our values and the accepted basis of our everyday reality.

"The contemporary reassessment of basic assumptions (truths) is a consequence of the growing suspicion that without some sort of fundamental change (in our assumptions), modern industrial society appears to be unable to resolve the socio-political and ecological dilemmas that beset us."

Harman also indicates the magnitude of the change that is needed.

He believes that we are experiencing "symptoms of a deeper malady." He indicates that "the change required is not simply a shift from one form of industrial society to another (such as capitalism to socialism) but rather a major change in the basic assumptions underlying both versions of industrial society."

Harman believes, relating to the way this change will happen: "It will be something as quiet as a change of mind, a change of mind that is bubbling up out of the unconscious depths, spreading around the world, changing everything." He also indicates that it is already beginning to happen without us really noticing it. It is happening in small groups, individuals and communities, which do not seem to influence as yet the thinking or policies in most large businesses or governments.

Further to his convictions, Harman believes that our search for meaning and purpose in life and work is closely related to the values that underpin our whole industrial society:

"The industrialized world, having lost any consensus on ultimate meanings and values, steers itself mainly by economic and financial signals serving as pseudo-values. . . . The macro-problem has its origins in basic assumptions related to scientific-based reality. Since (science does not give credibility to) inner experience, transcendent values have no power and materialistic values prevail."

To come to grips with our problems, Harman states:

"The key step in our bringing about change is eschewing the negative visions (of purely objective based thinking) to which we have unwittingly been contributing, and choosing a vision that benefits our inner purpose and that of those around us."

Dr. Harman clearly believes that we are in need of a complete "global mind change" in order to release our blockage, which involves the development of all capacities of our minds—including both the objective conscious and the subjective unconscious (higher consciousness) sectors.

b. David Korten[4]

David Korten is well known in relation to the concepts of globalization and the role of the multinational corporation in human and ecological development worldwide.

His views include: "Successful as capitalism has been in creating a mass consumer culture, the fact remains that its values are largely alien to our basic nature." In this sense he refers to the deeply held core human values that we possess as an essential part of our basic nature, and how out of step these are with the values that underpin capitalism as it is practiced today.

c. Hazel Henderson[5]

Hazel Henderson is an internationally respected futurist and evolutionary economist. In the midst of our present dilemma, she points clearly to the core of our problems:

"The debate about sustainable development has become a metaphor for a complex cluster of issues; but at its core, it is a debate about values and which cultural, social, technological and behavioral repertoires embedded in the various cultural DNA codes of the world's people actually contain the "programs" which may serve as the seeds for human survivability."

This appears to indicate clearly that the present "conventional" way of thinking, and the values on which it is constructed, no longer work, and we need to delve deeply to its core in order to find the "DNA programs" that can serve genuine sustainability.

d. Mary E. Clark[6]

Mary Clark expresses her concern for especially youth, related to their future and the key importance of meaning in life (as viewed in the United States).

She observes, "psychic uncertainty about their personal identity in a culture where community and personal bonds are continuing to weaken identity (owing to the commoditization of more and more relationships); where their autonomy is increasingly constrained by the needs of a national economy and global market over which they have absolutely no control, yet from which they see no escape; and especially where human meaning has been reduced to dollars and cents. There really is no other value being discussed in the national dialogue. It is hard to find a meaningful 'personal identity' in such a culture. People are only employees or employers, ciphers in a national accounting system. There is no other widely-shared community meaning."

Clark emphasizes in her book *In Search of Human Nature* that the role of culture and values is extremely important in discovering what and who we are.

e. E.F. Schumacher:[7]

Schumacher was a visionary economist who experienced a major transformation in his life as he moved from purely objective thinking to fully embracing spirituality and the subjective and subconscious higher consciousness aspects of his mind.

Some of his insights include:

"The purely quantitative approach (objective mind) misses out on everything that really matters."

He also believed:

"A civilization that deprecates the heart, which idolizes objectivity in the forms of scientism, positivism and rationalism, which bases the entire education on the notion that decisions must be taken without interference from the emotions, inevitably exposes itself to the dangers of unlimited violence. . . . Modern civilization can survive only if it begins again to educate the heart, which is the source of Wisdom."

To summarize his philosophy he states: "It is the philosophy of materialism which is being challenged and the challenge comes not from a few saints or sages, but from the environment."

Schumacher makes a clear connection between humanity (our thinking and values) and our interdependence with the natural environment as the basis for genuine long-term sustainability.

f. Ervin Laszlo:[8]

Ervin Laszlo, is a philosopher and visionary. With reference to the period of change in which we live, he views it in a hopeful light if we are willing to make deep-seated changes in our thinking and actions.

Laszlo states: "Our globalized technological civilization could break down in chaos and anarchy—or it could break through to a more humane and sustainable world. The choice between these possibilities will not be made by applying technological fixes or implementing strategies based on the same kind of thinking that created today's uncertainties . . . to master our destiny we need new thinking, new values—a new consciousness."

Clearly, Laszlo is convinced that a complete transformation in our thinking and values is essential, in order to provide the basis for fulfilling life and work, and a long-term sustainable world.

g. Albert Einstein:[9]

Albert Einstein needs no introduction. However, an important aspect of his thinking is perhaps little known. Einstein was a deeply spiritual man and believed that in order to solve our problems we need to consider subjective as well as objective thinking. Some of his most valuable statements include:

"No problem can be solved from the same consciousness that created it. We have to learn to see the world anew." Einstein obviously envisioned, even at that time, that there exists a serious problem in our world, and that the only way to solve it demands our embracing a new way of thinking—a new consciousness.

These beliefs in the importance of subjective thinking (embracing spirituality, creativity and intuition) are also evident in his view of science and the special human capacities he utilized.

In that regard he stated: "Imagination is more important than knowledge." Hence, we see the importance he attached to the subjective or subconscious aspects of the mind, where the depths of imagination are found.

Regarding spirituality Einstein stated: "My religion consists of a humble admiration of the illimitable superior spirit who reveals himself in the slight detail we are able to perceive with our frail and feeble mind." This is a profound statement for a person endowed with such a brilliant mind.

To highlight his views about everyday values in life, Einstein commented: "The ideals which have lighted my way, and time after time have given me new courage to face life cheerfully, have been

Kindness, Beauty and Truth. The trite subjects of human efforts, possessions, outward success, luxury, have always seemed to me contemptible." These are deeply meaningful humane words from a visionary who gained outstanding scientific fame.

The insights of these visionaries and many similar studies in this field point to the importance of deep reflection, the rethinking of our deeply rooted foundation of values if we hope to find genuine solutions to our dilemma. This appears to require some special human capacity beyond strictly objective thinking. This new dimension in our thinking, according to an increasing number of researchers, appears to be an essential ingredient in the successful lifting of the blockage which we are experiencing. It brings new insight into our deeply held core values which appear to affect everything----- how we think, work, relate to others, attitudes to nature, how we manage our lives and how decision makers manage organizations.

C. Main Question of Study

Where is the blockage that prevents us from dealing successfully with our most urgent human and ecological concerns? What does the blockage consist of, and how can we initiate the first steps to unblock our thinking, and allow sustainable universal values to prevail in organizations?

This main question is explored at a number of different levels. Firstly we deal with the relationship between our way of thinking and its association with our natural human capacities and the *deep* foundation of our root values. Next we move to the identification of positive values (ones that produce positive outcomes), followed by their role in the development of viable principles (truths) and policies. Finally we provide some guidelines and recommendations for personal and organizational transformation, based on positive sustainable values as their foundation. Lastly, we discuss an actual case study that has led to new understandings of commonly held root values across cultures.

D. Objectives

The main objective of this study is to explore the direct relationship between our blockage and our deep foundation of thinking and root values, and explore how rethinking and changing these values can formulate a foundation for sustainability.

Specific Objectives:
1) To provide insight into the foundation of our thinking and root values that underpin our present policies and principles. (blockage source).
2) To identify specific deeply held universal, sustainable values that positively affect daily life, work and organizational activities.
3) To identify emerging principles (truths) that are seated on positive, sustainable values.
4) To identify some emerging trends that show indications of emerging sustainable values as their foundation.
5) To provide some positive tools or recommendations for initiating a transformation process to a sustainable value base for both personal and organizational development.

E. Focus

This project, while global in perspective, is focused mainly on the Americas (including North, Central, and South America), and is directed principally toward young professionals working in smaller and medium sized organizations, although larger organizations can also benefit. The smaller organization sector is where the majority of the population is employed, or apparently (based on studies in this area) will be employed in the future, as well as the sector that provides the strongest basis for the stability of a community, region or country. The Americas is a large region of dramatic contrasts, spanning two continents, some of which can be summarized as:
-- contrasts between rich and poor populations;
-- contrasts in levels of industrialization;
-- contrasts in climate and natural resource base;
-- very importantly, dramatic contrasts in culture.

These contrasts affect how different individuals and organizations will approach this study. Within the organizational context, this study will focus principally on management aspects related to values, on principles that govern organizations, and how these are dependent on the deeply rooted values on which they are seated. In this sense the study provides significant insight into emerging new values and principles that are taking hold and affecting organizations and individuals in their daily lives.[10]

The dramatic differences in culture between North and South America needs to be emphasized, especially as it relates to values that underpin their worldviews. We experience literally two different realities, and two very different sets of values that underpin them. Here we have a significant learning experience, as we attempt first to understand each and then attempt to find some deep-seated common values.

The study is focused on three major areas of organizational development: social, economic and ecological. These different perspectives are examined in the light of the emerging positive values and the principles that evolve from these values. These in turn affect all policies and daily organizational practices.

In addition to the focus on organizations and the effects of emerging values on their functioning, a broad spectrum of readers should also find the essence of this study applicable to their own needs. In that regard, it should be mentioned that universities and community colleges are of particular interest due to the key role they play in preparing young people for the working world. With the fundamental reassessment of many of the values on which organizations are seated, these educational institutions will be examining their own teaching philosophies, curriculum content and teaching approaches. In addition, this study should be helpful to a wide personal-level readership, all those who are interested in gaining valuable insights into the emerging trends of today, and how they can affect their lives and work.

F. Limitations of the Study

Readers who have an interest in the topic of values naturally have certain expectations related to a study such as this one. Obviously the main foundation of the study involves a wide range of different aspects related to values. Therefore it is important to clarify the limitations of this study in terms of how it is focused and what these limitations involve for the reader.

1. The concept of values in this study draws from a number of disciplines related to this concept. They include philosophy and spirituality, psychology, ethics, and sustainable development studies. While the author has drawn on certain aspects of all of these disciplines to provide a solid foundation, the study itself focuses on the common values base that draws them together. Therefore the reader will find each discipline represented in some form, and the concept of values is an important common foundation in all the disciplines. This approach will undoubtedly create some controversy, especially for readers who have a depth of knowledge or interest in a particular aspect involved. However, that is also considered positive, as among the important purposes of this book is to provide food for thought and encourage further study.

2. This book is intentionally brief. The purpose is to attract a wide readership, many of whom (such as young professionals) have little time available to read in the fast-moving present-day working world. It is hoped that it will generate sufficient food for thought and motivation for readers to search further into their own particular area of concern.

3. As the book is directed toward a broad readership and cuts across disciplines, it is maintained as free of jargon as possible. To assist readers in providing definitions of certain concepts used throughout the book, a short glossary is provided at the beginning of the book.

4. The book is meant to form a bridge between theory and practice. Therefore its strength is not limited to one or the other, but it is hoped that readers will find ingredients that provide both theoretical food for thought as well as practical ingredients that can be helpful in their own personal lives and work.

5. The study brings out some emerging thinking related to deeply held values, and it is understood that some will create controversy. This is considered positive and not limiting in terms of the usefulness of the study. Exposing emerging changes in ways of thinking will

naturally create some discomfort. As this book is primarily directed to younger professionals, it is hoped that the stimulation of their own thinking (whether agreeing or disagreeing with some of the concepts) will assist them in selecting some of these concepts that concern them most and adapting them to their own experience.

6. While the study is basically directed toward "the Americas," the concepts, ideas and applications related to values are universal. It deals with commonly held values that go beyond cultures and countries.

Chapter II

EVOLUTION IN GLOBAL THINKING

A. The Scientific/Industrial Revolution

Throughout history, scholars tell us that human development has gone through only a small number of major fundamental transformations related to how people view the world and the beliefs that have given life meaning and purpose. This section outlines some events and thinking leading up to the most recent major change in human thinking, the present-day ongoing one, which appears to be affecting the course of our human development. It is believed by many visionaries that we at present are in the middle of the most dramatic "shift" in thinking, as described by Laszlo,[1] in over 300 years. Consequently it is helpful for us to view briefly the other major shifts that have led us to our present views on the world.

Let us first go back to the period before the Copernican revolution. During that time, lasting many centuries in Western European history, the Earth was viewed as the center of the universe, with the sun, moon and stars revolving around the Earth. This view was particularly comfortable for the religious leaders (Roman Catholic Church) who played an important role in all aspects of scientific studies.

Then came Copernicus. He was a cannon in the church as well as a lawyer and a respected Greek scholar. As the church was also the major centre for learning in that period in history, it was naturally the centre for astronomical studies. Following various decades of work and study, Copernicus's book *On the Revolution of the Celestial Spheres* was published in 1543. Some in the church felt these new ideas were almost heresy. The "dethroning" of the Earth as the center of the universe came as a shocking idea and difficult to accept, following centuries of belief in the Earth as the supreme center of all heavenly bodies. As a result, this book created great consternation in the church in general, especially in the studies of philosophy and social theory. It contradicted many long-held beliefs, including much of Aristotle's work, which had become elevated almost to the level of religious dogma. This new thinking associated with the Copernican revolution became known as Scholasticism.

Willis Harman[2] describes the period as a major change in thinking: "The implication was that man might not have such a special place in creation after all. . . . It was a heresy on a grand scale."

Next came the Scientific/Industrial Revolution. Like the Copernican revolution before it, this was a period in history when there occurred a major disruption or transformation in human perception of the world and the human relationship to it and to each other. The advocates of this "new science," which formed the basis of the Scientific/Industrial Revolution, were in fact attacking traditional ways of thinking, that is, Scholasticism. In contrast to Scholasticism the new thinking was empirical. That is, authority rested in observation and experimentation—the scientific method.

According to the "scientific" view, Harman[3] stated, "the universe is essentially dead, constructed and set in motion by the Creator, with subsequent events accounted for by mechanical forces and lawful behaviours." Since the beginning of the Scientific Revolution scientists have been studying these "mechanical forces and lawful behaviours." This scientific approach has also spread to almost all disciplines in society, where the scientific method is required in order for the particular discipline or activity to maintain credibility in society.

In this new view of the world of the Scientific/Industrial Revolution, the whole basis of authority changed. The new authority as such was "science." It meant seeking authority through scientific-based knowledge, and the application of this knowledge to control the Earth and its functioning. This meant a shift in what was considered human well-being—now associated with the "material" Earth, rather than a "future in heaven." That constituted *a total transformation in reality.*

This major transformation in thinking to a scientific-based reality, has affected all of us to the very roots of our own reality—our ways of perceiving, thinking, valuing, and doing.[4] The evolution of this new reality has passed through many stages, but has maintained its basic premise of "scientific" knowledge as king, and the key to human well-being and happiness.

However, major breakdowns and questions are now appearing as a result of some unexpected negative consequences related to the predominant scientific-based development model, which it cannot seem to solve. In an attempt to understand what is really happening today in the evolution of human thinking and our relationships to nature, an increasing number of visionaries and researchers are moving from the "margin" into being accepted as more mainstream thinkers, as it is becoming increasingly difficult to explain and "solve" the new problems using only conventional scientifically based principles. Thus we have entered a chaotic period, what appears to be a new major transformation in human perception of reality—from the purely scientific materialistic view of the world to including something else—which is still not clear in terms of a new model, but certainly seems to require the development of special human capacities for subjective thinking.

B. Modern Scientific Principles—A Brief Summary

The identification of our conventional values and "truths" are important to understand in order to be able to fully comprehend how they fundamentally differ from the new emerging values. Let us briefly summarize some of the principle beliefs or values that underpin our conventional way of thinking, as well as some key accepted "truths," all of which have been directly controlling our daily assumptions about what is important in life and work.

Our conventional value base and the assumed "truths" that have grown out of it have been for many years a source of controversy. During the past decade this controversy has accelerated with the increasing problems related to the environment and socially related issues.

The authors who have researched these issues are numerous. For the purposes of this study, following are examples of summary findings of authors working in this field, which are basically in agreement with the findings of many others. Readers will find some of these listed in the bibliography.

For example, according to Ervin Laszlo,[5] some important conventional "truths" include:

a. The Environment: The belief that the environment around us is an infinite source of (free) resources and an infinite sink of wastes.

b. Mechanical control: Twentieth-century civilization persisted in treating both its technologies and its natural environment as a kind of mechanism that can be engineered and reengineered.

c. Survival of the fittest: Based on Darwin's theory of natural selection, in society as in nature "the fittest survive." This is taken to mean that if we want to survive we have to be fit for the existential struggle.

(Laszlo states that this struggle extends to the working world, when he writes of the "struggle of competitors (win-lose) in the marketplace, states and entire populations are relegated to the role of clients and consumers.")

d. Value of humans: The value of everything, including human beings, can be calculated in money. What everyone wants is to get rich.

e. Cult of Efficiency: We must get the maximum out of every person, every machine, and every organization regardless of what it produces, and whether or not it serves a useful purpose.

f. Every person is unique and separate: Individualism is natural and means pursuing our own interests. We are in control of our own future, and everyone else is either friend or foe, at best linked to us by ties of mutual interest.

g. Everything is reversible: The problems we experience are temporary interludes, after which everything goes back to normal . . . all we need are tried and tested methods of problem solving.

In addition to these indications, Laszlo has summarized a few important prevalent truths that apply directly to our everyday life experiences:

    a. Nature is inexhaustible.

    b. Nature is a giant mechanism.

    c. Life is a struggle for survival.

    d. The market distributes benefits.

    e. The more you consume the better you are.

Another visionary who has contributed significantly to a better understanding of our present-day worldview based on scientific principles is Willis Harman.[6]

Harman summarizes them as follows:

1. We acquire knowledge only through the physical senses (using our intellectual capacity).

2. Our understanding of the nature of the universe is through empirical science—exploration of the measurable world.

3. Qualitative properties can all be reducible to quantitative ones.

4. There is a separation between the objective world (which can be perceived by anyone) and subjective experience, which is perceived by the individual alone in the privacy of his/her own mind. Scientific knowledge deals only with objective knowledge (and is the only one that has validity).

5. What we know as consciousness or awareness of our thoughts and feelings is a secondary phenomenon arising from physical and biochemical processes in the brain.

6. The evolution of the universe and of man has come about through physical causes (such as random mutation, natural selection). There is not justification for any concept of universal purpose in this evolution, or in development of consciouness or in the strivings of the individual.

7. Individual consciousness does not survive the death of the organism.

According to Marilyn Ferguson,[7] some conventional "truths" include:

a. Promote consumption at all costs.
b. People (must) fit jobs (not jobs fit humans).
c. Impose goals—top-down decision-making.
d. Fragmentation in work and roles. Emphasis on specialized tasks.
e. Aggression, competition, "business is business."
f. Work and play separate—work is means to an end.
g. Manipulation and dominance of nature.
h. Quantitative (thinking): quotas, status symbols, income, etc.
i. Strictly economic motives, material (related) values.
j. Rational—trust only data.
k. Emphasis on short-term solutions
l. Centralized operations
m. Subservience to technology.
n. Allopathic treatment of "symptoms" in economy.

According to David Korten,[8] some accepted "truths" or assumptions in our free market conventional society include:
a. Sustained **economic growth** is the foundation of human progress and is essential to alleviate poverty and protection of the environment.
b. **Free markets**, free from government interference or regulation, result in the most efficient and socially optimal allocation of resources.
c. **Economic globalization,** moving toward a single, integrated world market spurs competition, increases economic efficiency and growth, and is generally beneficial to everyone.
d. Localities achieve economic success by abandoning goals of self-sufficiency and aspiring to become **internationally competitive** in providing conditions that attract outside investors.

To draw together these findings, one can summarize them in terms of a composite person and the present conventional society into which we fit:

A person with conventional thinking believes that our objective mind and rational intellectual thinking is paramount in life and work, and the rational mind is capable of eventually solving all the problems and mysteries in our world. As a result of this belief, there is no credibility or place provided for higher human consciousness and its special potential for subjective "knowing." This also leaves the concept of intuition, inner fulfillment and meaning in life as irrelevant or nonexistent, as all meaning is seated totally in the rational, objective mind. Hence the concept of happiness in life and work depends on acquiring "things" and consumption in its full spectrum. The motivation to work is to earn money and buy things. This in turn provides status, power, control and happiness. The expression, "money talks" is appropriate, as everything considered worthwhile in life can supposedly be bought at a price. Therefore happiness and success is interpreted in economic terms. Accompanying this concept of success, life naturally involves pride in one's capacity to earn money and to show this through owning things and through associations with others who have done the same.

As a result, it is assumed that humans are by nature competitive, greedy and jealous of others who have more than themselves or have things they would like to have. Money has proven a good motivator. In addition, with this thinking, there is always the pressure to "get there first," no matter what may be the consequences for others. It is felt that strong individualism is a natural and valuable trait that makes it possible for competition and personal success to work well. It is believed that we are completely "architects of our own success and lives," so competitiveness is essential in everything, bringing with it such qualities as jealousy and greed. However, they are considered natural motivators for working hard and "getting ahead." On the other hand, when we feel threatened in our ability to succeed in the competitive world of winners and losers (because if I win someone else naturally loses), we may also feel anger and sometimes fear—even fear of failure.

The conventional system views nature as completely separate and unrelated to humans. This means that nature is seen as part of a big machine (Earth), with predicable laws (which can eventually be fully understood through scientific objective reductionist thinking), and have a logical predictable makeup that humans have the capacity to understand, control and manipulate as we wish. This means that nature can eventually come completely under the control of humans as we come to understand and dominate its secrets, so it can work in such a way that is compatible with human-made technologies and systems that satisfy the aspirations of a society with economic-related values.

This means that the concept of greed, and always aspiring to more wealth, can be satisfied, as there is no limit to economic growth once humans fully understand and control the mechanisms of nature. Also, having things and doing things that represent monetary success is considered admirable in society, and people possessing them are considered role models for others to follow.

In summary, these principles of our conventional scientific thinking can be very thought provoking, because we rarely stop to actually identify the principles that underpin our realities of the world. Even though we may personally not agree with all of them, they have become, for the most part, the accepted principles on which our scientific-based thinking and development models have been based for many generations. Each one of these principles of course deserves extensive study and provides much food for thought, but for our present needs they can provide an overall panorama for refreshing our minds of the basis for Western thought and the scientific mindset.

These are just a few examples of the "truths" and values that underpin the conventional system. Within this group in the overall population there are of course a broad scale of intensity of beliefs in these values. They range all the way from reluctant acceptance to intense belief, with its accompanying practices. These values and the system that practices them do not combine well with the emerging new values, as their success depends on "homogenization"—that is, it strives for its acceptance across cultures and countries—homogenous values, systems and practices. The people supporting this conventional values base mostly believe that it satisfies the genuine basic nature of humans. This values foundation, it now appears clear, is also the one which has been dominant in the development model that has resulted in the intractable problems that now exist and threaten the very existence of human life on Earth as we know it, as well as the natural environment on which we humans depend for survival.

Fortunately, we are also discovering that humans have some very deeply held values that are completely different from those underpinning the conventional model. This realization of the innermost nature of humans is a profound and all-encompassing understanding about the little-realized potential of human nature and our close connection with the natural world. It involves knowledge and wisdom that has existed for many centuries—but has remained largely dormant, especially in modern Western society.

This does not mean that some human characteristics underpinning the conventional system do not exist, but they may not be the dominant ones in human nature. It appears that they became more dominant when some positive values were not allowed to flourish during our 300 years of primarily objective thinking. Now it appears that this new transformation in thinking is allowing some dominant positive values to come forth, while the conventional negative ones will become increasingly weaker. This is truly a significant breakthrough in positive human development.

C. Visionaries

Throughout many centuries we find visionaries who have had a profound impact on the way of thinking in their times. Particularly since the Scientific Revolution, many of these visionaries have had a significant influence on the foundation for our present-day way of thinking (our view of the world), and the values that underpin our view of reality. However, our interpretation of the thinking of many of these pillars of society has sometimes become distorted, or at times has been incomplete. This has resulted in the formation of basic assumptions or "truths" that we are now discovering do not genuinely respect the essence of thinking of some of these visionaries.

This section provides a brief overview of a number of visionaries who have had a significant impact on our views of the world since the Scientific Revolution. It brings out some additional key insights into their thinking, which in many cases show their compatibility with the new emerging values and worldview. Also included are overviews of important recent visionaries who have adopted a worldview based on emerging values and related universal wisdom. They are considered new pillars of the "shift" in thinking toward a new foundation for our human well-being and the planet as a whole. These names were very difficult to select, as many "visionaries" exist, and additional visionary views are also recognized throughout the book.

1. Adam Smith (1723 – 1790)[9]

Adam Smith is a towering figure in the history of economic thought. He wrote the first comprehensive system of political economy, for which he is most famous, called *An Inquiry into the Nature and Causes of the Wealth of Nations*, 1776, but his previous book, *Theory of Moral Sentiments*, 1759, lays the psychological foundation for *Wealth of Nations*. At that time, the question of particular interest was: What was the source of man's ability to form moral judgments, including judgments on his own behavior, in the face of seemingly overriding passions for self-preservation and self-interest.

Smith's answer was: Present within each of us is an "inner man" who plays the role of the "impartial man," approving or condemning our own and others' actions with a voice impossible to disregard. This Smith refers to in *Theory of Moral Sentiments*. Smith saw man as a creature driven by passions and at the same time self-regulated by his ability to reason—and no less important—by his capacity for sympathy. This duality serves both to pit men against one another, and to provide them with rational and moral faculties to create institutions by which these dual struggles can be controlled and even turned to the common good. In the book *Moral Sentiments* he made the famous observation repeated in *Wealth of Nations*, that self-seeking men are often "led by an invisible hand"—without knowing it, without intending it, (to) advance the interest of society. This showed the dilemma that Smith noted as the "impartial spectator," which balances morality and reason. In *Moral Sentiments* he relied on the presence of the "inner man" to provide restraint and noted that each stage of development is accompanied by institutions suited to its needs. He said, "Civil government, in so far as it is instituted for the security of property, is in reality instituted for the defense of the rich against the poor, or those who have some property against those who have none at all."

Smith believed that the wealth of nations would grow only if men, through their governments, did not inhibit the growth by catering to the pleas of special privilege that would prevent the competitive system from exerting its benign effect. This is in sharp contrast with present thinking and practices, where special privileges and influence are sought through gigantism and globalization of organizations that in turn provide special relationships and influences with governments at all levels.

Smith also speaks negatively of the restrictive measures of the "mercantile system" that favoured monopolies at home and abroad. Smith's system of "natural liberty," he carefully pointed out, would not be put in practice if government is entrusted to or heeds "the mean rapacity, the monopolizing spirit of merchants and manufacturers, who neither are nor ought to be, the rulers of mankind." This thinking again contrasts with present thinking and practices, where globalized organizations feel it their right to wield enormous power to the point of in fact being the sector of society with the most influence and control over how a nation develops.

He also asserted that "sympathy" was a guiding emotion of human conduct. Related to this thinking, it was also during this period that the important question of the relationship between the ethical faculty (human nature) and the faculty of reasoning were considered important.

This is quite a different Smith from that portrayed by modern-day economists. Many now believe that his work needs to be carefully reexamined to provide insight into the more complete context of his philosophy, especially his genuine interpretation of the concept of the "invisible hand," his obvious belief in the "common good," his belief in human capacity for sympathy, and also the real meaning of the "impartial spectator." These new interpretations certainly bear new insights into what appears to be some deeply held sustainable values.

2. Pierre Teilhard de Chardin (1881-1955)[10]

Pierre Teilhard de Chardin was a French paleontologist and Jesuit priest.

He is one of the few visionaries in his time who believed deeply in the integration of pure science research and thinking with his spiritual vocation and convictions, in other words, the integration of science and spirituality.

Since early childhood, Teilhard was fascinated with nature and all the mysterious things to be found there. He studied in Jesuit schools, which lead eventually to his spiritual vocation as a priest. At the same time he maintained his fascination for the mysteries of nature, and finally studied as a paleontologist. Part of his work in this field included a six-year research period in China connected with the anthropologic studies related to the Piltdown man.

During these years, Teilhard became more convinced of the connection between science and spirituality. He used lessons learned from nature as a foundation for spirituality. He believed that Earth is a "living" body of complex interconnected organisms and matter, and imbued with spirit and energy. Teilhard believed that there is a common universal (cosmic) consciousness, which he referred to as "noosphere" (meaning mind), that involves human higher conscious-ness and brings harmony between all sciences and spirituality. He also believed in the evolution of the world, through consciousness, and that evolution has a certain direction, an "Ariedne's Thread," which draws us toward higher consciousness and thus integrates science and spirituality.

Related to this concept he asserted:

"My starting point is the fundamental initial fact that each one of us is perforce linked by all the material organic and psychic strands of his being to all that surrounds him."

Teilhard believed that the concept of evolution leads to a rise in consciousness of the whole Earth. From that standpoint he viewed that consciousness has a way of effecting the union of all—science in harmony with spirituality. Related to this thinking, Teilhard spoke of our present situation:

"We are at this moment passing through a change of age. Be-neath a change of age lies a change of thought."

Both the Roman Catholic Church and the science community were very critical of his work, as it contradicted or strayed signifi-cantly from the accepted thinking of the times.

Regarding evolution, Teilhard asserted (based on Charles Henderson's book) that, "the most sublime product of evolution is the human person, the individual uniquely aware of itself as a person, yet also aware of its interdependence with the whole."

"Our origin and ascent follow the same path taken by all the creatures of the natural world. Human consciousness (including a consciousness of God) is the culmination of nature's own movement through time."

Regarding science Henderson comments on Teilhard's beliefs: "As science in this century has emphasized the interrelationship and interdependence of all things, religion affirms the *unity* of all things, is itself the most solid evidence of a God who embraces all."

The most important work of Teilhard is *The Phenomenon of Man*. This book brought great controversy in both science and the church. Following is a quote that sums up Teilhart's beliefs about the relationship between science and spirituality:

"To outward appearance, the modern world was born of an antireligious movement: man becoming self-sufficient and reason supplanting belief. Our generation and the two that preceded it have heard little but talk of the conflict between science and faith; indeed it seemed at one moment a foregone conclusion that the former was destined to take the place of the latter. . . . After close on two centuries of passionate struggles, neither science nor faith has succeeded in discrediting its adversary. On the contrary, it becomes obvious that neither can develop normally without the other. And the reason is simple: the same life animates both. Neither in its impetus nor its achievements can science go to its limits without becoming tinged with mysticism and charged with faith."

3. Albert Einstein (1879 – 1955)[11]

Albert Einstein is considered one of the giants of science.

A German-American physicist, Einstein developed the special and general theories of relativity, the equivalence of mass and energy, and the photon theory of light.

His name is also closely associated with the advent of the atomic age, and he participated in the development of the atom bomb.

Einstein had a passionate sense of social justice and responsibility. This was demonstrated in various ways, such as:

1) He was a committed pacifist and believed in liberalism, beginning during WWI and increasing after WWII.
2) He joined other scientists after WWII seeking ways to prevent future use of the atom bomb, and urged the establishment of a world government for that purpose.
3) He believed in non-violence, and was an admirer of Gandhi.

Einstein was not an atheist. He believed in God, who "reveals himself in the harmony of what exists."

Einstein was also an accomplished violinist. He played regularly and carried his violin with him to all parts of the world as a way of satisfying his artistic and deep needs for inner fulfillment. He also enjoyed his sailboat and sailing as a source of peace and contemplation.

Thus we find a man who in addition to his outstanding scientific achievements, was also a deeply spiritual person, and believed in many of the emerging values that are coming forward today and are considered essential for long-term sustainability.

Some noted comments made by Einstein include:

a) "The moral influence which Gandhi has exercised upon thinking people may be far more durable than would appear likely in our present age, with its exaggeration on brute force. We are fortunate and grateful that fate has bestowed upon us so luminous a contemporary—a beacon to generations to come."

b) "No problem can be solved from the same consciousness that created it. We have to learn to see the world anew." These are insights Einstein had over fifty years ago that now relate closely to the dilemma of our way of thinking today.

c) "Not everything that counts can be counted; not everything that can be counted, counts." This statement shows our present-day dilemma of placing credibility only in things that can be measured scientifically.

Einstein obviously had a deep insight into our present-day dilemmas. He believed that a fundamental change in our values was essential—toward a new worldview, and new values imbedded in a new consciousness.

4. Mahandas (Mahatma) Gandhi (1869 – 1948)[12]

Gandhi was an outstanding leader of Indian nationalism and a prophet of nonviolence in the twentieth century. He is internationally respected for his doctrine of nonviolence to achieve political and social aims. He was a pacifist and believed in the sanctity of all living things.

Gandhi wrote widely concerning Western industrialization, urbanization, his distrust of the modern state, and total rejection of violence. He gained the highest respect from leading figures such as Albert Einstein, Martin Luther King and Swedish economist Gunnar Myrdal.

According to Gandhian economics, development must come mainly from "below," from the villages and not from "above," such as the central or state governments.

Gandhi asserted in reference to production and employment: "It is not mass production, but only production by the masses that can do the trick." He believed that mass production is only concerned with the product, whereas production by the masses is concerned with the product, the producers and the process. He asserted that the driving force behind mass production is a cult of the individual (personal and corporate profit). In contrast, he believed a locally based economy enhances community, spirit, community relationships and community well-being. Mass production, he was convinced, leads people to leave their villages to become cogs in the "machine."

He believed that goods are intended to last and must fit the precise conditions of a place, not standardized. He emphasized local production for local needs and gave preference for the preservation of social structures and the natural environment over purely economic considerations.

Gandhi believed in the principle of "swadeshi," which means local self-sufficiency. In this sense he believed the soul of India rested in the village communities, and foresaw a confederation of self-governing, self-reliant, self-employed people living in village communities.

The Swadeshi principle also indicates that whatever is made or produced in the village must be used first and foremost by the members of the village. Goods and services that cannot be generated within the community can be bought elsewhere. The village community should embody the spirit of the home—the extension of the family rather than a collection of competing individuals.

In Swadeshi, the machine would be subordinated to the worker; it would not be allowed to become the master, dictating the pace of human activity.

He believed that market forces would serve the community rather than forcing people to fit the market.

Gandhi said: "A certain degree of physical comfort is necessary but above a certain level it becomes a hindrance instead of a help; therefore the ideal of creating an unlimited number of wants and satisfying them seems to be a delusion and a trap. His famous statement was, "There is enough for everyone's need, but not for anybody's greed."

Therefore Gandhi viewed Swadeshi as a way for comprehensive peace: peace with oneself, peace between peoples, and peace with nature. He insisted that the global economy drives people toward materialistic success, resulting in stress, loss of meaning, loss of inner peace, loss of space for personal and family relationships, and loss of spiritual life. For Gandhi Swadeshi was the spiritual imperative.

Gandhi also believed that there is an intrinsic value in anything we do with our hands—for work by hand brings with it a meditative mind and self-fulfillment.

In addition to Swadeshi, Gandhi believed in two other principles: Sarvodaya and Satyagraha.

Sarvodaya means "upliftment for all." He believed that morality must underpin all human action. Society must strive for economic, social, spiritual and physical well-being of all. He favoured a holistic approach to well-being, and a total approach to community.

Satyagraha refers to nonviolence and nonviolent action as in fact a way of life.

This is not just an absence of violence. It requires self-discipline and self-restraint in respect to what Gandhi refers to as "the sensory urges and consumptions." It also entails respect for all beings and devotion to the values of truth, love and responsibility. It is a guide to building constructive processes from a position of inner moral strength.

5. E. F. Schumacher (1911 – 1977)[13]

Schumacher was a highly respected economist and philosopher. He was born in Germany, but lived most of his life in England. From 1950 to 1970 Schumacher was the economic advisor, and director of statistics for the National Coal Board in England. In addition, he had a distinguished academic career in Germany, England and United

States, but always believed that "an ounce of practice is worth a ton of theory."

He experienced a life of constant challenges, including questioning most basic assumptions on which Western economic and academic theory had been based. These questions included: "What are the "laws" that govern the 'science' of economics?; What is the true value of money?; What is the real worth of work?; What is the value of economic development?

Until 1951 Schumacher was an atheist and idealist with a restless mind whose earliest values had been very modern, based on speed, measurement, efficiency and logic of the Western world. It was much later that he understood that such criteria were too inflexible and totally incompatible with the more subtle "unconscious" rhythms of the natural world.

In his book *Guide for the Perplexed* he said, "The art of living is always to make a good thing out of a bad thing. This then leads to seeing the world in a new light." His life was a true expression of Gandhian nonviolence, of finding balance, or later, in Buddhist terms, of finding "the middle way." It could be said that Schumacher essentially followed the Gandhian search for truth, thus explaining his changing economic and metaphysical views. His speeches, articles and projects reflected these changes, all the way from Marxism through Buddhism and eventually to Christianity. His experience in Burma (now Myanmar) as economic development advisor to the Union of Burma in 1955 was a turning point in his spiritual and intellectual development, particularly relating to economic development in the Third World.

Schumacher became a Christian in 1971. This was also his formal renouncement of supremacy of the intellect and reason over the Christian virtues of compassion, forgiveness, unconditional love, the acknowledgement of a divine creator, and the integrity of all creation. Thus Schumacher became, following many years of reflection, a devout believer in spirituality.

Internationally, Schumacher's aim was to promote sustainable development strategies in the first and third worlds alike, including United States, Latin America, Japan and Russia. He saw fuel and food as the two basic necessities for survival and sustainability.

He believed all communities should strive to be as self-sufficient as possible in these two basic necessities; otherwise they would become economically and politically vulnerable.

He saw the dangers of economic dependence of agriculture systems on monocultures, and oil based chemical fertilizers. Schumacher became involved in forest farming and sustainable agriculture, and was a prominent member of the UK Soil Association.

Schumacher also founded the Intermediate Technology Development Group, whose aim is to give practical "tool aid" skills and education to poor rural communities in developing countries. He saw Western aid to poor countries simply served to increase their cultural and economic dependence, and increase the gulf between rich and poor, young and old, even within their own societies. He believed in respecting indigenous and cultural traditions, and providing them with skills and upgraded tools to achieve long-term sustainability.

Schumacher's recognition and fame came with the publication of *Small is Beautiful*, which focused not just on size, but his belief that twentieth-century Western society, whether agricultural or industrial, was living artificially on Earth's "capital" rather than on its "income." He believed that life could not provide sustainability on the increasing curve of production and consumption without material and moral restraint. In his book the message of "empowerment" (people power) had a strong impact worldwide.

Schumacher's interpretation of the "middle way" involves occupying oneself with things that can be changed—however small. It also means separating needs from wants; separating quality of life from quantity of consumption; wisdom from knowledge; production of the masses from mass production.

He was among the first economists to challenge the unqualified desirability of the "growth" concept. Schumacher's concept of sustainability automatically places the spiritual and material well-being of the people involved at the forefront of all policy and decision making.

In accounting and accountability areas, Schumacher believed in taking not only monetary but environmental and nonrenewable resource costs into consideration in policy making.

His strengths still lie in his ability to address problems at the systems level, and to communicate solutions simply and practically.

6. Willis Harman (1919 – 1997)[14]

Willis Harman was a visionary thinker, futurist and social scientist who had his initiation as an electrical and systems engineer.

Throughout his books, and especially in *Global Mind Change*, Harman continuously promoted the possibility for humankind to transcend the limits of outmoded thinking. He was a major force in helping people understand the role of business in transforming social consciousness.

He asserted: "I am convinced that the real action today is changing fundamental assumptions."

Related to changing assumptions, Harman was president of the Institute of Noetic Sciences from 1973 to 1996. Noetic refers to the Greek word "nous," meaning mind, intelligence, or understanding, and implies three ways in which we gain knowledge. These are:

a) the reasoning process of the intellect,

b) the perception of our experiences through the senses,

c) the intuitive, spiritual or inner ways of knowing.

The Noetic Science Institute is an example of a number of highly respected research institutions that provide for systematic study of these ways of knowing, which are basic to how we see ourselves, each other and the world.

Harman indicates that people often feel threatened by the awareness (conscious or unconscious) of impending change in their lives. The prospect that "truths" they have known all their lives might be superceded by some other belief can be especially threatening. Consequently, there is a tendency to "fight back," to oppose the change. Sociologists and historical researchers show that during similar revolutionary changes, we typically see increases in frequency of mental illnesses, social disruption and use of police to quell disruption, violent crime, terrorism, religious cultism, and acceptance of sexual hedonism. Harman indicates that these are all basically responses to the underlying anxiety and uncertainty to the unconscious threat of change. But societal change implies individual change, and it is that which brings on the sharpest anxiety.

Harman's book *Global Mind Change* explores the hypothesis that a change is taking place at the most fundamental level of the belief structure of Western industrial society.

In this book, Harman says, "the concept of unconscious beliefs and the extent to which they are capable of shaping or distorting our perceptions of everything around us is central to understand the global mind change."

Harman explains that a person's total belief system is an organization of beliefs and expectations that the person accepts as true of the world he or she lives in—verbal and non-verbal, implicit and explicit, conscious and unconscious.

The belief system he indicates can be conceived of as comprising "concentric" regions or shells. The outermost region is relatively accessible to conscious awareness and relatively easy to change, as by education. The intermediate level of beliefs are less accessible and more resistant to change. These contain beliefs about the nature of authority (trust and external authority). The innermost core of the belief system includes basic unconscious assumptions about the nature of the self and our relationship to others, and about the nature of the universe. Most go through life without changing in this innermost core.

According to Willis Harman the belief system has two purposes: need for a cognitive framework to interpret new experience, and need to ward off threatening aspects of reality. Our belief system, he indicates, is our way of making sense out of raw experience. The more closed (rigid, distorted) the belief system the more defense is needed against anxiety. As a general observation, Harman indicated that the typical individual is psychologically fragmented—the conscious mind makes one set of choices, while other fragments outside conscious awareness are choosing other things.

We believe, value, choose and know unconsciously as well as consciously, according to social scientists' research. The way we perceive reality is strongly influenced by unconsciously held beliefs. Cultural anthropologists have thoroughly documented how persons who grow up in different cultures perceive literally different realities.

Harman indicates that, "Western neglect of the realm of the subjective experience has had serious consequences in our confusion about values, for it is ultimately in the realm of the subjective, the transcendent, and the spiritual that all societies have found the basis for their deepest value commitments and sense of meaning."

Harman refers to a number of concepts related to the "subjective mind" that have created a great deal of controversy and are now beginning to be understood and accepted. An example concerns the concept of attention and volition: "the mind is to the brain as digestion is to the stomach. The brain is what is, the mind is what the brain does."

Volition is one of the most problematic of human experiences. Nothing is more central to the sense of self than the experience of volition—of "I choose," or "I decide." The apparent conflict between the sense of volition and the deterministic assumptions of positivistic science is one of the oldest problems in psychology. "Does free will exist?" is a common formulation of the puzzle.

In deterministic science, free will would seem to be no more than the feeling associated with a deterministic action. That is, I act in a way determined by all the external and internal forces acting upon me, and feel it is my choice to do so.

Regarding creativity and unconscious knowing, Harman states that we "know" in the unconscious mind much that is not ordinarily accessible to the conscious mind. He states that unconscious knowing is a far more pervasive aspect of experience than is ordinarily taken into account. Research in "biofeedback" training discloses that we "know" unconsciously, for example, how to relax muscle tension, change brain waves, alter heart beat or blood pressure, change blood flow and skin temperature—but we are not aware of this knowing until the feedback signal is provided. With our unconscious mind we know how to carry on mental activity that we can't do or even understand with the conscious mind.

This includes the creative process. Creativity and intuition are terms we use to refer to those occasions when unconscious knowing is made accessible to the conscious mind. (So also are aesthetic and spiritual experience.) In inner creativity Harman indicates there are at least three actors:

a) The conscious mind, which wants to know.
b) The creative/intuitive mind, which knows.
c) Another part of the unconscious, which for whatever reason chooses to block or partially block access.

One of the most powerful techniques for dissolving the resistance and releasing the creative abilities is that of affirmation (expression of self-fulfilling beliefs) and inner imagery. This technique has been used successfully in many organizations.

Harman believes, based on multifaceted research, that there appears to be no conflict between "mature" science and "mature religion" (spirituality based on perennial wisdom). Indeed he says we must seriously question whether we have a mature science as long as such conflict appears to exist.

In summary, Harman has contributed significantly to the deeper understanding of our subjective mind and its relationship to our present dilemma.

7. Ervin Laszlo (1932 --)[15]

Ervin Laszlo is considered today as the foremost exponent of systems philosophy and general evolution theory, as well as noted for his work in futures and management fields.

Laszlo has held a number of significant positions and responsibilities, including being the founder and president of the Club of Budapest; director of the General Evolution Research Group; director of International Peace University in Berlin; administrator of Interdisciplinary University in Paris, as well as directing systems science and futures studies at various universities in Europe, United States and the Far East.

Laszlo believes that, "The future is not to be forecast but created. What we do today will decide the shape of things tomorrow."

He believes that, "today's transformation is not just economic, it is a civilization process—part of a long-term evolutionary trend . . . and this process has now reached the limits of the planet; it is 'globalizing'. Economic globalization is part of it—but only a part." Laszlo believes that this evolutionary transformation will go beyond economic globalization, to pave the way toward a shift in civilization—an era of *macroshift* (the name of his book). This macroshift, he believes, will be rapid, spread to all parts of the world and involve all aspects of life.

Laszlo believes that established present-day values, vision and behaviors have become useless and even dangerous. This means we must change the way we see the world, value the world, and how we behave in the world. This macroshift is sensitive to human values, perceptions and actions. It can be guided with foresight and new understandings, and has great promise, as well as dangers. He believes that, "to master our destiny we need new thinking, new values—a new consciousness."

Laszlo states, "A Macroshift is a process of societal evolution in which the encounter with the system's limits of stability initiates a BIFURCATION: an era of transformation."

Laszlo believes we will embrace a new planetary ethic.

He states that "values and beliefs determine the way we perceive the world, and suggest the ways we prioritize the responses to our perceptions. They affect almost all areas of our judgment and behaviour."

According to Laszlo, planetary ethics can be divided into different sectors:

a) Private ethic: our personal ethic reflects our unique background, heritage, and family and community situation.

b) Public ethic (morality): this ethic is shared in the community, ethnic group, state or nation. It reflects group culture, social structure, economic development and environmental conditions.

c) Planetary ethic (universal morality): the ethic of the human family as a whole. Universal morality is an essential part of private and public morality.

Universal morality respects the conditions under which all people in the world community can live in dignity and freedom, without destroying each other's chances of livelihood, culture, society and environment.

His planetary ethic summarized is: "Live in a way that allows others to live as well."

In the context of a planetary ethic, "the pleasures and achievements of life are defined in relation to the quality of enjoyment and level of satisfaction they provide rather than in terms of the amount of money they cost and the quantity of materials and energy they require."

Based on this philosophy, Laszlo provides a basic rule of thumb for each of us: "Envision the consequences of your action on the life and activity of others."

8. Herman Daly (1938 --)[16]

For the past thirty years Herman Daly has been one of the pioneer economists who has questioned the viability of conventional classical economics.

He worked until 1994 as a senior economist in Environmental Department at the World Bank, where he helped to develop policy guidelines related to sustainable development. Presently Daly is professor of Ecological Economics at University of Maryland. He is considered the "guru" of the Ecological Economics movement.

Among his many books, Daly co-authored, with John Cobb, Jr., *For the Common Good: Redirecting the Economy Toward Community, the Environment and a Sustainable Future* (1989). This book has won several special awards in Europe. It is considered an important critique of modern economics, and shows how economic growth is intricately linked to the ecological limitations of the Earth, and exists as a subsystem of our ecological whole Earth system.

Daly and Cobb assert that sustainable economic growth is simply no longer an option. They outline the limitations to purely economic-based growth, viewing the Earth as a complete system on which all human activities are dependent. Therefore economic growth is viewed as a subsystem of the whole Earth ecological system. Following this thinking, they stress that economic growth needs to be carefully controlled by the limitations of Earth systems. This means we need to change our "thinking" related to the relationship between the role of economics on the one side and the realities of nature's limitations on the other. This requires a rethinking of the present classical economic assumptions related to economic growth and ecology.

Daly believes **qualitative** development is possible and "desirable" to continue, and that it "enhances the people's lives without increased throughput and hence without increasing the impact on the natural environment."

Daly states also: "It is impossible for the world economy to grow its way out of poverty and environmental degradation. . . . As the economic subsystem grows it incorporates an ever greater proportion of the total ecosystem into itself and must reach a limit at one hundred percent, if not before." This is contrary to conventional economic thinking, which views no limitations to economic growth, thus not taking into consideration the limitations of the ecosystem as a whole.

With reference to conventional economic growth and globalization versus internationalization, Harman states, "globalization, when examined, turns out to be unfettered individualism for corporations on a global scale. . . . Globalization even undercuts our ability to deal with irreducibly global problems such as climate change, because nations are not able to carry out any effective national economic policies." Daly explains that internationalization, on the other hand, refers to "the increasing importance of international trade, treaties, alliances, etc., between nations. Inter-national means between or among nations. . . . Globalization refers to global economic integration of many formerly national economies into one global economy, mainly for free trade and free capital mobility. . . . It is the effective erasure of national boundaries for economic purposes."

With reference to economic policy related to ecological tax reform, Daly recommends a policy to use "taxes as a tool to shape a more efficient economy that uses fewer resources, pollutes less, and satisfies more human needs, including meaningful work. It involves shifting the tax base from labor and investment to resources and pollution, in effect taxing "what we have less of" rather than "what we want more of." In other words we should "tax bads, not goods.'"

Regarding globalization and the military, Daly comments: "Military observers seem not to have paid much attention to how globalization blurs the issue of national defense as it erases the economic importance of national boundaries . . . as their boundaries lose significance, then do we really need to defend those boundaries? . . . Do we imagine that national boundaries will long retain any political or cultural significance once their economic significance is gone? . . . Can the industrial part of the military-industrial complex globalize while the military part remains national?"

These are questions that provide much food for thought, as visionaries such as Herman Daly provide new insight into the human and ecological consequences of our conventional economic-based development model.

In addition to these visionaries, some economists and specialists in various disciplines have also been considering the importance of both objective and higher consciousness thinking. One of these think-ers is David Korten.[17] In relation to science and reason he states:

"That which cannot be observed and measured, such as spirit and consciousness, came to be excluded from consideration by sci-ence—and therefore from the scientific perspective does not exist." Korten is referring to the separation or delinking of objective and subjective consciousness during the Scientific/Industrial Revolution, and only objective thinking became accepted as having validity.

Another well-known author, Richard Tarnas,[18] wrote in *Passion of the Western Mind*:

"Our psychological and spiritual predispositions are absurdly at variance with the world revealed by our scientific method." This clearly indicates his concern related to the importance of the develop-ment of the whole person –(both objective and subjective thinking), which a purely scientific method does not seem to recognize.

Another well-known visionary who has gained much respect and prominence in the world of new thinking is the economist Ken-neth Boulding.[19] In recognition of the importance of the spirit, he stressed:

"When humans reached self-awareness and learned to think rationally, we became instruments by which 'Universal Mind or Mind at Large,' could more sensitively adjust and synchronize the course of creative process . . . Spirituality involves the spirit and 'spirit' is a code word for what lies at the deepest levels of consciousness. . . . Spirituality, as distinguished from religious dogma, is a kind of con-sciousness, one that is characterized by a 'noetic' sense of unity and ultimate reality, the fruit of which is compassionate, unconditional, universal love."

This whole concept of expanding recognition and acceptance of subjective consciousness thinking, in addition to objective scientific thinking, as valid, has opened up a whole new "reality"—pushing the envelope so to speak. This new unfolding reality views subjective, "higher" consciousness as an extremely valuable and often untapped source of an additional way of "knowing." Many scholars also believe that we all have the capacity to reach this deep higher consciousness in our unconscious minds, and to draw this deep wisdom into our conscious minds.

This leads to a whole new way of looking at our beliefs or values as we begin to accept both objective realities as well as subjective consciousness realities, which together form our foundation of deeply felt values.

D. Viewpoints—Young Professionals[20]

These views from young professionals provide some insight into indications of questions and concerns, as well as what appears to be some subtle changes taking place in especially younger working professionals. Following is a brief summary of the results of a survey completed in both North America and Latin America.

This questionnaire was directed mainly toward one group—the young professional sector of our society. The reason for this is that they represent a large group that has much at stake in getting to the root of our dilemma. They have many years of work ahead and want their lives to be as productive and fulfilling as possible. They also represent an important sector of the working world from which will come our decision makers of the future.

Following is a very brief indication of some of the typical concerns and questions we hear today from young professionals in both rich and poor countries. I am sure readers can add many more from their own experience. It should also be noted that some young professionals live happy and fulfilling personal and working lives, but there is an increasing current of concern evident in surveys that show that an increasing number of people are beginning to question the merits of the present conventional "system." The following questions demonstrate these deeply felt concerns. They provide an important window into a much deeper level of doubt related to the present system, and the areas where it is breaking down.

Some of these questions are more notably found in the highly developed countries of the North (and a small group of elite from the South), while others have their origin in the developing countries of the South. In addition, some questions are common to both North and South. Please bear in mind that the group from which most of these questions came represents young professionals from different regions of the "Americas," including North, Central and South America.

CONCERNS AND QUESTIONS:
YOUNG PROFESSIONALS

A. The North: Highly Developed Countries, North America

1. I feel something is missing but can't explain what it is. I am not finding that my life and work are providing worthwhile purpose and meaning.

2. I feel I am on a rapid "treadmill" because of all my work obligations and responsibilities. How many responsibilities and long hours of work can a human take?
But to keep my job I have to stay on the treadmill.

3. Why do so many feel that we live with two sets of values —one at work and a different one at home?

4. What is money worth if I have no time and energy left to "live" —to enjoy my family, friends and participate in my community?

5. Why do most of us experience problems of stress? And the situation seems to be getting worse, and resulting in burnout and other health problems.

6. We seem to measure everything in monetary terms. How can we put a monetary value on things like relaxation, time with family and friends, a walk in the forest, or a beautiful sunset?

7. Personal safety and security are increasing concerns. We see a global picture full of wars and violence. This creates worries, as we see increased violence in our own regions.

8. We are told that everything will be fine if we keep buying things. This makes the economy strong, we are assured. Most of us live on "plastic," which often puts us deeper in debt, and we often find it difficult to make ends meet. And yet, at work we are obligated to keep up with the going fashions in clothes and cars, etc., to be

accepted as modern. How many things do we need to be happy, or does owning material things really provide happiness? We sometimes wonder.

9. Job security does not exist at any level. Layoffs are frequent and downsizing and mergers of companies are common. As well, many new jobs are on contract basis without benefits or security of continuity. How can we plan our lives or buy a home without job security? At the same time companies expect us to dedicate ourselves totally to our job.

10. Opportunities for good jobs are becoming much more difficult. To find one of the few well-paid jobs you need to be highly educated and skilled. On the other hand, most jobs are now in a much lower pay range, with very little opportunity for promotion. How are we supposed to be motivated to do our best in this situation?

11. We often worry about healthy food with all the new pollutants and diseases showing up. We see more new chemicals and products being sold every day that are supposed to make our lives better. Our health and whole lives depend on healthy, safe food, safe water and clean air. What are we to believe of what we are told?

12. What is "progress" in reality? We see a small elite group earning millions of dollars (and often with questionable ethics), while the rest of us are struggling to "stay afloat." Is that progress?

B. The South: Developing Countries, Latin America

1. Our one immediate worry is finding reasonably paid work. It used to be that a university degree assured us of a well-paid job. This is no longer so. Now even most international companies are offering lower salaries for graduates than previously, and jobs are scarce. How can we plan our lives without the security of a good job?

2. We worry about the loss of our human-based cultural values. We value highly our families and human relationships at work. How can long working hours and the need for a family life combine? We

do not want to lose our quality of life and deeply held cultural values, but it seems a condition for "modernization."

3. What is the value of modernization and progress if only a very few become very rich, and the rest are struggling to survive? Meanwhile, poverty is also increasing. We were assured that the new international free trade agreements were supposed to provide us all with well-paid jobs. What has happened with these new democratic ideas?

4. How can we feel any tranquility with our terrible safety and security problems—kidnappings, robberies, violence, and murders? Our personal safety and that of our families is a constant worry, especially in the mega cities where it is critical. It is the worst we have ever seen in our lifetime.

5. What is happening to our farms and food supply? We are importing basic foods even though we can produce enough better quality food ourselves. We used to be mostly self-sufficient in basic food, and now we are not. What has happened?

6. Our water supply is a huge problem. What has happened to our rivers and lakes that used to provide us with safe water? Now people talk about water shortages in many regions, as well as deep concerns about air and soil pollution. What natural resources are we leaving for our children and grandchildren?

7. We often look to the North as the land of opportunities and a positive model to copy. But are we willing to give up our deeply rooted human related cultural values and embrace the economic-related values of the North? Now we are not so sure.

These are indeed difficult questions. Many of them represent concerns of a wide spectrum of society, including the business sector, different levels of governments, educational institutions, as well as local communities and individual groups in civil society. An example of this is shown in broad surveys completed by Paul Ray[21] in the

United States related to social and values issues. There have been some attempts at trying to come to grips with some of these issues through attempted policy changes in some business and governmental organizations, directing more attention to human needs as well as ecologically based concerns.

When we look at typical organizational mission statements, or principles and policies, most organizations now have statements related to the importance of "human resources" in their organizations. Also, most organizations have included language referring to concepts relating to the importance of participation, empowerment, sustainability, environment concerns, stakeholders, etc., only to mention a few.

One would conclude, when reading these obviously good intentions in giving the human aspect a higher priority in organizations, that they would translate into a major transformation in practices that focus on more human-based priorities. However, in spite of the laudable words, it seems "business as usual" is still the norm (with a few notable exceptions), with only a few superficial attempts at actually putting into practice policies that give priorities to the human and ecological aspects of organizations.

Words vs. Practices

What is really happening? Why are the good intentions seemingly coming to nothing? Where is the blockage? These are the questions we are attempting to answer.

Firstly we need to examine layer after layer of policies and principles, which contain given "truths" in which decision makers have believed and operated for many generations. Then we need to go further, underneath these principles, to examine the very values on which our "system" is seated. Here lies the root of the system—the foundation of our organizations, or more precisely the deeply held personal values of the decision makers themselves who control these organizations and their policies.

At this root level, we have other new discoveries. Even though we sometimes find diverse values among decision makers, the ones that always seem to dominate are the ones that are related directly to conventional economic-based values, where the human and ecological aspects are not a priority. This tells us something about the present problems and why they are worsening.

We seemingly have a mismatch between the values that underpin principles and policies and the words or language used in organizational statements and marketing.

The apparent changes in policies, which reflect the importance and priority of the human and ecological side, have not penetrated to the root of the organization. Traditional economic-based values still prevail, which translate into principles based on these values. The policies that follow then naturally will contain the ingredients of these purely economic-based values and principles. From that point the actual practices will translate into ones that respect the values that underpin them—no matter what words or language is used.

This is a very worthwhile revelation! It seems to confirm that most decision makers at different levels continue to believe in conventional economic-based values, and consequently the interpretations of the policies reflect those values. So the new "sustainable language" is still interpreted through conventional economic-based values.

No wonder we see only rare cases of transformation in organizations!

Whole System Illness

We must now recognize that we have a whole system that is unstable and unsustainable. We also recognize that we have new positive, sustainable policy language in organizations, but it doesn't work because the values on which the policies are seated have not changed to be able to implement sustainable policies. Therefore this next step involves the need for insight and understanding of firstly which values produce positive sustainable policies and practices, and which ones produce the conventional negative results. In other words, we need to learn which values result in only purely economic-related policies (which would continue the broken down system) and which ones produce policies and practices that provide priorities for human and ecological concerns, not just economic.

Thus we are entering a new way of thinking about what has

gone wrong, and that it is essential to rethink organizations at the *root*—that is, to rethink those deep values that can provide a new foundation for principles, policies and practices—in other words, change course to a new, viable pathway. This will need the input of all the members of an organization. Therefore, as with most major transformations in society, the process must begin with each one of us, in our own personal lives. Then we bring these values to our work, whether we are decision makers or employees, or individuals in the civil society.

This study is meant to assist readers firstly in their personal search process, to identify those desirable values that we all strive for, but sometimes are hidden or forgotten for a long period of time. Following that, we need to gain insight into how these can be applied to our personal life, our community, and finally to our work and organizations in general.

I am certainly very aware of the fact that one cannot, and should not, try to change the mind of the reader. But hopefully this study will provide much food for thought, and that through a process of genuine reflection readers will be able to identify their own deeply held positive values, and from that standpoint be able to construct their own viable path to a fulfilling and happy life. In this process, daily life and work will be positively affected, as these newly discovered values will begin to form a new view of life, and new universal "working values" in organizations at all levels.

Chapter III

Values Overview[1]

Our overall dilemma or blockage points to a worrisome situation linked to human activities on Earth and the way we as humans think. We clearly need to study the role of humans in the whole development process, and to learn what humans really need to be happy and productive. This means looking at human nature and the way we think, leading naturally to our deeply held values which provide the basis for a fulfilling life.

Presently we are living in a period of dramatic change—a period of chaos—where conventional structures, business and development outlooks, and even the human role on Earth are going through a period of controversy, questioning and change. Conventional assumptions, or "truths," based on conventional values are breaking down. New emerging values are slowly unfolding (or being rediscovered), and societies, especially at the community level, are going through a process of examination and questioning of conventional thinking, while at the same time rediscovering often forgotten values. This process is being pushed by concern for worsening social, ecological and economic conditions, a dilemma where conventional "solutions" do not seem to be working, and the situation is threatening our very human existence in the longer term.

Thus it appears that to locate the deep roots of our blockage, we cannot avoid examining the very depths of our thinking—where we find the source of our deeply held personal values. This can be a very painful process, as it touches the very core of our own identity. It is also very complex, as the concept of values is interpreted in many different ways depending on our own background and experiences.

A. What Are Values?

The whole concept of values is one that has been studied by many visionaries and scholars. The insights of these scholars, relating to how values are linked to different aspects of our thinking, includes research involving many fields, such as values and science, values and psychology, values and perennial wisdom, values and business and universality. This section helps to clarify some of the confusion related to the term "values" when viewed from different readership perspectives.

The concept of values in this study refers to a number of deeply held beliefs (universal values) about the nature of human beings, beliefs about nature and beliefs about how we relate to the larger context (universe/God/the spiritual domain).

Values include our basic ways of perceiving what is true, and what we value in life. For more clarity, values in this study have been divided into three different groups:
   a) Values related to the self—these are beliefs about the essence of human nature.
   b) Values related to family, work and community—these are beliefs concerning our relationships with others.
   c) Values related to nature and the universe—these are beliefs about the nature of our natural environment and the broader context of the universe, and how we relate to our whole universe.

The concept of values thus enters every aspect of life, work, attitudes and our everyday behaviors. Values, it appears, thus affect all human activities on Earth today and for the future.

Different Value Levels

Many interpretations of concepts related to different values levels have been taken into account in this study, and many are very complex. However there seems to exist among the works of many scholars a common thread that leads us to the need to examine our deep inner consciousness to more fully comprehend what is meant by "universal" deep level values. This concept is expressed in a very accessible form by Willis Harman, describing the different "levels" of the mind using concentric circles to depict our different levels of thinking, so to speak, and the depth of the different values we possess.

Following is a simple diagram based on Harman's description of our different levels of thinking and accompanying values.

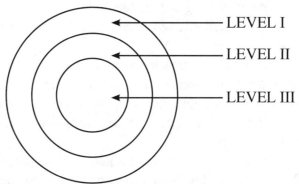

Level I: Outer Level: Conscious Thinking (values)
-- Our visible world—what we see, touch, and measure scientifically
-- Logical, objective thinking
-- Easy to change beliefs (values)—through education and life experiences

Level II: Intermediate Level: Subconscious Thinking (values)
-- Intermediate values/beliefs, less accessible and more resistant to change
-- Involves level often worked with in psychotherapy
-- Includes instinctual drives, repressed memories, automatic functions
-- Includes some more superficial cultural beliefs/values (point added by author), such as certain habits, and aspects related to preferences in music, food and entertainment

These values are strongly associated with what we often refer to as "cultural values" and are ones that can create significant misunderstandings where people from different countries/regions work together.

Level III: Supraconscious Level: Deep Inner Core Thinking (values)
-- Innermost core of belief system—higher consciousness—most of "perennial wisdom."
-- Basic unconscious assumptions about the nature of self, relationships with others, and about the nature of the universe.
-- These beliefs usually remain unchanged through life.
-- Included in this level are: creative imagination, intuitive judgment, feeling of purpose and meaning, inner peace and happiness, aesthetic sense, and SPIRITUAL SENSIBILITY.

From this brief summary one becomes aware of the complexity of different levels or layers of values, and which ones are closely associated with our cultural upbringing, as well as which ones exist as deeply rooted values that are common to all humanity, crossing all cultural lines.

For readers who have interest in further explanation of how these different levels of values can manifest themselves in a country, examples can be found in a study undertaken in Mexico by the author. Please refer to *Modernizing Mexican Management* in the bibliography.

The level of values on which this study is mainly focused is the deep Level III, which most visionaries refer to as our deep human consciousness. These deep values are believed by many scholars to have a profound influence on how we interpret Level I and II values, and consequently are considered paramount to our capacity to understanding genuine sustainability, and all the behaviors, attitudes and actions that are associated with everyday life and work.

As a result, if we are to gain insight into the roots of our blockage, we will need, it appears, to delve into the identification and meaning of these Level III values as a starting point. Many scholars refer to these as *universal values*. Once these values can be identified and understood it will be easier to identify the depth of the blockage for each organization, decision maker or individual in work or life in general. It is possible that in some cases only superficial changes need to be made (Level I or Level II values). However, from experience in many cases to date, attempts at changes to these more superficial levels have not proven very helpful, as the actions do not seem to demonstrate a fundamental removal of the blockage in thinking that allows genuine "sustainable" universal values to prevail. In other words, if the deep Level III values are not examined and rethought where necessary, the resulting essence of the behaviors and actions that follow will not be sustainable in the long term. Somehow it appears we have to delve to this deep level to unblock the deeply held unsustainable values.

B. Human Mind Capacities

The complexities of our deeply held values form the central core of this important sector of the book. Here we examine the root of our thinking, and it would appear, the deep source of our blockage. Now that we as humans have virtually taken control over much of the management of life on Earth, it is imperative that we look at ourselves and our innermost values to understand what needs to be done to redirect our thinking, values and actions toward long-term sustainability.

Before discussing specific positive personal values, it is important to firstly examine some of the inherent capacities that it appears we have all had from birth, according to studies such as the comprehensive work of the United Nations, the Earth Charter.[2] These special capacities are put to use in everything: how we think, our attitudes, our behaviors and our actions. However, differences appear related to which capacities are developed in certain cultures and which are left to languish. Some scholars, such as Roger Walsh,[3] consider the imbalances in development of some of these capacities the root cause of much of the present imbalance in our human development and behavior, resulting in the social and ecological deterioration that we now experience. These special capacities also appear to have a direct relationship to our full comprehension of the deeply held values that we possess.[4] In other words, to fully understand our deeply held values, we need to balance the development of our special human capacities. These concepts are discussed further later in the chapter.

We are now beginning to more fully understand these special capacities, and how each one has different levels of development in each of us as individuals. Some of these capacities may be overdeveloped, and others hardly developed at all, depending on the importance attached to a particular capacity in our culture or upbringing, and the society in which we live. It is now becoming better understood the need for balancing the development of these capacities for a well-balanced and fulfilling life.[5]

According to the United Nations Earth Charter, these special human capacities are described as:

MAJOR HUMAN CAPACITIES[6]
a) Intellectual capacity
b) Higher consciousness capacity (spirituality)
c) Artistic capacity
d) Ethical capacity

a) Intellectual Capacity

Historically, from the time of the Scientific/Industrial Revolution in highly industrialized Western countries, the importance attached to intellectual development of the general population has been a high priority.[7] This has produced a dramatic development through its association with scientific discovery and associated sophisticated technologies. Within intellectual capacity is included our capacities for reason, our objective interpretations of our reality, and general logical thinking. As a result the development of our intellectual capacity has become top priority in every area of Western human development, in the process placing less or little priority on other human capacities. Scholars such as Roger Walsh[8] are concerned that we have overdeveloped this capacity at the expense of the other capacities, creating an imbalance in our personal development. This seemingly has been the case in most of the industrialized Western world. Other regions of the world, and some small cultures within the highly industrialized West, where industrialization was slow or not dominant, have placed more importance on other human capacities. For example, it appears that indigenous people[9] in most countries that have not embraced modern industrialization have not placed the same priority on developing this capacity, and have instead been able to preserve centuries old capacities in higher consciousness and spirituality.

On the other hand we see the highly industrialized West, which reveres intellectual capacities and objective thinking, give little credibility or attention to the human capacity for higher consciousness.

b) Higher Consciousness Capacity

This capacity, it appears, is gaining importance in the highly industrialized countries, but is also the one that is controversial and generally still least accepted and developed.[10]

Higher consciousness is probably one of the most difficult capacities to understand, yet an essential capacity for all human beings to develop in order to live a meaningful life. This capacity has been highlighted previously, but it is important to emphasize here that it is one of the most important capacities we possess.[11] Every day more research appears showing the capacity of the human mind over and beyond the things we see and touch every day. This includes the capacity for expanding the human mind to embrace the essence of spirituality in its broad sense, to gain genuine wisdom associated with the full comprehension of universal values, as well as deeply felt inner peace of mind and genuine purpose in life.[12]

Comparing this capacity with our intellectual capacities, we find some important contrasts, such as: the difference between logical thinking and deep feeling; between logical thinking and deep reflection; between reason and passion; and between the mind and the heart. It should also be understood that this whole capacity for higher consciousness does not discount the important role of intellectual-based capacity. However, it appears that higher consciousness penetrates to a different level of the human unconscious, much as Harman describes as the "inner ring" of the mind.[13] It is also this capacity apparently that makes it possible for us to fully comprehend universal human values and to feel genuine purpose in life.

In addition, it is through higher consciousness it seems that we can fully comprehend the direct link and interdependence we have with the natural world.[14]

Ancient traditions, which often have a highly developed capacity for higher consciousness[15] and spirituality, are teaching us much about our capacity for higher consciousness that existed in our early history, and the capacity of humans to perceive realities beyond what we can physically see and touch. This capacity, it appears, we all have deeply embedded in our innermost mind, and appears to be absolutely essential to fully understand and put into practice the positive values essential for "rebalancing" human development on Earth.

Many scholars also believe that we can "pull" some knowledge and wisdom from our deep unconscious mind, where our higher consciousness is located, to our conscious mind, and from there benefit from this deep source of "knowing." Techniques to access our higher consciousness are discussed later in the study.

c) Artistic Capacity

This capacity is closely linked to the human capacity for higher consciousness, as that capacity is needed for a highly developed artistic capacity.[16] Artistic capacity, in addition to being directly related to many different forms of artistic expression, such as found in renowned musicians and artists, also includes our deeply rooted sensitivities. For example, we may not be able to sing or paint pictures, but have a deep sensitivity to different aspects of nature—that is, our sense of awe and humility in experiencing nature's beauty and complexity, which is beyond human capacity to understand.

Some of the most ancient cultures of the world have developed populations with a highly evolved artistic capacity, to the point where they are still held in awe today.[17] Most of these cultures did not embrace the Scientific Revolution when it was at its height, and many have been considered "underdeveloped," and consequently not viewed as "modern" by the West. In recent years many researchers and visionaries from the highly industrialized West have been studying these cultures anew, and are recognizing the importance of the development of artistic capacities,[18] and how it provides a balance to the highly evolved intellectual capacities (and objective thinking) in the West.

d) Ethical Capacity

Human ethics is another of our special human capacities. Some scholars[19] now consider that we have an innate capacity to differentiate right from wrong and good from bad. This continues to be a controversial issue, but an increasing number of scholars now believe that the human capability for knowing intrinsically what is right is a genuine human capacity. The development of this capacity is naturally closely associated with a healthy upbringing and positive family life. Related closely to this capacity we find the important and deeply held value—love.[20] It involves the incredible capacity of humans for compassion, generosity, joy and forgiveness, among other positive human values. Love as a value is discussed in detail in the next chapter.

All of these important human capacities together form a strong foundation for comprehending and absorbing the positive values that are described later in the study. This foundation provides a framework for positive attitudes and behaviors that we all possess, once we allow ourselves to develop them fully.

C. Values, Beliefs and Ethics

The concept of values has been defined in many different ways. As indicated previously, the term values, in the context of this study, is perceived as a number of deeply held beliefs about the nature of human beings, beliefs about nature and beliefs about how we relate to the larger context (universe/God/the spiritual domain).

Among scholars, values and beliefs are often used as interchangeable terms. Therefore, for the purposes of this study the terms are being used interchangeably.

However, there appears to be more of a difference related to the connection between values and ethics. While values are considered to be at the very root of how we view ourselves as human beings and our role on Earth, the concept of ethics is often used as an interchangeable word for values. This has caused confusion. However, some scholars are now differentiating between these two concepts. These two concepts are related, but ethics in fact appears to depend on some basic underlying values. Ethics thereby appear to be formed on top of an assumed base of values that underpins them. In other words, we begin with a foundation of values, and ethics is a concept seated on top of these values.

Ethics is also referred to as morality by some scholars. One of these scholars who describes these relationships, as well as referring to a composite ethic as "morality," is Ervin Laszlo.[21] Regarding values and beliefs, Laszlo says:

"Values and beliefs determine the way we perceive the world and suggest the ways we prioritize the responses to our perceptions. They affect almost all areas of our judgment and behaviour."

This seems to clarify the idea that values form the foundation, and ethics is based on this foundation of values. Laszlo goes on to explain the problems we encounter in the broader society relating to local interpretations of society with our different cultures and customs. His view is that "in the wider context of society, individual values and beliefs are unlikely to conform to a common standard."

Regarding this broader-based problem of cultural differences he states: "If mutually consistent values and beliefs are not imposed 'from above' a further factor needs to be present: This is a shared ethic; the acceptance of a common morality—a planetary ethic."

In other words, Laszlo is speaking of a basic set of values that are common to all cultures, and on these we can build a common ethic, or foundation of commonly understood values. Out of this common foundation would then grow another level, one which involves diversity of cultures, and an additional set of ethics particular to an individual culture, but in harmony with the deep-level common values.

Laszlo's definition of a planetary ethic is:

"A planetary ethic respects the condition under which all people in the world community can live in dignity and freedom, without destroying each other's chances of livelihood, culture, society and environment." This clearly respects diversity of cultures, at the same time promoting an overall planetary ethic based on commonly held values.

In this regard Laszlo adds: "A peaceful and sustainable world is not built on eliminating cultural differences but by cooperation that makes productive use of them."

Thus is appears that when we search for cooperation between cultures and countries, or within organizations, we in fact, consciously or unconsciously, look for common "planetary" or universal values that we all agree on as a starting point. In this way we do not depreciate the culture of either side, but utilize commonly held values (and ethics associated with them) as a foundation for cooperative efforts.

This study basically focuses on this universal foundation of values, which underpins "planetary" ethics, no matter what culture is involved. In other words, this study views universally held values as the foundation stones, and "planetary" ethics, as described by Laszlo, are seated on these universal values, and are common to all cultures.

Therefore, in terms of cross-cultural understandings and agreements on basic values that underpin agreements and projects, it appears we need to reach deeply to the level of "planetary" or universal values and ethics to find common ground for understanding and formulating sustainable working relationships.

This search for commonly held values and ethics is in fact what happens (often unconsciously) in long-term sustainable organizations where different cultures are involved. Some insights into how this can happen are found in examples of cross-cultural organizations today, described in Chapter VII.

D. Ethics and Business[21]

One sector of society that has experienced considerable difficulty in this close relationship between values and ethics is the business sector, and most especially organizations that operate in the international arena. The concept of ethics in business has become a difficult problem. Typically a company will interpret their concept of ethics from the viewpoint of their own culture or country. How often have we heard the statement, What is ethical in our country doesn't seem to be ethical in another country, or alternatively, what is considered ethical in another country (as viewed through our ethical lens) is not ethical in ours? How can we do business when we have different yardsticks for measuring ethics?

This is certainly true, as each culture has its own interpretation of ethics based on the particular values that underpin its ethical beliefs and practices. Several researchers have provided insights into this problem, and the challenges and complications it poses for us today in an increasingly interconnected world. Examples of a few of these studies and insights include:

a. Harry Lane[22]

"The least clear aspect of social responsibility for managers may be in the domain of ethics. . . . Ethics is the study of morals and systems of morality, or principles of conduct. . . . It is concerned with human consequences associated with decisions and actions, not solely profits."

"Business students and managers generally have not been trained to think about ethical issues as they have been trained in the frameworks and techniques for functional areas of specialization."

b. Stephen Covey[23]

"The view we have of ourselves affects not only our attitudes and behaviours, but also our views of other people. In fact, until we take how we see ourselves, and how we see others, into account, we will be unable to understand how others see and feel about themselves and their world." Covey stresses that we must understand ourselves, our own values and ethics first. Then we can better understand the thinking, values and ethics of others. This he views as essential in finding common ground in our cooperation with and respect for people who think differently from ourselves.

c. Hazel Henderson[24]

"We need to clarify the roles and responsibilities of business, governments at all levels, and the civil and informal sectors of society. What "codes of conduct"(ethical conduct) are socially responsible corporations accountable to?"

This is one of Henderson's great concerns, in a world where common codes of conduct seem often not to exist, and the most powerful tend to impose their own profit-based codes.

However, Henderson is also hopeful, as indicated in the following quote:

"Today we see cultural diversity and biodiversity necessarily reemerging to challenge economism."

In other words, she views the increasing concern for cultural diversity and biodiversity (natural environment) as positive, which is gradually challenging "economism," referring to purely economic-based codes of conduct, as practiced today.

d. David Korten[25]

"When a cultural field emerges as a consensual expression of shared experience, values and aspirations of the members of a society, it serves as a deeply democratic mechanism for achieving social coherence. But when a small group is able to manipulate the society's cultural symbols and values to serve its own narrow ends, the process of cultural reproduction can become deeply undemocratic and destructive."

Korten is referring to the imposition of the economic goals and ethics of large multinational organizations on countries with which they do business, and the often resulting negative outcomes. Each country has its own culture and ethics that suit that culture, and the imposition of another narrowly based economic one from outside, according to Korten, is proving extremely destructive for healthy human development.

e. Peter Brown[26]

"Nowhere does Locke limit the scope of obligations to compatriots. He talks of our obligation to preserve all humankind, and this obligation creates a transboundary frame of reference for evaluating the conduct of nations. It is therefore a cosmopolitan theory of morality (ethics) in which each person is a global citizen."

Brown emphasizes that one of our most respected visionaries (Locke) believed long ago that we have a moral responsibility for actions that affect not only our own home region, but also all other regions or countries with whom we have contact. This confirms, based on Brown's studies, that even many years ago, a visionary perceived the necessity for clear universal ethical behavior no matter where our organizations or governments have interests.

Therefore it appears we need to go to the deep foundation level (beyond cultures) of values to find common ground—an examination of what are known as "universal values," where everyone is in agreement on some basic values and "codes of conduct" that are universally accepted.[27] Once these values are identified, a universal ethic naturally evolves that is based on these universal values. Achieving this basic step is one of the most important challenges today. In this regard, it is encouraging to note that a few organizations and even some countries are taking this seriously.

E. Universal Values and Perennial Wisdom

To discover values that surpass cultures and countries (universal values), we need to transcend vast differences in religious faiths and all great religious traditions.[28] This has been attempted for example during the Parliament of Religions event, held in Chicago in 1993, where religious leaders from fourteen of the world's most important religions met and produced a commonly held set of universally held values.

For many years scholars have been aware of the fact that religions and traditional beliefs and practices have a common root. This concept was developed in depth by Aldous Huxley[29] through his book *The Perennial Philosophy*. In studying the many religions and beliefs of the world and their history, Huxley found that they have basically two aspects: each religion has one or more *exoteric* or public forms. These are characterized by rituals, dogma, history and literature, and places of worship. All of these aspects are very diverse, depending on the culture or region. On the other hand, each spiritual tradition, according to Huxley, tends to have an *esoteric* aspect, which usually involves some sort of meditative discipline that draws a person beyond physical reality into the higher consciousness of the individual. Huxley found that all of the esoteric traditions are essentially the same and are based on some form of universal spiritual experience. This common universal core of higher consciousness is sometimes referred to as "perennial wisdom." It also appears that every human being has the potential to gain access to this esoteric level, usually through some form of meditative discipline. This expands the human mind beyond the realm of concrete objective realities into a new subjective realm where we can experience our deep human consciousness, and a world where we can expand our deep understanding or wisdom.

It appears now that we need to access our higher consciousness to fully comprehend universal values

"Perennial Wisdom" can thus be described as deeply seated unconscious human "knowing." This we combine with our "conscious" knowing, forming a deeply rooted foundation for understanding "universal" values that surpass all cultural boundaries.

This is the level to which Huxley and others such as Ervin

Laszlo, Willis Harman and E.F. Schumacher[30] all agree we need to reach to genuinely comprehend universal values. In other words, we need to develop our higher consciousness if we hope to find a genuine inner feeling of happiness and meaning in life, and to fully comprehend our connection with our natural environment.

F. Perennial Wisdom and Science

One of the most controversial issues involves the deeply held views and principles underlying modern science. On the one side we have principles and values related to the rational, conscious mind, and on the other side we see many scholars who believe deeply in the importance of our higher consciousness as expressed in "perennial wisdom."

Willis Harman[31] through much of his life studied the connection between perennial wisdom and its compatibility with science. In his book *Global Mind Change*, Harman indicates that, "science has not, is nowhere near, and presumably never will "prove" the inner understanding we refer to by the term "perennial wisdom." Perennial wisdom in turn, is not, and presumably never will be, articulated in a form such that it can be tested in a scientific manner. It may be, however, exemplified in a life, and 'proved' by living it. The best scientific knowledge available would seem at the least not to contradict it, and at most to tend to support it."

As a scientist Harman was convinced that science and perennial wisdom can work together. He concluded that, "not only has it now become clear that perennial wisdom is compatible with all the world's spiritual traditions, since it is at the heart of each, but the supposed conflict with science is turning out to be not as real as had been earlier assumed."

A renowned scientist, Albert Einstein also believed deeply in the need to draw on our deep consciousness to be a good scientist, as well as have a fulfilling life. He apparently saw no conflict between science and perennial wisdom.

Einstein stated:

"The most beautiful thing we can experience is the mysterious. It is the source of all true art and science. He to whom this emotion is a stranger, who can no longer pause to wonder and stand rapt in awe, is as good as dead: his eyes are closed."

Science and Access to the Human Mind

Related to the human mind, as Harman points out, it is a well-known fact that only a small part of our total mental activity is conscious—the greatest part being outside our conscious awareness. He explains that we can think of our conscious awareness as being a narrow "visible spectrum" between the "subconscious" and the "supraconscious." Harman also indicates that access to our supraconscious level is facilitated by attention to feelings, emotions and inner imagery. This is often achieved through some kind of contemplation or meditation. These aspects are all compatible with perennial wisdom.

Harman also stresses that, at the same time we are attempting to access our supraconscious, we also experience "resistance," to knowing ourselves. He states that "the ego self is threatened by the existence of the "real self" (found in the supraconscious) and throws up a variety of smokescreens to block our awareness of our "true center." In the end, for integration the ego self must become subservient to the "real self."

Related to this concept Harman states: "Belief systems serve two powerful and conflicting sets of motives at the same time. One is the need for a cognitive framework to interpret new experience—to know and understand and act responsively. The other is the need to ward off threatening aspects of reality . . . we may also distort (raw experience) if necessary to preserve the illusion of order. . . . The typical individual is psychologically fragmented. While the conscious mind is making one set of choices, other fragments of the mind, outside conscious awareness, are choosing others. Our perceptions, values, attitudes and behaviors are influenced far more by what is going on in the unconscious mind than by what is easily accessible in the conscious mind."

Consequently, we need to take the unconscious mind seriously, because here lies the deep foundation for universal wisdom and values.

Supraconscious (Unconscious) to Conscious Mind

To put Harman's findings into a perspective, it is encouraging to think that it is and has been possible for humans to access this incredible well of wisdom housed in our unconscious minds. As Harman has indicated, this pulling of wisdom from our unconscious (supraconscious) to our conscious minds usually requires some form of meditation or contemplation, and is something we are all capable of achieving.

How do we know if we have accessed some wisdom from our unconscious mind?

Firstly, it should be pointed out that it is a different experience for each one of us, but specialists in the field indicate that most of us already have had some "living" experiences that indicate we have had some experiences that have come from our unconscious mind. These are things that go beyond our logical, objective thinking. Examples of these include: intuition about some experience or decision; a "gut" feeling about something that defies logic or explanation; a sense of awe when seeing an unexpected beautiful sight or scene in nature; a sense of human smallness or weakness when confronted with the power of nature. These are only a few examples that many of us have experienced, and when thinking further we may discover that a number of different aspects of our thinking involves the unconscious mind, such as thinking about the real nature of humans, our relationship with nature and how we depend upon it just to breathe every day, and even our need for purpose and meaning in work and life.

As a result, it appears we have progressed much further in our transformation to new thinking than we may realize. We now know that we can access the incredible store house of our unconscious mind (if we wish to), and benefit from the wisdom and new meaning and purpose in life it can provide. We are also beginning to identify these deeply held values that are being pulled out of the unconscious mind and finding them a positive foundation for new human relationships as well as our feeling of importance of nature and the Earth as essential for our existence.

From a slightly different perspective, the psychologist Roger Walsh[32] summarizes the concept of perennial wisdom, which he refers to as "perennial philosophy":

"We are discovering that underlying this vast array of practices, traditions, and theologies and beliefs, is a common core of wisdom and practices. Beneath the surface we find a deeper wisdom, not usually recognized but hidden in the depths of each and every one of the great religious traditions, a wisdom known as "perennial philosophy," and the perennial psychology, which encompasses a set of perennial practices."

Walsh divides his term "perennial philosophy" into four main statements relating to the nature of reality—what we as humans live every day. These statements have also been expressed by other visionaries, in many different forms, but all refer to the concept of perennial wisdom.

These statements include:

i) "This physical world we live in and see and touch is not all there is to reality; that underneath it—at its source—is another world, a sacred world, a world of spirit, or consciousness or mind."

ii) "We as human beings partake in this world. We are rather like amphibians. We have a part of our life and being in the world we see and touch, but in a deeper part at the core of our being, at the center of our minds, at the center of our awareness, we experience this other sacred realm, and we partake of it and we ARE it."

iii) "We are capable of KNOWING this other realm. If we train and develop the mind sufficiently, if we hone our awareness, develop our attention, refine our perception, then we can come to know this reality directly for ourselves."

iv) "Coming to know this sacred realm and coming to recognize it as ourselves is the highest good and the highest goal of human existence—that it is the means by which we can best serve ourselves and others."

Thus is appears that the world of science and spirituality, viewed through the eyes of a highly respected psychologist, could meet in common recognition of a higher consciousness in humans, thus comprehending "perennial wisdom."

G. Wisdom and Knowledge

The use of our intellectual capacities alone, it appears, will result in only a superficial understanding of deeply rooted universal values.

We need to develop our higher consciousness to penetrate to a deep understanding of what "wisdom" really means and to fully comprehend the essence of deep-level values. Thus we begin a new path, using both our intellectual as well as our higher consciousness capacities.

Thus "wisdom" requires an understanding of the fundamental differences between wisdom and knowledge. In our society today, we value knowledge very highly, and knowledge is usually viewed as the key to success and a happy life. Knowledge is a concept that requires our full intellectual and rational capacity, a capacity that is highly developed today, especially in the industrialized countries. Knowledge today has been organized in very sophisticated forms through many different technologies, which has made it readily assessable to the largest part of the educated populations.

On the other hand, wisdom we cannot comprehend through the intellect alone. In addition, it requires the capacity for higher consciousness. Thus, in the process of developing wisdom we are utilizing the full spectrum of the human mind—both the objective conscious aspects coming through the intellect and the subconscious subjective aspects coming through higher consciousness.

When applying this concept to our deeply held values, it now appears that the values related to our conventional economic-based "system" are ones that have been developed using our intellectual and reasoning capacity only, but new sustainable values are emerging through the development of our higher consciousness, in combination with our intellect. Therefore it must be emphasized that it appears higher consciousness, which comes through the unconscious mind, is needed to fully comprehend the wisdom inherent in sustainable universal values. But it is very encouraging to realize that this is a capacity that we all have, and is now being rediscovered and developed.

To summarize, Walsh[33] has offered a more specific comparison of the differences in meaning between knowledge and wisdom:

"Knowledge requires information, but wisdom requires understanding;"

"Knowledge informs us but wisdom transforms us;"

"Knowledge empowers, but wisdom enlightens;"

"Knowledge is something we have, but wisdom is something we become."

Another example of a visionary who struggled with the connection between the objective mind and higher consciousness was the famous economist and thinker, E. F. Schumacher.[34] He had an outstanding career, through much of which he believed only in the power of the intellect and the human capacity for reason, objective scientific reality, and was of the firm view that that was all there was in our world.

He stated in his book, *This I Believe*:

"I don't think it was arrogance that made me think that at long last we had discovered the only possible method for acquiring valid knowledge—the scientific method, and that therefore people who adhered to pre-scientific faiths or beliefs were simply behind times, to be pitied rather than despised."

But through time, he had a dramatic transformation in his thinking and view of our reality. This process began quietly and gradually produced a total transformation in his perception of reality and the world. It is an incredible story of discovery of higher consciousness. Here is a very small window into his process of transformation.

"I cannot claim that there was some dramatic conversion. . . . No, someone suggested to me that I could greatly improve my health and happiness by devoting fifteen minutes a day to certain relaxation and concentration exercises—which were explained to me. . . . From then on everything began to change. . . . Happily, the modest practice of allowing some degree of inner stillness to establish itself—if only fifteen minutes a day to start—led to unsuspected discoveries . . . the inward parts started to react and in fact to 'burn' as soon as my mind found itself in contact with the real thing—what shall I call it?—with Truth?"

"This inner organ with its indwelling spirit of Truth is really the most wonderful thing. It tells me whether something is the Truth . . . sometimes long before my reason is able to understand how it 'could' be such."

Schumacher's new revelations as a result of contact with his higher consciousness explain his new insight relating to distinguishing True from False: "I mean distinguishing True from False with regard to the only question that we cannot sidestep—the question of what to do with our lives—which obviously depends first of all on what we think we are."

These words of Schumacher show us what can happen in a very simple way, even for a person as brilliant and successful as he was.

Stories such as these may provide some encouragement to all of us to examine our own thinking.

Roger Walsh[35] also believes (as indicated earlier) that presently our minds tend to be "underdeveloped" or "immature," and we do not recognize our true potential and true nature. Walsh indicates that through perennial psychology (involving higher consciousness) it is possible for us to "restart the growth process."

In addition, Walsh's work related to our "underdeveloped" mind appears to provide some insight into the apparent "imbalance" we seem to have in the development of our own thinking—that is, highly developed objective aspects of the mind and poorly developed higher consciousness or subjective aspects. In today's world, it would appear that the "imbalance" has become so severe in some areas that it is beginning to manifest itself in our attitudes and behaviors toward human and ecological aspects of our lives. The question is: Can we really hope to have inner peace and fulfillment in our lives and understand our direct link with our natural world without a balance between objective and higher consciousness thinking?

This whole field of psychology-related studies has been extremely important during the 300 years following the Scientific/Industrial Revolution. Other eminent personalities, such as Sigmund Freud,[36] Erick Fromm[37] and Karl Marx[38] have had a great deal of influence on how we perceive our reality and the deeply held values of human beings. Some of their work, such as that of Freud, have become the center of controversy, as ever larger numbers of people are questioning some long-accepted "truths" about human nature, and how science and spirituality can find common ground.

Many other far sighted visionaries and scholars have emphasized the importance of recognizing our higher consciousness as essential for coming to grips with our problems. Some examples of these visionary statements are:

Albert Einstein:[39] "No problem can be solved with the same consciousness that created it. We have to learn to see the world anew."

This refers to his clear indication of the necessity to access another level of consciousness—our deeper (higher) consciousness, if we hope to find a viable solution to our problems.

Ervin Laszlo:[40] "We are attempting to cope with the conditions of the 21st Century with the thinking of the 20th Century. . . . We must not only think in a better way: we must ACT. This implies that we must feel, perceive, and get involved in events morally, emotionally and humanly." . . . "Ultimately, such a shift (in human thinking and acting) lies in changes in hearts and minds, in the values and conduct of us all."

In these statements Laszlo refers to changes in our thinking that go beyond the purely objective mind. In these changes he refers to accessing our higher consciousness in which is located the human aspects related to deep-seated morality and values.

Vaclav Havel[41] stated in a speech to the US joint session of Congress: "Without a global revolution in the sphere of human consciousness, nothing will change for the better." In this statement as well, "human consciousness" development is considered essential if we are to solve our deep-seated problems.

This process of rediscovering the incredible potential of the human mind, especially the potential of higher consciousness, and its relationship with deeply felt purpose and meaning in life and work is now considered by many researchers to be one of the most positive movements for improving human well-being in both developed and developing countries.[42] This is beginning to provide a foundation of values that can result in positive human actions and for redirecting the human behaviors that are presently threatening future generations. In other words, it can begin to release us from our blockage.

The study of deeply held values forms the foundation for the whole process of rethinking we are experiencing. In this process we are all learning together as we struggle with "letting go" of values that have created our problems, conserving ones that are positive, and at the same time embracing again ones long forgotten. This is often a painful and complex process. At the same time it is also an exciting and fulfilling one, as we begin to see "light at the end of the tunnel" and we begin to perceive that our deeply held values are at the root of how we feel and think. Once we begin to examine these values we can begin to see the direct connection between them and a new way of thinking, and acting. It is hoped that by taking this initial step in actually identifying these positive emerging values, it will assist readers in the process of assessing their own. It is expected that some values will create controversy, but that is healthy, as we wade through this period of chaos in search for a new meaningful and positive future.

Chapter IV

EMERGING VALUES

A. THE SEARCH FOR SUSTAINABLE VALUES

The search for positive, sustainable values has presented one of the most difficult challenges of this study. This challenge has required many years of research into experiences and studies that have taken place around the world, including different disciplines related to the study of values, such as philosophy, religion, psychology, ethics and indigenous studies. This has also included as an important component the need to transcend cultures and find commonly held universal values that are considered positive in all regions of the world.

Many studies exist in this field, but the challenge has been to draw them together in such a way that we may actually begin to identify specific positive values that are easily comprehensible and can be agreed upon by all so that we are all "on the same page." This has included valuable international studies, such as the Earth Charter,[1] which is global in its scope. Other examples of studies include extensive surveys such as those undertaken by Paul Ray,[2] the Harwood Group,[3] World Values Survey,[4] as well as The Institute of Sathya Sai Education, New Zealand,[5] the work of the Parliament of

71

Religions,[6] and UNESCO.[7]

This whole process began with studying practices in the working world, including large and small organizations as well as local community practices, and separating out the ones that have shown themselves to produce positive results from the ones that have had negative consequences.[7] Underneath the practices in these organizations are found, of course, the policies on which the practices are based.

This concept we can all relate to in our own experiences, as in one form or another we have been involved in jobs or practices at work or in our community that seem to be based on ideas or policies that we believe are not viable, and afterwards have resulted in negative consequences. Therefore we often experience different ways of thinking—in other words, sometimes coming from different sets of values. These situations create real confusion and frustration, but are very common, and are the results of practices that are based on policies that need to be thought through carefully.

As a next step, beyond the policy level in organizations, it was necessary to identify and examine the assumptions or principles that underpin the policies. At this point one begins to see more clearly the real thinking or assumed "truths" on which the policies have been based in the first place. From that standpoint it becomes quite clear which beliefs or values underpin these principles that form the very root of our thinking both at a personal as well as at an organizational level. Therefore, from the examination of the principles, we soon arrive at deep-seated beliefs or values that underpin the principles and affect the whole process. Here lies the ROOT—the root values, the basic building blocks so to speak for all our thinking, attitudes, behaviors and actions.

The following step in this search process involved separating the values into two groups—the ones that have had positive outcomes, and the ones that have resulted in negative practices. The positive values, naturally, we want to preserve, and the negative ones we need to rethink. This step sometimes led to examining often "forgotten" values that have proven valuable for positive human development over thousands of years. Finally, combining all of these values (positive and rethought ones) began to form the beginning of a new, sustainable base of "universal" values (transcending cultural differences) that could be helpful as a guide or foundation for positive human development.

Today, studies on the topic of values, and especially "universal" values, are now taking place in very diverse fields, extending from philosophy and religions to the sciences to economics and business. Many of these different views, as has been noted in different sections in this book, have been taken into account in this study. One wide-ranging international study is the comprehensive work completed by the United Nations and published as the Earth Charter,[8] a document that is accepted by all cultures and countries as an agreed upon set of values and principles underpinning a positive human role on the planet.

The Earth Charter states:

"The most important influences shaping the ideas and values in the Earth Charter are contemporary science, international law, the wisdom of the world's great religions and philosophical traditions, the declarations and reports of the seven UN summit conferences held during the 1990s, the global ethics movement, numerous nongovernmental declarations and people's treaties issued over the past thirty years, and best practices for building sustainable communities."

The Earth Charter, combined with examples of other international studies, such as the ones mentioned above, have thus served as a broadly based framework of positive values on which we can build.

For this basic framework to work, it has also become clear that the whole process of examination of values requires beginning at the personal level first, with the examination of our own deeply held personal values and beliefs. That forms the foundation for all the following steps—rethinking relationships at home and at work, attitudes to nature and the universe. Then at a practical level we need to rethink the values related to organizations. At each step a new solid foundation of positive values needs to be formed. Once that happens it appears that long-term positive outcomes become possible. In other words, if the foundation is positive and solid (value base) the rest of the organizational decisions and practices will very likely be solid and sustainable for the long term.

The complexities of our deeply held universal values form the central core of this important sector of the book. Here we find the root of our thinking, and it appears, the deep source of our blockage. Now that we as humans have virtually taken control over much of the management of life on Earth, it is imperative that we look at ourselves and our innermost values to understand what needs to be done to redirect our thinking, values and actions toward long-term sustainability.

B. EMERGING VALUES OVERVIEW[9]

Emerging values in this section have been divided into groups to provide more clarity as well as show the connections that exist among the values. These groups are:

-- Values Related to the Self:
These values show our deeply felt beliefs concerning the very nature of human beings, and how we perceive the role of humans in everyday life and interpersonal relationships.

-- Values Related to Family, Work and Community:
Building on the self, these values relate to how we view our family relationships and responsibilities, work attitudes, expectations and responsibilities, and finally values related to our relationship with our local community where we live and belong.

-- Values Related to Earth and the Cosmos:
These values show our perception of the role of nature in our lives, how it is linked to our everyday well-being, our work and our attitudes and behaviors in everyday life. It also includes our perception of outer space, the cosmos, and how it is interconnected with our lives, as well as its importance in comprehending the concept of a meaningful life, including spirituality in its broad sense.

C. PERSONAL VALUES: RELATIONSHIP WITH SELF

(i) Love: An All-encompassing Value[10]
"Perennial wisdom" encompasses the value "love" in its broadest sense, and most of our deeply felt personal values are housed under the umbrella of love, that is, interconnected with and imbedded

in the concept of love. Most also have an interpersonal aspect. Love involves two important aspects: love of others (including all living beings and nature) and love of self. Both are essential for a healthy and meaningful life. Let us examine some of the values that grow out of love in the light of their depth of meaning related to our intellect combined with our higher consciousness.

Undoubtedly the greatest and most complex of human values is our capacity for love. But the concept of love is often misunderstood, as it is often limited to the narrow concept of romantic love.

Love in its all-encompassing meaning forms the foundation for most of our positive human values, and is often associated with compassion in the sense of consideration for others. Love also includes a number of other values such as joy, kindness and generosity, and forgiveness, among others.[11] [12] [13]

One may ask: If love is human nature at its essence, why are we often seeing the manifestation of the opposite characteristics around us?

Why do we see so much conflict and humans killing each other?

Why do we see so much mistrust, selfishness and greed—looking out for our own self-interest?

Why do we see so much violence in general?

Many scholars over the years have studied these contradictions, and the results of these studies have often been controversial.[14] It appears that much of the controversy relates to the different interpretations of human nature.[15] Since the Scientific Revolution particularly, there has evolved the concept of man as being motivated only by his personal self-interest, as well as being in a constant struggle and competition for survival, based on much of the work of Darwin.[16] These beliefs have been central to the philosophies of the most modern Western industrial societies.[17] However, during the past two to three decades especially, it has become clear that the policies and practices that have grown out of these philosophies are being questioned as many of them have become destructive to our human well-being and that of the whole Earth. As a result we are seeing within scholarly communities, and among many visionaries, as well as in civil society, a new quiet but dramatic questioning of conventional thinking related to the nature of man and our role on this Earth.[18] This has grown into a far-reaching force, which is beginning to question conventional "truths" about human nature.

This particular study is a part of this new rethinking of our reality. At the heart or foundation of this transformation, which Laszlo[19] calls a major "shift" in thinking, lies our newfound understanding of the nature of human beings—one that places the human element in a positive light based on the concepts of perennial wisdom. This new thinking, therefore, is based on a philosophy that takes into account our human capacity for high consciousness, or spirituality, in addition to intellectual capacities. This "new thinking" seriously questions many of the values upon which conventional thinking is founded.

Hence we can now speak of love as one of the most admirable of qualities that humans have shown to possess.[20] But what has gone wrong to produce the negative human responses we are experiencing in society?

According to studies in the field it appears that our capacity to love is a value that we all possess, but we are experiencing blockages that have not permitted love to flourish. According to some scholars these barriers in our lives include: fear, greed, anger, jealousy and pride[21]—values linked to our conventional thinking. These are incompatible with love and thus seem to block the development of our positive human attributes. Many of these blockages we can easily identify from our own experiences in life, and most people still consider these as natural human characteristics that we have to live with. This is the main conventional view, and many organizations have policies designed to encourage or control some of these human tendencies, depending on their affect on the organization's economic success.

Returning to love as a complex and core value, another of its major components involves compassion. Compassion involves our natural desire to help others—without expecting anything in return. Combined with this value is kindness and generosity, as these two values are essential for us to genuinely feel compassion for others, especially the ones less fortunate than ourselves.[22] Showing love is an act of giving of oneself from the heart for the benefit of another person without expecting anything in return. This act of love has for many people also helped them to rediscover other positive values of their own. It has often "brought out the best" in people, so to speak, enriching them in ways never imagined—such as increased kindness, generosity, empathy and forgiveness. It has been instrumental in many cases as the catalyst for "service" to others and to the community.[23] Service has often acted as a type of therapy in this transitional trans-formative period in which we live, where helping others has proven to be the catalyst for bringing out other positive values that we had either not been aware of before or values that had laid dormant for many years.

These sometimes almost unconscious or dormant values related to love surround us every day and seem to appear almost unexpect-edly at times of great crisis or tragic events. For example, we can all recall times when we have felt quite overwhelmed and even surprised by the natural goodness of people (often complete strangers) when there occurred an emergency, such as we have seen in cases of natural disasters such as floods, earthquakes or horrific storms. These experi-ences seem to demonstrate that we humans must inherently possess values that are not necessarily apparent in everyday life, but exist and may lie dormant for long periods.

Joy is another aspect of love, and we all have the capacity to feel joy. This seems an obvious statement, but much depends on how we define or think of the word joy. The meaning of joy can be very superficial, such as enjoyment that can come from acquiring new consumer goods. This is the aspect of joy, and "happiness," that our conventional value system tells us is true happiness and joy. However, many people are no longer finding joy in acquiring "things," and are looking inward to try to find something else that gives them joy related to a deeper meaning.[24] This exercise is related to the human need to search for a deeper meaning in life through the awakening of our inner consciousness, and the joy that comes from inner peace, tranquility and depth of meaning in life. This type of joy usually comes quietly but with tremendous impact on everything we do. This profound joy we feel, for example, in interpersonal relationships, or our apprecia-tion of nature and its many awe-inspiring gifts.

Therefore, joy in our everyday life often comes from small, ordinary things that together are a part of an incomprehensible whole.

Things such as a beautiful sunset, a walk in the woods, or simply a small kind act from a stranger are examples of things that can bring joy. In addition, of course, we have the great events in our lives, such as a birth, a marriage, a birthday, a special holiday, all of which involve other human relationships to make them full of joy.

(ii) Self-respect[25]

For us to respect ourselves we must basically feel that we are worthy people. We have to feel that we are basically good, have intrinsic value, and fulfill a valuable purpose in this life. We need self-respect and confidence in our own worth before we can genuinely feel respect for others. Here we often feel socially related blockages as we struggle with deeply felt self-esteem and self-image. The world outside often places value on aspects that have little relationship to our own values on which our self-respect is seated. This can cause confusion and stress, when we live with conflicting values—often one set of values in our world outside, and another within.

(iii) Purpose and Personal Discipline

In our thoughts, we need to feel a sense of personal purpose in life. This gives meaning to all relationships with others as well as a sense of a positive future. The concept of a positive future brings out a sense of purpose for contributing something useful in society, and this provides personal fulfillment at the same time. All relationships and activities resulting from this bring with them a natural sense of responsibility for one's behaviors and actions in order to make positive things happen. Combined with this value comes a sense of personal discipline, a value that Gandhi considered extremely important.[26] Personal discipline is essential in everything we do. Without personal discipline, all the positive behaviors and actions, and the feeling of deep meaning itself, will eventually falter, and the results are often deep disappointment and loss of confidence in and respect for ourselves—we may begin to doubt our sense of worth. Consequently, personal discipline goes hand in hand with a deep sense of purpose in life.

(iv) Truthfulness or Honesty[27] [28]

This value is related first and foremost to how we view our-selves—are we really allowing ourselves to see our true self, or are we covering up something that we do not want to expose to the light of day because we are ashamed or fearful or hurt when it is men-tioned? Once these aspects are pulled out of their hidden place in our minds (or we may be fortunate and not have these deep-seated concerns) and examined, we have come a long way along the path to being genuinely truthful to ourselves. Even for those of us who think we have no deep-seated concerns, it is amazing the things we learn about ourselves, and our deep beliefs, when we confront a cri-sis or very unpleasant situation. This examination process is a very important one, as the concept of "knowing thyself" is essential for inner tranquility and peace of mind, as well as our ability to develop meaningful relationships with others, and being truthful and honest in these relationships.

The concept of honesty or truthfulness is one that is highly val-ued in everyday life, and especially in the working world. It creates tremendous problems when one or more people begin to doubt that the concept of honesty exists in a particular situation. This doubt has led to destroyed human relationships as well as serious work-related problems. The relationship between truthfulness and trust forms an indispensable bond. It is the glue that allows us to live and work together in society harmoniously and provides the foundation for realizing common goals. The value of trust is discussed more fully later.

In the working world, some of the most complex problems have arisen when the legal system and its regulations have collided with our moral understanding of truthfulness or honesty. The common expression of something being legal but not honest has highlighted the difficulties of trying to legislate honesty in the sense of morality in its broadest sense. Obviously, morality can come only from within the human being. Thus we often have a clash between a person who is morally honest on the one side, and another who is not, but can legally hide behind the laws in the judicial system. Presumably the laws have been written by honest people, but it demonstrates what can happen when morality enters into the legal picture for interpretation from different perspectives. This indicates the importance of decision makers being morally honest if our organizations and institutions are to work positively for the benefit of all the people who are affected by their decisions.

Another complication arises in organizations that work across cultures. What is considered honest in one culture may be different in another. This difficulty naturally creates monumental problems. To solve the problem organizations have to try to understand the cultures of both countries, and search into their deep values to find some common ground—basically universal values that are common to both. From that point they can come to common understandings and establish agreed-upon values (and common meanings) and policies that do not undermine the culture of either country. This process has had success in a number of cross-cultural country issues where differences occur.

(v) Trust[29]

The concept of trust has two important components for each of us. One is related to how much we trust ourselves and the other is related to our trust of others.

It may seem a strange phenomena, but one of the values that provides us with a strong and positive foundation is our capacity to trust ourselves, that is, our thinking, and our behaviors. If we feel secure and confident within ourselves as human beings it is likely we will also trust ourselves in terms of how we view another person, how we judge others, and our behaviors in many different kinds of situations. On the other hand, if we are uneasy, unsure of how to react to a situation or person, we sometimes doubt or trust our own capacities. This can lead to anxiety and further doubt and insecurity. Therefore, our capacity to trust ourselves appears closely related to our other values, such as self-respect and self-worth, which create confidence in oneself and one's reactions.

Trusting others has an additional dimension. Trusting someone leaves us open to a more vulnerable situation—we are as such in the hands of another person, because if we trust that person, many of our own feelings, attitudes, behaviors and actions will be dependent on another person with whom we are linked in a trust relationship.

When that person upholds our trust, we both benefit tremendously in a deeply felt mutual human relationship. If, however, as happens in some cases, a person does not uphold our trust, we feel hurt and vulnerable. At times such as this, our strength to withstand the situation, and our ability to maintain our faith in the basic goodness of humans, depends very much on the solidness of our other deeply felt personal values.

We cannot live full and happy lives without trust. Every relationship depends on trust, whether it be family, friends, work or our community-related activities. Therefore trust has to become a vital value for a fulfilling and meaningful personal as well as working life.

(vi) Nonviolence[30]

This human characteristic is one that creates a great deal of confusion in its interpretation. Therefore it deserves special attention.

In essence nonviolence is not just the absence of war, or dislike for war, as is often the assumption. It has a far deeper meaning, and is related to a nonviolent way of thinking, nonviolent attitudes and behaviors every day.

Nonviolence begins basically with how we think and how we approach everyday life. Do we see life as a constant competition for survival, where we need to fight for everything we have in life, and accept life as a win-lose battle? Or do we believe in cooperation, dialogue, and a willingness to resolve differences?

Historically probably the best known advocate of nonviolence was Mahatma Gandhi,[31] and he was followed later by other highly respected visionaries, such as Martin Luther King. One of Gandhi's three most important principles, satyagraha, or nonviolent direct action, is in fact a way of life, not just an absence of violence. He believed that to carry out nonviolent actions one needed to be disciplined. This means self-restraint in what Gandhi called "sensory urges and consumptions." This also means respect for all beings, and a devotion to the values of love, truth and responsibility.

As Ela Gandhi[32] (Mahatma Gandhi's granddaughter) wrote, "The Gandhian way is gaining ever more support as people find it gives guidance in both how to resist destructive processes and how to build constructive ones from a position of inner moral strength."

Today Gandhi's thinking is gaining new relevance as we are going through a process of dramatic change at the very essence of our being—the examination of our fundamental personal values, and moving toward non-violence as a natural human attribute. The "Gandhian way" also has Love as its central core and as the essence of human nature.

(vii) Humility[33]

Humility flourishes in an environment where love exists, and is an essential value that is closely related to our respect for nature and hence for all living beings. We are conscious of the fragility and insignificance of humans when experiencing, with a sense of awe, the complexity, enormity and beauty of the world around us. This humility is essential for our everyday lives, in all our interpersonal relationships and as an extension of our close relationship with and respect for nature as our source of life. It is a value often considered within our conventional thinking as a weakness, and one that often causes concern today because people may have a tendency to take advantage of us, and perhaps use this "advantage" to become "successful" economically in the shorter term. This thinking tends to trap us in a whole web of negative human characteristics, such as greed, jealousy and pride, which appear to have contributed to our present dilemma.

Nevertheless, humility does not mean acting without intelligence. It does mean that we need to learn to listen carefully to consider other points of view, and sincerely try to understand the reasons for the differences of opinion. It also means nonviolence in thinking and behavior, as dialogue is considered essential to resolve conflicts and differences of opinion.[34] And finally it means that we allow our faith in the inherent goodness of human beings to come to the fore. Indeed, humility is essential for love to flourish. We should remember that some of the most respected and admired visionaries have mostly been humble people, in spite of their vast knowledge, wisdom and international recognition.

D. EMERGING VALUES AND WAY OF LIFE

The key emerging values evident in this transition period also lead us to examine what we usually refer to as "our way of life." This involves gaining new insight into how our deeply rooted human values play out in our everyday way of life. To summarize some aspects, following are a few significant ones that can provide food for thought:

i) Intrinsic right to life:[35] All our thoughts, attitudes and behaviors show our intrinsic belief that our way of life must be mindful of the intrinsic rights to life for others. This becomes a sort of lens through which we reexamine our present-day attitudes and behaviors, before any actions take place. This belief has dramatic implications for everyday living, as the needs and inherent rights of others become part of our thinking and concern in all our daily decisions and actions.

ii) Satisfy needs, not wants:[36] This forms the essence of responsibility for living within limitations of nature, controlling greed, and finding creative ways of living this belief during this transition period when most of the people surrounding us may be still in the "wants mode." Most are finding that small quiet examples in everyday thinking and actions are the place to begin to have an impact. Little by little these increase and gradually change our whole way of thinking and acting in all aspects of life. We also tend to "infect" others with our way of thinking.

iii) Spiritual dimension in life:[37] This refers to spirituality in its broadest sense—a higher consciousness, that is the capacity of humans to perceive unseen and deep realities beyond the world we can see and feel. It is at this deeper, innermost level that we find the real feeling of peace and inner tranquility. This is where we sense real meaning and purpose in life and work, and where genuine depth of relationships share common ground. It is this world of the unexplainable, where we often sense that "there has to be something more" to working and living than just making money and spending it. The wonderful aspect of this deeper spiritual world is that we as humans all have the capacity to experience it through the development of our natural capacity for higher consciousness.

iv) Being vs. doing:[38] Presently we live in a world where only "doing" seems to be highly valued. We are constantly busy "doing," not only during the working day, but also in our free time. How often have you been asked: What did you do last weekend? Your answer will usually involve happily reporting some "doing" activity, which in turn draws an appreciative and interested response. But if you spent the weekend reading or listening to music or walking in a quiet landscape you will probably respond, "I didn't do anything," even though the weekend was very important to your inner feeling of quiet and tranquility. This balance between "outer world activity" and the "inner world being" is essential for our human happiness and fulfillment, and we need to find time for both if we hope to restore the essence of positive human values and behaviors—to make "the outer world activity" balanced with our "inner world being."

v) Wisdom: The concept of wisdom is often confused with knowledge, as has been described in the previous section. We have knowledge in abundance, especially with the explosion of new technologies over the past three decades. However, it appears that we have been suffering a severe shortage of wisdom (which includes higher consciousness) to accompany all the new knowledge, in order to ensure its positive use.

Roger Walsh[39] identifies the main existential and spiritual issues in life that involve developing our higher consciousness combined with knowledge to form genuine wisdom. He summarizes our most important issues as:
-- finding meaning and purpose in our lives,
-- managing relationships and aloneness,
-- acknowledging our limits and smallness in a universe vastly beyond comprehension,
-- living in inevitable uncertainty and mystery,
-- dealing with sickness, suffering and death.

These major issues in life, as identified by Walsh, can only be fully realized through development of wisdom—the combination of higher consciousness and knowledge.

Striving for wisdom therefore appears essential for humans if we are to achieve true happiness, fulfillment and a meaningful life. In order to develop our capacity for wisdom we must then search beyond the present-day technological world, which reveres knowledge, to the inner world of our higher consciousness in order to acquire the understanding and insight essential for wisdom. We now know that it is within human capacity to achieve.

vi) Future generations:[40] If we believe in the dignity of humans and our fundamental right to life, then we must also feel an instinctive sense of responsibility for the rights of future generations to have the same opportunities as ourselves, that is, to have a healthy, natural environment and an adequate supply of natural resources for their benefit. This responsibility becomes a lens through which all human activity is viewed, and decision makers take seriously into account in project planning, as well as all of us involved in the development of our own communities.

There is another aspect of future generation responsibility not often mentioned in this context. This deals with our responsibility for education and "formation" of our youth.[41] This responsibility falls principally on parents, demonstrated by their own values shown through their attitudes and behaviors. However, the surrounding community needs to demonstrate similar values consistent with our emerging values. In this way the children and youth in general receive a consistent approach to what are considered acceptable values, attitudes and behaviors for them to emulate. This responsibility for youth also extends to interpersonal relationships, both at the family and community levels, providing a solid grounding for the young as they venture out into the broader society.

This responsibility is a complex one, as our conventional thinking places pressures especially on efficiency and time and the need to possess as many things as possible.[42] This draws parents into long working hours, and often frustration in not having sufficient time with their children, plus the exposure of children to many negative values that may not be compatible with their parental values. Parents need to be very creative and dedicated to their families in order to instill positive values in their children that may not be in rhythm with conventional values. History has shown the deeply engrained values of the young are the ones that they draw on heavily when they themselves become parents.

In conclusion, the values we tend to "value" most are naturally the ones that are associated with what is "valued" in society.[43] These provide us also with our motivation in work and daily life. Today in our conventional society these values are naturally associated with the consumer society. Therefore all our ingenuity and energy is mostly directed toward the things that this society considers important. This also means that the human characteristics that are dominant and accepted as normal parts of everyday life include such characteristics as pride, greed, jealousy, fear and anger. These characteristics have become common in our society and have formed barriers to allowing the natural human values related to love, for example, to come through. Therefore it appears that when we begin to shift our values at the deep personal level, then we consciously or unconsciously begin to change what we "value" in society. Once this happens our motivations in life and work begin to change as well, and society gradually begins to place value on new aspects. This shift is already beginning in some areas as people continue to question conventional values. This whole shift in what society values naturally affects our everyday motivations and goals, as well as our organizational goals, allowing our positive emerging values to come forward, and at the same time weakening and overpowering the negative aspects. Thus, during this transition period we may tend to live in "two realities"—one that mostly satisfies the conventional system on which our livelihood mostly depends at present, and the other parallel one of emerging new values and purpose in life in the long term, toward which we are moving.

E. PERSONAL VALUES: RELATIONSHIP WITH FAMILY, WORK AND COMMUNITY

This section, concerning the emerging values that are considered positive within the family, our working life and the community where we live, is really an application or an extension of our personal values as described in the previous section. Readers will find this foundation penetrating all aspects of thinking and behaviors in a broad spectrum of human experience and behavior.

(i) Relationship with the Family[44]

a) Love and security: As we grow from infancy to childhood, our first contact is with our parents and other members of our family. It is within the family unit where we develop the essence of our values from the time we are very young. Most medical researchers believe that the most sensitive formative years are from birth to about three years of age. These are the years when children, through the love and security of parents and family, form their basic sense of emotional security, and where they sense their first almost unconscious sense of deep values. These are transmitted unconsciously at times from the parents and family members through their love and behavior toward the child. Specialists tell us that we should never underestimate the importance of these early years for the child's sense of security, love and healthy emotional development.

b) Ethics/morality:[45] As children grow the family becomes the first social situation where they learn to interact with other human beings—feel love, feel protected, and the first feelings of what is right or wrong. This concept of right and wrong becomes very important in the child's relationship with other children as well as older members of the family and in the school environment, and forms the basis for a solid foundation of positive values.

c) Self-discipline and cooperation:[46] Developing into school age the child learns to interact with others, learns cooperation, consideration for others, and socializing in general. This also means developing self-discipline, and thinking before acting. Taking responsibility for their own actions naturally follows, and learning to help others becomes a normal part of everyday life. The values passed on to children during this period, specialists tell us, are important in forming the core of their values in later life. The family especially, combined with school life, clearly are the foremost places for establishing positive values that will affect their future interpersonal relationships, their work, their relationship with their local community, and their sense of self-discipline and responsibility when they relate to the world outside.

(ii) Relationship with Work

a) Self-confidence and self-discipline:[47] Following our early experience within the family unit, school and community comes what is often a traumatic experience, that of our first job. This usually represents the first time that we are "on our own" so to speak. This is a time when we draw very much on the values we have learned from home in respect to our attitudes and "work ethic." Now our basic values are being tested for the first time. For the first time we do not have parents to protect us if something goes wrong. We have to find our own path—learning about new environments with often strange or different ways of thinking from what we are used to. Our personal self-confidence and sense of self-discipline will be tested. We must feel confident that these differences do not negate our own values, but realize that different people have different values and we need to find ways to understand them and to accommodate the differences. This requires a high level of self-confidence and self-discipline as we search for commonalities in values. This builds integrity of character for the future, as experience shows that situations will arise where our values will be questioned and we are tempted to compromise them.

b) **Tolerance, trust and cooperation:**[48] We will need to learn tolerance of others who think or look different from ourselves. There are many different cultures in the world, and each deserves the same basic human respect. Through tolerance we also learn to cooperate with others in order to do our job, learn respect for others and trust them, including authority, and feel confident enough in ourselves to ask someone when we need help. We learn that we are one small but important part of the whole, and want to feel fulfillment in contributing our part to the success of the whole, whatever be the organization or situation. Here lies the essence of the human need for dialogue and cooperation, in place of conflict. Here also lies the situation where commonly held "universal" values are found that everyone can agree on and can be used as a foundation for future behaviors and actions.

c) **Fulfillment:**[49] As we gain experience we begin to realize that work provides many different needs, in addition to making money to spend. These human needs often become the markers for continuing in a job or moving to an alternative where they can be met.

Here often lies the problem during this period of transition—

moving from thinking about work as essentially a way of earning money to work as an essential part of our emotional well-being and feeling of fulfillment in life.

In recent years many scholars have studied the concept of the changing role of work, and why work is considered such an important part of our lives.

Conventional economics considers work as a cost on the financial statement. The cost of work is compared to the cost of technologies or machines, and whichever is most "cost effective" is selected. This places the concept of work in a purely economic box. The motivation in work is considered basically to make money, and the organization employing us provides expectations of our work being economically profitable.

This concept of work is changing. This has brought us to study anew some of the wisdom of such economists such as Schumacher, who brought out some enlightening concepts about work from the Buddhist point of view, which seems to provide some valuable food for thought in our process of thinking about the real human importance of work.

Schumacher[50] explains that Buddhist thinking takes the function of work to be threefold;

i) it gives a person a chance to utilize and develop his faculties.

ii) it enables a person to overcome his ego-centredness by joining with other people in a common task.

iii) it brings forth the goods and services needed for a becoming existence.

Schumacher also explains the Buddhist concept of leisure. He states that "to strive for leisure as an alternative to work would be considered a complete misunderstanding of one of the basic truths of human existence, namely, that work and leisure are complementary parts of the same living process and cannot be separated without destroying the joy of work and the bliss of leisure.

"The Buddhist sees the essence of civilization not in a multiplication of wants but in the purification of human character. Character, at the same time, is formed primarily by a man's work. And work, properly conducted in condition of human dignity and freedom, blesses those who do it and equally their products."

Schumacher indicates that "If a man has no chance of obtaining work he is in a desperate position, not simply because he lacks income, but because he lacks this nourishing and enlivening factor of disciplined work which nothing can replace."

These concepts of work may on one side seem rather strange, but on the other side seem to point to many of the concerns and frustrations working people often feel today. Some of these were brought out in the survey at the beginning of the book, which indicated the dissatisfaction so often related to work, and the need for meaning in our everyday activities, as well as the need to have a common values base that is compatible with both work and personal life.

The concept of work as a positive and fulfilling activity is also closely related to the size of the organization. In order for workers at all levels to feel a part of the whole and able to participate and contribute to their fullest is very closely associated with how we as humans relate to the concept of size.

As Schumacher says, "There are three things healthy people most need to do—to be creatively productive, to render service, and to act in accordance with their moral impulses. . . . In a big organization our freedoms to do so (act according to our moral impulses) is inevitably severely restricted. Our primary duty is to stay within the rules and regulations, which although contrived by human beings, are not themselves human beings. . . . The bigger the organization, the less is it possible for any member of it to act freely as a moral being." He goes on to conclude that often "big organizations behave immorally, not because the people inside them are immoral, but simply because the organization carries the load of bigness."

Therefore one can conclude that the large organization is beyond "human scale" and hence not sustainable for the long term. Its size means that it cannot provide basic human fulfillment based on the thinking of Schumacher [51] and other visionary scholars today. Even more concerning is that the very principles on which it rests naturally tend to be not human or ecologically focused or balanced, but focused on purely economic-based values and shorter term profit maximization. As a result we have large-scale organizations that do not have genuine sustainable criteria at their root when selecting their product or service's major focus, as their basic values do not include a foundation of sustainable values on which to build a genuinely sustainable organization, including the objectives and policies that follow. This would suggest the eventual transformation of large unsustainable organizations into medium and small sized independent entities. This is an important topic that requires in-depth studies of its own.

d) Empowerment: This concept is a much used term today, but it had its roots many decades ago as a concept related to the natural human need to feel some sense of meaningful participation in the workplace and how the work was done.

Schumacher related the loss of empowerment to the development of large-scale organizations in which people lost their possibility for empowerment.

In his concern over the problems of bigness and the human aspect in work, Schumacher stated:[52]

"On a small scale people's power (empowerment) can be mobilized but when the scale becomes too large, people's power becomes frustrated and ineffective." People's power refers to the need for human beings to participate meaningfully in an organization where their contributions are fully recognized and utilized. A few larger organizations that are aware of the real value of human beings for their viable future have managed to rethink their organizational structures and incorporate some smaller independent units. However, as Schumacher pointed out with reference to size, the difficulty lies in the corporate control that invariably still exists over all these smaller units.

Today the concept of empowerment and new emerging work-related values are "bubbling up" in many organizations. Working people are looking for working life that respects their deep values and provides a source of meaningful and genuine participation, and a feeling of fulfillment in these efforts. Thus work provides an essential part of a complete and happy life.

(iii) Relationship with Community[53]

The concept of community is one that appears at first sight easy to understand, but once we begin to gain insight into its meaning in the context of our changing world, it becomes complex and begins to take on new and important meaning.

In essence the concept of communities where we live has existed for many centuries, but the meaning of communities for human well-being and viable development of regions and countries has changed dramatically, especially over the past three decades.

Why are communities important for human happiness and viable development? This has been a topic of much controversy, and one that has been much discussed in both the public and private sector. Perhaps the simplest way of tracing its function in society is to provide an overview of the role the community has played over the past recent history.

a) Traditional and present-day communities: Prior to the dramatic explosion of development in the fields of communication, transportation and world trade, communities were relatively stable. They provided a sense of belonging and a sense of security for the inhabitants. In fact they formed the backbone of stability in most countries.

With the advent of modern technologies, whole populations have been drawn into mobility. Modern transport, new communications and other technologies have drawn massive numbers of people from rural to urban areas. Farming has become largely nonviable except for large industrially run enterprises, and opportunities are located principally in large urban regions—the metropolis. Economics and large-scale thinking began to take priority over all other human considerations. Schumacher was concerned about this development many years ago.[54] He believed, "This idolatry of giantism, is based on modern technology, particularly as it concerns transport and communications. It has one immensely powerful effect: It makes people FOOTLOOSE."

This footlooseness of a large part of the population in the West has affected profoundly the concept of communities. These have been broken up as people search for new opportunities in cities where they have no roots. Everyone has become mobile. This concept has been accelerated by the advent of unrestricted trade (usually referred to as free trade). Country borders are being erased and much of the work in many countries depends a small number of gigantic companies or consortiums, and work in one region or community can depend on markets on the other side of the globe. This situation has created what we call a "stress" or "risk" society.[55] People have lost control of their sense of security and control over their lives as a whole. People live with uncertainty in work, and uncertainty in their home life, with no traditional community or family support systems. It is a mobile, individualistic society.

The largest percentage of trade today is financial, requiring country governments to place top priority on the requirements involving world trade-related issues (such as paying their interest on international debt) while the majority of the populations, especially in the developing countries, are becoming more marginalized. The consequences of these events have been the breakup of local communities, increased social unrest, un/underemployment and the rise in underground employment, crime, and a general lack of personal safety. This social insecurity and instability in turn has begun to affect governments, concerned with capital attraction, and the vicious circle of further increased poverty, insecurity and further breakdown of communities, due to the dire economic necessity, and the need to go where jobs may be found. This has also lead to increased central control to manage public unrest.

We live in a world where giantism in all its forms is the controlling force in society, with the accompanying disintegration of the communities and families that provide the foundation for local, regional, and country stability and long-term viability.

Fortunately, many visionaries, local leaders, and a large part of civil society are beginning to recognize the vital importance of communities, and their need to recover control over their own lives and development.

b) Emerging communities: Gradually communities are becoming aware of their key role in society, related both to personal well-being as well as their role in establishing stable employment and self-sufficiency on a broader scale.

A highly respected economist and international development visionary, David Korten,[56] in his book *The Post Corporate World*, stated:

"One of the greatest challenges is to create caring communities that nurture our wholeness. Wholeness and coherence in one's own life and relationships are essential foundations of both individual freedom and the coherence of society. These in turn are the products of loving relationships that nurture our individual and collective capacities for civility."

Korten's views clearly place deeply felt values at the foundation for the development of sustainable communities. These views are becoming more common among an increasing number of visionaries. It appears that the formation and nurturing of healthy communities forms the foundation for healthy social and economic development, as well as the restoration and conservation of our natural environment. This means that communities are being recognized as filling a broad-based new and vital role in both a fulfilling life for individuals and families, as well as forming a foundation for sustainable governance of related regions and countries.

Based on experience and research in many countries, the community level is the key and initial level of governance essential for viable development. It has been shown that the more local control communities have the more stable and socially viable is the community, and the region that groups of communities form.[57] This seems to be the case whether it involves rural, village or urban settings. However, important differences do exist in the development of sustainable rural and urban communities. Urban communities are growing very rapidly, especially in developing countries, where mostly rural, poor populations are flocking to large cities in search of work.[58] Many studies now exist describing both rural and urban sustainable community development, but the limitations of this study will not expand on the details of this development—but will focus on the values that underpin sustainable communities. Apparently the solidness of the values that underpin healthy communities is vital to produce positive local activities, which in turn provide the upper levels of government with positive development models, as well as establishing a sound basis for social stability and viable economic sustainability.

c) Values and sustainable communities: Sustainable communities possess a number of values that are characteristic of the majority, with some differences due to their rural or urban settings and the economic strength of each. These values flow from a composite of wisdom that has its roots in universal values. Consequently, for most communities in the process of rethinking their roles, the participants individually will need to reexamine their personal values at a deep level to develop a commonly held set of values applicable to the whole community. This provides a foundation that can result in sustainable processes and viable results for the longer term.

Based on the work of a number of researchers,[59] some important values related to sustainable communities are discussed below. Many others can also be included, but for the purpose of this study a brief summary that directly reflects sustainable values are included.

1. Participation and responsibility
2. Solidarity
3. Lifelong education
4. "Common good," and ecology
5. Nonviolence and dialogue
6. Service

1. Participation:

The participation of all its inhabitants is essential to make the community strong and thriving. This requires development of mutual respect, cooperation and compassion—for the benefit of the whole community. This participation also brings out the human satisfaction of helping others—making it a better place to live, and creating a sense of belonging and responsibility to help keep it viable and thriving.

People living in communities are becoming more aware of the responsibilities that accompany full participation and forms the basis for the privileges and rights of all community members. Communities increasingly are finding ways of regaining control over their lives—in the sense that they have renewed control over their community economic development projects, and their ecological conservation and social issues. That also means controlling the financial resources earmarked for the community, and a responsibility for their positive outcomes.

This may seem a giant step back, as the tendency in our conventional development model has been toward more centralization of control at higher levels of governance. This has left communities to languish and the inhabitants to lose interest as their rights gradually disappear and they lose control of their lives. On the other hand, the changes that are now occurring are indicating a total change from the conventional thinking related to the role of communities in society.

2. Solidarity:[60]

This includes the development of mutual respect among all members of the community; cooperation and dialogue related especially to agreeing on a common purpose; consideration for different views; development of strength and cohesion that accompanies a focus on a common purpose; and a strong sense of responsibility and self-discipline needed to achieve the goals set together and to feel commitment to put forth one's best efforts for the benefit of all the members of the community.

3. Lifelong Education:[61]

In addition to ensuring the best quality education possible for children and youth, communities need the facilities for its members to have opportunities for lifelong education. This is particularly important at present with the rapidly changing world scene as we pass through this period of transition. To make well-thought-out decisions for the local community requires a good level of global knowledge, creative ideas, and the strength and courage for sound planning to carry the plans to fruition. Education also encourages increased participation, local job opportunities, self-confidence and proactive tendencies. It also places the community in a stronger and more effective position when dealing with issues at higher levels of governance.

An additional development related to lifelong education is concerned with the fairly recent development of new types of "global communities" via electronic communication. This has brought together people with common concerns and interests from many locations and broadened our knowledge of how our local regions can benefit from global solidarity and new knowledge.

4. "Common good" and ecology:[62]

All plans and activities at the community level have the purpose of contributing to the common good (benefit) of the whole community. This often involves issues affecting neighbouring communities, for example where natural resources such as water may have a common source that must be shared. In some cases even several communities need to work together for the common good of all and at the same time each remains as self-sufficient as possible.

The conservation of natural resources in general, as well as environmental issues, usually involves several communities as they are often sharing a common resource or protecting and restoring a common resource. The whole ecological area is recognized as an essential part of everyday life and must be cared for as an important aspect of the common good.

The concept of common good often extends to the economic development area. For the most part communities strive to be as self-sufficient as possible economically, but projects can sometimes prove more beneficial for everyone if two or three communities cooperate on a project for the economic benefit of all. In this way development decisions are kept at the community level, with horizontal-based equitable agreements.

It should be noted that in the process of project planning the aspects of ecological and social feasibility are considered as top priority before the economic feasibility is taken seriously.

5. Non-violence and dialogue:[63]

All participants in community projects have an inbuilt understanding of cooperation for their common benefit. Conflictive attitudes and behaviors are not considered sustainable, and it is important that each member at the personal level has developed values such as nonviolent thinking and behaviors, and dedication to dialogue as the way to solve differences. Dialogue among community members has shown itself to be a key to consensus-based decision making and long-term sustainability.

6. Service:[64]

The concept of service to others is considered a natural outcome of positive personal values and solidarity. This concept of service, as indicated earlier in the text, means giving of one's time and knowledge (without pay) for the benefit of the whole community. Service, as well as bringing positive results for community projects, brings members closer together and brings out common values and aspirations for themselves and their families.

Within the concept of service the important personal value of love plays a huge role. One of the values that is associated with love is compassion. It is considered central to the concept of service. In practice, service requires the capacity to work with a very diverse group of people, often coming from diverse backgrounds and cultures, and often directed to those most needing help in some form. This concept of service as giving of oneself for the benefit of others is considered a human need that we all possess—our need to give to others without expecting anything in return and feel a depth of meaning and purpose to life in the process.

In conclusion, central to this new role of communities for a viable lifestyle and development, deeply held sustainable values provide the solid foundation of these communities, which in turn form the core for social, ecological and economic stability for regions, countries, and globally.

F. PERSONAL VALUES: RELATIONSHIP WITH EARTH AND THE COSMOS[65]

(i) Earth systems and human thinking

Whether we like to accept it or not, our existence depends on Earth systems combined with complex elements located in outer space. The very air we breathe as we read this page is part of a complex and little-understood natural system that links us and our survival inextricably to the Earth and the cosmos.[66]

Much has become known through science about how our natural systems work, but the scientific knowledge related to how this complex mosaic is interconnected still remains largely a mystery. However, most of our human actions have been seated on our singular dependence on the objective scientific approach, and the way of thinking that accompanies it.

It is through this intellectual scientific mindset that we basically approach all our problems, even those related to the natural world and its systems. Consequently the explanations for our ecological deterioration on Earth and outer space changes, and our responses and "solutions" are proposed using the same singular objective science-based mindset or way of thinking.

What happens to this scientific criteria if we expand the approach to involve our capacity for higher consciousness in addition to the objective intellectual approach?

Thomas Berry provides his summary of what we are discovering:

"Science is discovering a new version of the "enchanted" world that was part of the natural mind for most of human history. Since the loss of this worldview in the last three hundred years is arguably at the heart of our current environmental crisis, its rediscovery may be the key to an eventual solution . . . this missing link between scientific breakthrough and the general consciousness."

A new way of thinking appears to be developing that creates a new perception of reality, resulting in a new way of understanding our reality, and valuing of that reality.

This new understanding and thinking means that:[67]

a) Linear thinking becomes integrated thinking (the whole spectrum of interrelated aspects).

b) Reductionist thinking becomes holistic—moving from studying the smallest, most isolated part or object toward its new reality, where all the aspects that influence its function or use are taken into account, including the often unconscious influence of the observer on the object. That is, we the observers are really part of the observed and unconsciously interact with what we observe.

c) Intellectual objective thinking becomes broadened by considering subjective, higher consciousness experience and "thinking" as also valid, both of which are necessary for arriving at viable solutions compatible with the complexities of nature and the universe as a whole.

This change in approach transforms how we perceive the total realities of Earth and cosmos systems, and as a consequence how we approach our responsibilities as being part of the whole system, and not just a spectator.

Let us now examine some of the key areas where our conventional thinking has resulted in unexpected consequences to the natural environment, and then look anew at these problems through transformed "systems" thinking. This transformation in thinking (including both our higher consciousness as well as intellect) appears to be the key to restoring and preserving our awesome Earth systems and the cosmos to which we are linked.

(ii) Human wisdom and Planet Earth[68]

Human "wisdom" as described in this study comes from the combination of our intellectual capacity combined with our higher consciousness capabilities. As a result of this combination our perception of the Earth and outer space surrounding it totally changes, and we recognize a different reality of who we are and how we fit into the whole picture.

We begin to see the Earth as a living system composed of many subsystems—everything interconnected and interdependent. We see ourselves as an integral part of this whole, as imbedded in the whole system, and dependent and interdependent on the whole. We look in awe at the complex and little-understood incredible Earth systems that are so delicately balanced in order to provide the conditions that make our lives possible. This harmony which exists is often hidden as we go about our everyday work and lives.

The awe-inspiring complexity of this whole phenomena has for example been directly experienced by a number of astronauts. Some tell us that they have returned to Earth as transformed people. Their experiences have had a profound effect on them—a true experience of their higher consciousness. One example of an astronaut who was truly transformed is Edgar Mitchell.[69] When he returned he founded a new scientific-based institution dedicated to studying phenomena related to higher consciousness—moving beyond conventional scientific boundaries in research (pushing the envelope so to speak), and attracting some of the most respected scientists from around the world.

It is interesting to note that many of the highly respected scholars and visionaries in the field of transformative thinking come from science-based disciplines. Something new and positive is clearly happening in the science world. Unfortunately however, the sector that is still the most convinced of the conventional mindset and values that underpin it is found in the large-scale business and economics sectors. These are also the sectors that still control our major economic development activities, and have the major influence on government policies and major media organizations. But even in these sectors we see some positive rethinking bubbling up from the bottom of organizations, most especially in the smaller-sized organizations. This smaller-scale business sector is also the sector where the majority of employment opportunities are or will be developing in the future, and is viewed as a vital sector for positive transformative thinking.

Returning to "alternative thinking," a current is also bubbling up throughout the scientific community. A clear example of this concerns the formation of the highly respected scientific group in 1993 called the Union of Concerned Scientists.[70] This organization consists of 1,670 leading scientists from 70 countries, including 102 Nobel Laureates.

It states: "A new ethic is required. This ethic must motivate a great movement, convincing reluctant leaders and reluctant governments and reluctant people themselves to effect the needed changes. . . . A great change in our stewardship of the Earth and the life on it is required if vast human misery is to be avoided and our global home on this planet is not to be irretrievably mutilated."

They also indicated that human beings and the natural world are on a collision course, and that this may so alter the living world that it will be unable to sustain life as we know it.[71]

(iii) Earth and the cosmos—human responsibilities

The responsibilities of human beings as an integral part of the whole Earth and cosmos can only be fully comprehended, it seems, with the combination of our capacities of intellect and higher consciousness. The responsibilities themselves, on the surface, appear to be a repeat of numerous documents related to environmental studies. But the aspect that is new is the "lens" through which we look when considering these responsibilities. This new emerging mindset, which includes both intellect and consciousness capacities, forms a new lens to fully comprehend the significance of the new values that ensure our continuing life on Earth as we know it.

a) Earth systems: protection and restoration: There is no doubt among even conventional thinkers that we have many damaged ecosystems, worrisome climate change, and loss of a significant number of species and life forms. Some restoration work and new laws have been put into place in a number of countries, but often not evenly applied. Many of the results have been disappointing due to the fact that the principles under which they operate still conform to the conventional mindset. In other words, the values on which they are seated are unsustainable conventional ones. As a result, economic-related priorities in most situations still take precedence over ecologically related considerations. Nevertheless, there are also some encouraging signs in the examples of a few communities organizing to form stiff resistance to economically lucrative short-term projects for some groups, but which have a significant ecological downside for the majority and for the community in the longer term.[72]

In the emerging mindset, we all have the serious responsibility of placing priority on restoration of damaged systems, as well as halting new activities that are significantly ecologically damaging, especially in the longer term. This is a huge challenge and not an easy one.[73] It means taking a new approach to all our activities, in which ecological and social aspects are taken seriously and given equal weight (and sometimes higher) to economic-related aspects. This turns conventional thinking upside down, where economic aspects take priority and longer-term ecological and social aspects are usually considered once the activity or project is well-developed economically.

b) Renewable and non-renewable resources:[74] The Earth and outer space system supply us with a number of vital resources essential for life on Earth. Most of the renewable resources are indispensable for human life. One of these is air— a delicate and complex mixture of elements essential for human and nonhuman life forms. Without air we die very quickly. Other critical renewable resources are water and soil. As we know, only a very small percentage of water on Earth is sweet water, or potable. Its supply is already becoming critical in many arid regions. The same problem holds true for soils. Nutritious food depends directly on healthy soils. To produce food we need fertile soil (in addition to clean water), and presently worldwide we have a severe erosion and chemical pollution problem reducing daily the amount of arable healthy land, as well as destroying subsistence farming for millions of inhabitants.[75]

Another important renewable resource includes sea life of all kinds, which has been the principle food source for millions of people for thousands of years. This system has been confirmed as being at the point of collapse.

Considering even the indispensable resources for life—water, air and soil—these depend directly on the health and survival of our broader natural environment. Therefore, the human element becomes vital in conserving these resources. To receive fresh water (rain) we have to have an abundance of forests; to have unpolluted air we need to stop polluting it with our many sophisticated products and industrial processes; to have fertile soil we need to genuinely take care of the soil and not pollute it with chemicals, nor starve it from needed water. Thus it appears that everything we need to do to have a viable life is in fact in human hands to control. We as humans now basically control the healthy supply of our essential renewable resources—so it is also in our power to protect and restore them—if we wish.

Why aren't we doing so? This present critical situation, some visionaries have noted, is *slow suicide*.

It appears the answer to this important question is: Our conventional mindset does not fully understand or accept the direct connection between our vital elements for life, our natural environment and outer space, and human everyday actions. Here one sees the seriousness of the need for transforming the mindset, that is, combining our highly developed intellectual objectivity with our higher consciousness in order to fully comprehend what we are doing.

The non-renewable resources are in a different category. These resources cannot be replaced, so that once used up, there simply are no more. It seems difficult to believe that we continue to use these resources as rapidly as possible with few concrete plans for alternatives.[76] To conserve these resources as long as possible, the emerging view involves an absolute strict control on their use (with accompanying changes in lifestyles), and at the same time focusing on developing alternatives to substitute when they are finished. This means basically that we can use these resources only at the same rate as we can develop viable alternatives.

(iv) Nature and responsibilities for the future

a) Precautionary principle:[77] In essence the precautionary principle indicates that decision making involving the natural environment should be approached with caution. That is, if an activity does not have credible scientific proof that it will not harm the environment in the longer term, it should not be carried out. The concern underpinning this principle is that if we cannot confirm for certain the ecological effects that will occur as a result of an activity or project in the longer term, we cannot take the chance of being wrong, possibly resulting in unknown catastrophic environmental damage.

This precautionary outlook has not, in most cases, been the practice in the past, or at best considered only short term, involving local ecological consequences. This thinking demonstrates a conventional mindset focused on short-term economic-based objectives, where ecological considerations are secondary and do not fit easily into the short-term profit-maximization policies.

In the future, emerging values require the precautionary principle to be taken seriously for all planning of activities and projects—whether local, national or global. It serves as one concrete way of preventing further damage to the natural systems before activities begin.

b) Projects and planning:[78] Under the conventional guidelines for development projects, major considerations involve three main areas: economic, social and ecological. Of these, the economic considerations take priority and the social and ecological considerations usually have a minor role once the overall economic plan is in place and the project is well-advanced.

In addition, the whole conventional approach to planning, and the mindset that accompanies it, naturally involves the intellectually based quantitative, objective scientific approach. Therefore, even in projects where social and ecological aspects are taken into account, the qualitative side that is needed to understand fully these two aspects does not fit the quantitative, economically focused mindset. For example, the social side, related to the effects of a project on human beings and their lives, usually refers to "standard of living" data (which refers to monetary income). On the other hand, the transformed mindset would consider "quality of life," which takes into account a host of qualitative factors that do not "count" in a conventional approach. An example of this is the limited thinking in long-term consequences that occur when uprooting inhabitants of communities by a project, and leaving the inhabitants rootless, even though most may eventually find some form of alternative work elsewhere (often in city slums).

On the ecological side, due to the conventional short-term economic approach, usually only fairly immediate and localized considerations are taken into account. This has proven to be a mistake, and it is only after the fact that there is a realization that natural systems are interconnected and very complex, that other regions and natural systems are affected, and that all these systems function on a very long-term time scale.

With the emerging values, which take both the intellect and human higher consciousness into account, we begin to consider the three major aspects of planning in a totally different light. These transformed aspects include:

i) Economic aspects: projects take into account the long-term needs of the majority of the local population as major beneficiaries.

ii) Social aspects: consider the long-term "quality of life" as the main criteria for decision making.

iii) Ecological considerations: the precautionary principle is applied.

Thus development of new activities and whole projects are approached through a different lens, which takes into account the whole natural system and humans as an integral part of it.

c) Cosmos (outer space), science and higher consciousness: Outer space, or the cosmos, is a concept that is becoming more important to us every day, as we learn more about the complex problems of, for example, climate change. We are becoming aware of the fact that human activity on Earth is affecting outer space elements and the complexity of systems that together control the climate we experience on Earth. This whole complex system appears to have a huge capacity for absorbing man-made contamination and alternations in Earth's natural systems. But there is, it has been confirmed by scientists, a limit to cosmos' capacity to absorb pollutants and alternations in our natural systems.[79] We apparently have reached that saturation point. As a consequence, for example, we are experiencing erratic climatic behaviors in all parts of the world. Much has been published on this topic, and deep concern is evident in many sectors of society, but major changes in human behavior and activities still appear very limited.

The whole complexity of outer space is still little-understood. From the human consciousness perspective, many astronauts have had profound experiences in outer space travel as they have tried to combine their scientific knowledge with their outer space experiences. Many have been deeply affected by what they describe as the incredible mystery of seeing our Earth as it appears from tremendous distances; to perceive the incredible harmony that has to exist among the many complex systems that affect the Earth, and make it habitable for humans. Many have had unforgettable reactions to these experiences that are outside their intellectual reality. That is, the human higher consciousnesses of these people have been opened, and with that, these new realities begin to make sense. There must be "something" beyond human intellect at work in us to be able to comprehend these experiences and new realities.[80]

The Earth and outer space are closely linked, and form a continuous vibrant interaction and harmony of systems. The Earth is really a complex series of systems and subsystems that are imbedded in each other and in their functioning. As a result the Earth and outer space systems are really "alive" with continuous movements and interactions to provide the intricate harmony which results—to make life on Earth possible. Thus the connection between science and higher consciousness becomes real—and we can in fact develop much broader and deeper in our scientific work if we can accept that higher consciousness, a capacity that we all possess, really exists. This acceptance of the value of higher consciousness to understand our place in these complexities of Earth and outer space systems also makes us realize how we as humans are a very small, dependent entity compared to the vastness, complexity and power of the whole universe. From this realization comes the roots of our reverence for Earth and outer space systems, and from here comes our humility as humans in the light of the enormity and complexity around us. This humility then affects all our earthly activities and demands our respect, including what should be our very cautious and thoughtful use of outer space, as we realize the mystery of where we are fortunate enough to exist, as well as our enormous responsibility in caring for these systems in our everyday lives and activities.

d) Lifestyle changes:[81] Major changes in our view of "reality" involved in development of our capacity for higher consciousness as well as intellect has significant influence on our daily lives. Briefly indicating some of the most significant ones, noted below are some contrasts to conventional thinking. These changes include:

i) Our priorities in life -- from accumulating things toward human relationships and meaningful work as the main source of human fulfillment. This is basically a change from quantity to quality.

ii) Simplification of lifestyle -- toward simplicity and comfort (or simple elegance as Satish Kumar describes it), shown in quality of food and basic everyday living comforts, fulfilling work and activities, and significant importance attached to interpersonal relationships.

iii) Service -- a need to serve or help others without expecting anything in return.

iv) Non-violence -- in thoughts, attitudes, behaviors, relationships and practices, and belief in dialogue.

v) Deep respect for nature, with conscientious participation in reducing consumption, reusing items and repairing items for reuse; and as a last resort recycling items that we do not need or cannot be reused.

vi) Reactivation of creativity in doing things in new ways. This leads to proactive and positive attitudes and activities.

These are only a few of the examples in major lifestyle transformation that are beginning. It is important to note once again that all this begins from our own personal perspective. Genuine changes come from a combination of individual and group-based living examples. This takes patience, creativity and determination to succeed.

In summary, the values we are seeing emerge are deeply embedded in universal values, which go beyond cultures, and therefore have been comprehended and accepted by people of many different countries, cultures, groups and organizations. Many of these values have been quietly in existence for thousands of years, but many have been left dormant and are now being rediscovered and newly valued as we search for alternatives to the conventional system breakdown, and the very survival of life on Earth.

To completely comprehend these emerging values, the concept of the human capacity for higher consciousness (or spirituality or higher self) needs to be accepted and developed as part of daily life, and combined with our natural intellectual capacities. A reader who accepts only a purely intellectual approach to values will find these universal values as "nice but unrealistic," and rather questionable, as most do not fit with the conventional objective world view. Therefore, for the reader who has not accepted or utilized as part of daily life his/her special capacity for higher consciousness, the application of these values and our human dependence on and interconnection with nature and its systems will have a huge hurdle to cross before the values really make sense. But indications for this hurdle being crossed are very positive. These emerging values in some communities are already beginning to provide much food for thought and inner questioning, especially at the personal level, as the conventional mindset and values are showing more signs of breaking down. This inner questioning is positive and forms the initial stage in a positive path toward awakening our higher consciousness. It is usually a slow process, so patience is important as the questioning becomes more persistent and new insights to new realities begin to appear.

Values and the Human Mind

1. Individual Values – influenced by country culture and background.

2. Universal Values – moves beyond cultures to include all humanity.

3. Human Mind – Interpretation of Values

4. Conscious/Unconscious Minds – Balance between two minds (thinking) essential to fully understand universal values. The foundation for genuine sustainable thinking and behaviour.

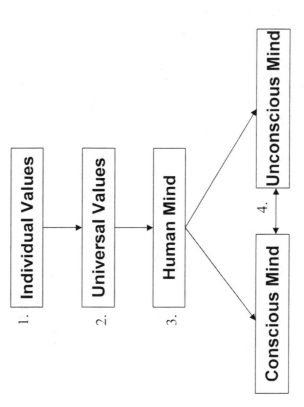

Figure 1

Summary Chart – Emerging Values

Self	Family, Work, Community	Earth, Cosmos
1. Love 2. Self Respect 3. Self Discipline 4. Meaning/Purpose 5. Honesty 6. Trust 7. Non-Violence 8. Humility	1. Family: love, ethics, security, self discipline, cooperation, trust 2. Work: tolerance, cooperation, self-discipline, trust, fulfillment, employment 3. Community: belonging, solidarity, cooperation, self-discipline, non-violence, service, education	1. Interconnectedness 2. Diversity 3. Spirituality 4. Ecological Dependence 5. Respect 6. Precaution

Figure 2

Chapter V

EMERGING PRINCIPLES

A. INTRODUCTION

The previous chapter, Emerging Values, laid the foundation for "sustainable thinking" based on universal values that form a solid foundation for sustainability in its broadest sense. The next step involves the "translation" of these emerging values into principles or "truths," which form the basis for all policy making, beginning with individual sustainable thinking, attitudes and behaviors. In other words, the principles or truths that we consciously or unconsciously hold, either as individuals or in organizations, are the ones that control the decisions we make and how they are implemented.

This move from the values level to the principles level is a complex step, as it is essential that we have already gone through a process of rethinking our own deeply seated values and have readjusted the ones that are not sustainable.

Figure 4 outlines the different steps we need to go through to assure sustainability in both thinking and practice. The first step, as noted, begins with the foundation values level. The step that follows, the principles level, is seated on these sustainable values outlined at the values level. It is at this level, as has been mentioned previously, where we see some of the blockages that we are experiencing. In other words, we have arrived at the stage of recognizing that the principles that underpin our policies need to be re-examined and rethought based on our rethought values. This is a fairly recent development, as we have usually depended on trying to change policies without looking at the foundation of principles on which they are seated. As a result, policy changes have been either inadequate, or interpreted through accepted conventional principles that we have felt were solid and true. This has resulted in blockages related to expected outcomes.

This chapter thus moves us from the deep values level to the principles level. Here we begin to see how these principles or truths affect everything we think or do, both at a personal level as well as at the decision-making level in business organizations, governments and universities.

1. Overview Chart: Transformation Process

Organizations typically pass through a number of different organizational levels in their search for the root of particular problems. Through many years most have found their blockages located at an early stage, like faulty practices or policies of the organization. However, today something new is happening, and the depth of the dilemma appears much more complex. The search for blockages and answers requires delving deep into the very root of an organization—the deep values foundation of the organization.

Figure 4 (at end of chapter) shows the different levels through which organizations pass in their process of examination and transformation. The illustration incorporates a linear focus in examining these steps, as it is the way of thinking most of us are accustomed to viewing. However, there are obvious interconnected concepts as well as interdependent factors that a linear illustration does not show. (Figure 5 shows this interconnected systems approach.)

Figure 4 is meant to provide the reader with a simple panorama of the different levels an organization needs to examine in order to identify and establish a solid foundation of values on which a viable long-term organization can be seated.

Figure 4: Steps

1. PRACTICES: Practices includes all the activities that are visible every day. All these activities rest on the underlying policies of the organizations.

2. POLICIES: All organizational practices are seated on policies that underpin them. These policies can be written or commonly "understood" by all, depending on the size and organization involved. These policies control the manner in which activities are carried out, and the attitudes and behaviors that characterize the organization.

3. PRINCIPLES: Principles underpin all policies. They are often understood as assumptions or truths that most accept as unchanging and common to all in a region, culture or country. These basic principles or truths in modern Western society have for the most part formed a common foundation for organizational thinking for many decades. Thus they are generally accepted as the natural way of thinking, and therefore not usually questioned in organizational changes.

4. UNIVERSAL ROOT VALUES: At this point organizational and personal (decision maker's) thinking meets. In other words, the deeply held personal values of decision makers form the foundation for principles. These root values make us who we are (including decision makers) and affect all human activity on earth. The root values level is also the most sensitive one, as it affects the essence of our view of human nature, and how we live, think and act every day, as well as our views on the relationship between humans, society and nature in its broadest sense. This becomes visible in both personal and working life. This is the key level, where deep examination and transformation are needed. New emerging values will then filter up and influence all the other levels to the practices level.

5. CONSCIOUS/UNCONSCIOUS MIND: We are accustomed to viewing the world from an intellectual, objective standpoint, using only our conscious mind. We now know that we as humans have several powerful inherent capacities related to the unconscious mind as well, namely the source of our higher consciousness "knowing"

and our deep inner intuition and knowledge. The development of both these capacities is essential to fully understanding the new emerging values. The careful balance in the development of these capacities is thus essential for attaining a genuine sustainable value base that results in human activities that foster human fulfillment and respect for the planet.

6. FUTURE, LONG TERM: This aspect can be viewed from two different perspectives.

i) All human activities have long-term consequences for the future. All future generations will in some way feel the consequences of our activities today. Therefore organizations need to identify with and take responsibility for these long-term consequences as part of their principles, and not a consideration following practices.

ii) From the perspective of emerging root values, all future consequences become a natural inbuilt consideration from the out-set, when we have a balance between the development of conscious objective and unconscious higher-consciousness thinking. Therefore the future long term is taken into account before any policies or activi-ties are planned as part of a new values foundation. This means that all our practices have a "built in" sustainable lens, so to speak. This provides a basis for assuring the formation of policies that result in practices that are positive for future generations.

Thus we have on the one side practices (based on conventional value base) that have often-unintentional consequences for the long term. On the other side we have emerging values that have built-in long-term controls that provide a foundation for sustainable long-term practices all the way from their root value foundation through all the levels, and finally to all our everyday activities and thinking.

Interconnected Systems Thinking (Figure 5)

This perspective, part of which we experience almost daily, provides an all-encompassing panorama that includes the full range of complexity of our thinking and actions in relation to the different levels described in Figure 4. This includes the aspects of interdepen-dence and interconnectivity, which in reality exist among the different aspects of transformation in thinking and activities. Systems thinking is a term that has not been specifically used in this book, but is one that commonly describes the interrelationships described in many sections. Visionaries and researchers in the field of sustainability have emphasized that systems thinking provides a sound basis for sustainable long-term planning and actions. Readers will note the importance of root values as the foundation for a balanced mindset that underpins all aspects of systems thinking and sustainability.

In summary one can conclude:
a) Human activities (practices) ultimately depend on deeply seated personal values.
b) Deeply held emerging values that extend beyond cultures (to include all cultures), to be fully comprehended, require a fine balance between the development of conscious objective thinking and higher consciousness thinking.

Concept of Principles

The concept of principles is often understood more readily using other words such as assumptions or "accepted truths" about how our world works and how we relate to it.

Principles as such we are often not conscious of, but are considered "understood" truths that everyone assumes to be correct, and the way everyone else around us naturally "thinks."

In the Western, highly industrialized countries these principles basically evolved following the Scientific/Industrial Revolution[1] as foundation principles for modern scientific and economic development. During this time some principles have taken priority over others. In organizations, the policies that have evolved from them have proven very successful economically from the standpoint of dramatic technological advances, as well as the development of a sophisticated consumer-based monetarized society. However, basing our development focus on these principles has also brought to light many difficulties that we do not seem to be able to solve. These difficulties have included both social and ecological breakdowns, as well as significant economic distribution dilemmas. These problems are becoming increasingly worrisome, and the decision makers have mostly attempted to solve them by making some adjustments to policies, but assuming that the basic principles on which their policies were seated remained sound. Unfortunately that has not been the case, and now we are faced with a serious situation that threatens the whole balance between human activity, social stability and the natural environment. Therefore we are in a situation where the principles themselves are being questioned.

This chapter examines some new emerging principles that have grown out of the universal root values discussed in the previous chapter. Many scholars, visionaries[2] and concerned individuals are beginning to accept that the time has come to rethink the roots of our conventional principles in search of answers to our seemingly intractable dilemmas. It is hoped this study can begin to provide a new foundation for rethinking our principles or truths, and following that, form a new foundation of principles beneficial for decision makers in policy formulation.

Today we are in the middle of a period of chaos, in which conventional principles are being questioned, but as yet we do not have in place a solid base of alternative principles to replace them. However, indicators show that a new positive path or direction is beginning to become clearer every day. This requires careful rethinking of the conventional principles that underpin our policies and practices if we hope to come to grips with our present unsustainable behaviors and activities, at all levels—personal, organizational and government.

There is no doubt that this section will create controversy and provide food for thought, as the very foundation of conventionally accepted truths, which have been held as untouchable for hundreds of years, are being questioned and rethought.[3] In order to provide the reader with a common starting point, it is important to emphasize again that the emerging principles are seated on the emerging values outlined in the previous chapter. These values form the ultimate foundation for all our thinking from which the new truths or principles evolve.

The reader undoubtedly will perceive some of the following principles as positive, that is, ones with which they agree, while others may seem rather strange. In either case it is important to always relate each principle back to the root values on which they are based.

This chapter is one that can have a dramatic impact at both the personal as well as the organizational level. Often decision makers are unaware of the inherent conventional principles that control their thinking. It can be unsettling for many to accept that their once solid and comfortable foundation of conventional assumptions or truths is being questioned or doubted, and that they will have to go through some deep personal-level rethinking and soul searching if they hope to transform their organization into a long-term sustainable operation. We are at a crossroads. Some decision makers and individuals will undoubtedly continue "business as usual," with no desire to look at root causes of our dilemma, nor to worry about the longer-term consequences that may result. Others, especially in the younger sectors of society, are beginning to see that even their own lives could be seriously affected if we do not make a major transformation and redirect our thinking to a deeper level.[4] This means a fundamental reexamination of our own values and utilizing the powerful human capacities we all naturally possess. This recognition of the necessity to utilize our vast human capacities, including our intelligence as well as our higher consciousness, is essential to fully comprehend and embrace the new emerging principles. This is the new world, where subjective wisdom as well as objective knowledge become part of our expanded understanding of ourselves and the world around us.[5][6][7]

In this change process, some readers may try to make sincere but superficial adjustments, utilizing only their well-developed intellectual and objective thinking capacities, but this will not be enough for a complete transformation, as many of the unsustainable conventional principles will remain intact. To be able to differentiate at a deep level between conventional principles and emerging sustainable principles will require a major transformation in thinking, involving first the values that underpin the emerging principles, and secondly opening a new path or direction where sustainable principles naturally fit. Thus begins a path to genuine progress, resulting in new rethought policies and practices.

The emerging principles are set out in three main groups—social, ecological and economic. These groups and the principles within each are all interrelated and interconnected, so the reader will sometimes experience what may appear to be duplications as one fits into another, and indeed some aspects need to be treated together. However, for simplicity and in an effort to provide clarity, separations have been made. In each category the emerging principles will be briefly stated, followed by a short explanation of each. This will provide a context for reflection on new "truths" that are evolving from the universal values that have been discussed. With the adoption of these new truths or principles, one's own personal attitudes and behaviors are naturally altered. This will affect every aspect of life and work at a personal level. At the organizational level, these new emerging principles will affect directly the policies of the organization, which depend on these principles as their foundation. Consequently, the lens through which decision makers develop policies is thus transformed, resulting in policies that are finally seated on a viable foundation of values and principles for long-term sustainability.

B. EMERGING SOCIAL PRINCIPLES[8]

1. Human beings are basically good, and have an inherent dignity. All humans have a basic right to life, and deserve respect and opportunity to utilize their full potential. Guaranteed human rights and fundamental freedoms are essential for all:[9] [10]

This principle fundamentally changes our conventional view of human nature, from a self-centered competitive individual to one who is by nature loving, cooperative and concerned with others.[11] [12] This emerging principle is meant to nurture and support these positive characteristics that we all apparently possess at a deep level. This results in accepting basic human rights to life and the need for a fulfilling and meaningful lifestyle. In addition, it also upholds the natural sense of responsibility each person feels to contribute his/her part, and feel a sense of responsibility for one's own actions.

2. All humans have the right to equitable use of natural resources, and it is our duty to prevent environmental harm while protecting the rights of people:[13] [14] [15]

Natural resources are "common" resources provided by nature, so we all have equal rights to their usage, as long as that usage does not negatively affect the basic rights of humans. This indicates that we also have some restrictions on our use of these natural gifts.

3. Diversity of cultures, languages, ideas and tastes are natural and healthy:[16]

This applies also to diversity of life forms in nature, which are linked to human diversity. Humans are part of the whole panorama of life on Earth. Therefore human development provides for diversity, just as we have diversity in nature. This diversity includes not only differences in cultures, languages and ethnic groups, but also differences in our ideas and our tastes. Therefore these differences must be honored and respected, and policies attempting homogenization of ideas and tastes are considered contrary to the basic principle of diversity. We see this homogenization related closely to the development of enormous global-level corporations where common products and ideas are introduced to many different countries and cultures with the hope of acceptance of common products and ideas. In a sustainable world, on the contrary, we search for commonality of only some key universal values, which are interpreted in local cultures according to their own cultural diversity. In this way we honor common root values at the same time as diverse tastes, cultures and languages.

4. Our way of life shows nondiscrimination in gender opportunities,[17] and the equality of opportunity for all humans to have a sustainable way of life:[18] This requires changes in present-day, often-wasteful lifestyles in wealthy societies especially to ensure equitable rights for all, including access to nature's resources and ecosystems. Alleviation of poverty is essential for a sustainable environment and a sustainable way of life for all.

In this process of poverty alleviation and equality of opportunity we have a huge challenge.[19] Based on experience in many poor regions, at the practical level, one of the keys to initiating and promoting this process at the community level involves the recognition of the contribution of local populations and the important role of women.[20] Their capacity for taking on responsibilities in carrying out local level projects, and in the process improving significantly the lives of local families, has been dramatic.

The concept of equality also means a major change in affluent lifestyles, where many of us are using much more than our fair share of Earth's resources.[21] We must allow the poor also to have their fair share of natural resources as an important basic human right.

5. We believe in tolerance, nonviolence and peace:[22]

Most humans by nature are peaceful and tolerant, and have a natural desire to cooperate and enter into dialogue to settle differences.

This principle requires much deep and sincere contemplation, as we live in a world that shows many opposite signs to tolerance and nonviolence. But once we accept the genuine nature of humans, then many major changes occur in how we think and behave. One dramatic example of an exercise in transformation and forgiveness was the war-torn and violent South Africa followed by the Truth and Reconciliation Commission Hearings.[23] Here people who had committed or were victims of terrible atrocities finally came to the point of forgiveness, and a transformation of values and behaviors. But a process such as this must be very thoughtfully planned, especially considering different cultures. It also requires a carefully planned follow through process in order for it to have long-lasting benefits, as many people are exposed to a world outside that shows intolerance and violence as a norm.

6. Social and economic justice is essential for all humans, allowing all to achieve a secure and meaningful livelihood:[24] [25] [26] [27]

There are great variations between countries and regions related to social and economic justice. The poor countries have the greatest changes to make, where most people wake up each morning with the perception of having no or very few rights in their daily life. In order for people to live secure and meaningful lives they have to have confidence that they have the same protection and justice as the rich. Even in some rich countries the poorer sectors of the population often suffer from somewhat similar challenges, where the wealthy have many economic and social justice advantages.

7. Education, both formal and lifelong, as well as universal health care are basic societal requirements in order to live a life of dignity, peace and fulfillment:[28] [29] [30] [31]

Education and health care are essential for all people, not only to find work and support a family, but also to live a life of dignity and fulfillment. This means that these two aspects form an important responsibility for governments at all levels in providing for the "common good" of the population. These two aspects also affect directly the social costs of governments, as it affects both employment and productivity capacities, as well as the high costs related to health issues for everyone. This is especially true in poor countries where disease and poor health have had a devastating effect. On the education side, the lack of the basic education and work-related skills has proven a serious obstacle in assisting communities in valuable types of development projects.

8. Work is essential for more than providing income for a decent living. Work is intrinsically valuable to fulfill fundamental psychological needs such as sense of personal worth, purpose and fulfillment in life:[32] [33]

Unemployment over long periods of time has had devastating economic and psychological effects on large sectors of populations. In rich countries the unemployed mostly receive social assistance of some sort so most can continue to live modestly, but they often lose their sense of self-respect and self-worth. In poor countries people are generally quite resourceful as there is no "safety net," so if one does not work one does not eat. It is that simple. As a result, most of these people find ingenious ways of eking out a living, usually in the underground economy.

9. Development projects of all kinds must respect the need to provide harmony and balance between sociocultural and ecological aspects on the one side and economic aspects on the other. Full participation and a high degree of self-sufficiency at the community level is essential:[34] [35] [36]

The first two aspects must be well thought out (including the values that underpin them) and in good order before economic aspects can be considered sustainable. This is a complete reversal of the present tendency, where priority is on the economic side, and social and ecological aspects are usually secondary considerations once the economic aspects are in place. In addition, this harmony is rooted in stable communities, which are as self-sufficient as possible, and citizens participate fully in the development and conservation of their local communities.

10. All actions, plans and behaviors must take into account long-term consequences and future generations:[37][38]

The future of our children as well as the future of the natural environment and natural resources are at stake. Future generations have the same right to a natural environment, resources and opportunities that we enjoy today.

We live in a world of short-term thinking and "instant gratification," with little concern for any longer-term consequences of our actions. But as we begin to see ecological breakdown, people are beginning to understand that nature is "long term," and if we destroy it we in fact are restricting our own lives, and that of future generations.

C. EMERGING ECOLOGICAL PRINCIPLES

1. Earth is a complex living system composed of many interconnected and interdependent subsystems:[39][40][41][42]

All of these systems are essential for all life on Earth, human and nonhuman, even though we do not fully understand all their functions.

This concept of interconnectivity is strange for us in many ways, as we are accustomed to thinking that to understand something fully requires breaking it down into its smallest component parts and studying each part in detail, isolated from all others. This concept is slowly changing as we are learning that in nature as well as in humans each part and its function are intertwined with many other parts and functions. So if we do not study the system as a whole we can never understand the characteristics and functioning of the individual parts.

2. Protection (preventing harm), conservation (limiting use) and restoration (correcting damage) of our ecological systems and natural resources is a fundamental human responsibility:[43][44][45][46]

These responsibilities must be reflected in all our attitudes, behaviors and actions.

This begins at the personal level with how we conduct our individual, family and community lives. We accept that human activities in total (economies) are a subsystem of the "whole" (universe) and are totally dependent upon it for our survival. Therefore it is accepted that we must learn to live within the limitations of the whole.

3. Social and ecological limitations control economic development:[47] [48]

These three aspects of development are totally interlinked and interdependent. All economic development, including production, consumption and reproduction patterns, must be in harmony with nature's regenerative capacities in order to be genuinely sustainable in the longer term.

We have been accustomed to seeing ourselves as separate from nature, and thinking nature itself would somehow regenerate and look after itself. Now we are gradually accepting that all living beings are interconnected to nature in some way—our very capacity to breathe air depends on nature every minute of the day. So it goes without saying that if we disregard the fact that nature is absolutely essential for us to live, we in fact limit our own lives when nature cannot function correctly. Many scholars now believe that we have already "overshot"[49] the limits of nature to regenerate itself in a number of areas, as we are experiencing breakdowns in our natural systems and resources, which has never happened before. We as humans cannot deny this any more. The problem is now: How do we go about repairing the damage done, and how will this change our lifestyles? We have to each make a very personal decision about our future.

4. The Precautionary Principle must be respected in all human activity:[50] [51]

Our knowledge of nature is limited in many areas, and long-term consequences are unknown. Nature is very complex and its future viability is at stake unless we act with precaution. This Precautionary Principle is also extremely important related to research and development and introduction of life forms such as genetically modified organisms (GMO) into the environment.

The Precautionary Principle really means that if we are planning an activity or action and we are not sure about its long-term consequences to nature, then we should be very cautious in implementation. The idea is that we cannot take the risk of being wrong. It could mean irreparable damage to nature—on which we depend for our lives. One example of this is the introduction of genetically modified organisms into our natural environment. Once they are introduced, they cannot be taken back if they have some longer-term negative affect on nature. The truth is that no one knows for certain what the long-term affects of GMOs are even though the short-term affects seem minor in most cases. The central point is that we are playing with complexities in nature we do not fully understand and one mistake could in fact threaten the whole human food base, and indeed our life on Earth as we know it.

5. Renewable natural resources should be used only at the rate at which nature can regenerate them and contaminates can be fully absorbed:[52] [53] [54]

Indications are that we are already "overshooting" nature's capacity to regenerate, which is evident every day in pollution of air, water and soils—the very essentials for human life. As for non-renewable resources, when they are finished, they cannot be regenerated, so it is essential for us to find viable alternatives as quickly as possible. This transition is proving difficult as the short-term economic motive has as yet such a powerful sway on decision making, and has taken precedence in most cases over the ecological longer-term realities.

Nonrenewable natural resources usage must be strictly controlled, with special emphasis on finding alternatives, especially to sources of energy, which are not highly polluting, toxic or hazardous, such as nuclear energy.

6. Biodiversity is a natural and extremely important aspect of nature, and links humans directly to nature:[55] [56] [57] [58]

Diversity provides the basis for a sustainable natural environment and the future health of the planet for human life. Biodiversity in nature is imperative to conserve if we hope to maintain a viable natural environment. Here we see the tremendous complexities of interdependency and interconnectedness of natural systems, of which we are a part, much of which we do not understand or take seriously. But now that serious ecological breakdown is becoming more obvious by the day, we are beginning to show more respect for its intricate systems and realize how little we really know about how nature works.

7. Understanding nature and its systems requires integrated "systems" thinking (as opposed to linear reductionist thinking):[59] [60] [61] [62]

This requires not only our intellectual capacity but also the development of higher consciousness to fully comprehend the mystery and awe humans sense when trying to understand the complexities and beauty of the natural world.

Systems thinking opens up a new world of human capacity for new sensitivities and experiencing fulfillment and peace of mind—an essential capacity to develop for us to fully be convinced of the ability of humans to live in harmony with the wonders of nature.

8. Lifestyle and nature's limitations are interlinked:[63] [64] [65]

Our way of life must respect the limitations of nature, as well as our responsibility for allowing others equal access to nature's bounty. This means a lifestyle that is frugal, simple but "elegant" in quality, and provides personal fulfillment.

To achieve this will mean a transformation of thinking, especially in the rich countries that are already using a very disproportionately large part of our natural resources. In these countries an altered lifestyle can still be comfortable, but not wasteful. In total terms we recognize that human systems are subsystems of the Earth and the whole universe.[66]

9. We believe in the principle of "the polluter pays":[67]

This means that taxation systems focuses on "taxing" the polluter, and "crediting" the nonpolluter. This is a very controversial topic as it is questions the wisdom of conventional thinking. Our economic system in most highly industrialized countries provides a wide range of rather unnoticed "subsidies" that support environmentally questionable activities. This means that the final price we pay for a product is not the "full price," but a subsidized price. The principle involved here is that all production should firstly reflect the full cost, and secondly discourage ecologically questionable activities while encouraging and providing benefits for activities that are ecologically positive.

10. Independent ecologically related research (which is seated on sustainable values) is vital for our capacity to understand the consequences of our activities and find sustainable solutions:[68] [69] [70] [71]

This research must be independent of any vested interests in order to provide full objectivity, transparency and accountability in its results.

We are experiencing a trend where the credibility of much research is being questioned depending on who is paying for it. Research in which economic-vested interests are directly involved, and seated on conventional economic-based values, can rarely be fully credible, as the motive of the funding source is naturally directed toward financial benefits for the funding organization. The results of the research naturally need to provide some positive economic potential to be considered cost effective. In these cases, which are becoming more common, the credibility of the research is often questioned. Reliable research, as society requires (based on sustainable values), is free from a restricted agenda, and without any "strings attached." Results are thereby respected as having not been influenced by any nonsustainable motive. Presently the public is often confused as research results sometimes provide very contradictory results related to the same issue. This is a serious dilemma, as many research institutions and universities are very limited in their funding, and have accepted funding from "for profit" businesses, mostly with accompanying monetary-related agendas. Significant transformation in thinking about the seriousness of research needs to take place to ensure transparency and utmost adherence to sustainable principles and values. This is an area where we have lost important respect and value—research is our lifeline to continue learning about this marvelous and complex world in which we live.

Ecological sustainability in the long term depends on promoting study and open exchange of reliable knowledge, as well as widespread application of that knowledge.

Global ecological problems require sharing of all knowledge that can be of assistance in contributing to our common goal of conserving and restoring a damaged planet.

At present there is developing a considerable store of valuable knowledge related to nature and its systems. However, that knowledge needs to be brought out into mainstream society in order for it to be seriously considered in planning ecologically related aspects of every activity in a community or country.[72] This distribution of knowledge should also become an integral part of all educational institutions in all their programs, and become imbedded as part of all sustainability thinking that can form a sound foundation for all disciplines.[73]

Open sharing of this knowledge is especially important between rich and poor countries, where the funding for ecological studies is very limited. Once economic knowledge becomes part of ecological knowledge, we are on the path to a sustainable development approach.

D. EMERGING ECONOMIC & POLITICAL PRINCIPLES[74]

1. Economic and political principles are focused on human and ecological well-being:

Quality of life is related to quality of human relationships, quality of products needed for human health and well-being, and quality of human activities and communities.

On the contrary, the present neoclassical dominant economic principles are themselves completely interconnected within their own core, and seemingly the human and ecological factors need to fit somehow around these principles, and are subservient to them. Therefore this needs to change to provide the central core of economic principles as completely interconnected with a human and ecological focus. Therefore we view the concept of progress as one in which human and ecological well-being is central, and economic progress is dependent on how human and ecological well-being can be maintained for all.

2. Economic principles should promote development that is equitable and sustainable in the long term, balancing social, ecological and economic factors:[75] [76]

This means planning and assessment of social and ecological consequences in the longer term, as well as the equitable distribution of benefits to all participants.

This way of approaching economic planning and activities will require long-term thinking in place of our present short-term norms. This focus on long-term planning will naturally bring to light longer-term impact on human development and distribution of benefits, as well as related ecological consequences. Thus it will provide the basis for a much more balanced and equitable playing field than at present.

3. Democratic institutions that guarantee transparency and accountability in governance, participation for the people, and equal access to justice for all must be promoted:[77] [78] [79]

This is considered indispensable for a genuine democratic society, and involves the meaningful participation of all stakeholders.

Transparency and accountability have in recent times shown themselves to be extremely complex to control in a globalized world. Many of the most powerful institutions that support and promote unrestricted globalization have evolved without basic regulations that serve as checks and balances on their activities, thus leaving a situation where transparency and accountability aspects are limited. This situation is not considered sustainable. In a democratic system all sectors of society are stakeholders or direct participants in institutions that have a global reach, and not just left to a small group who tend to benefit from unrestricted control in the global marketplace.

4. All economic development requires considerations of "size." Human scale organizations and projects are essential for sustainability:[80]

The principle of "human scale" thinking is the size that provides the basis for humans to work together for maximum participation and fulfillment. It is also the scale that provides the basis for stable, healthy communities—the foundation for stable and sustainable societies.

This also includes a major development focus on local, regional and national levels.

The concept of "human scale" as the ideal places us in direct contrast to the conventional principles related to globalization and the larger the scale the better. Another aspect to this principle involves the focus and location of development—now we believe that the most important core of development projects should be at the local community level. This type of development focus provides a basis for satisfying the long-term human needs related to the importance of family, solidarity, belonging and human relationships at the community level in general. This human scale development focus is considered essential for long-term social stability and genuine qualitative and quantitative progress.

5. Each sector of society has a special role with their distinct and interrelated responsibilities. These sectors include government, private sector, and civil society:[81] [82] [83]

The integration of these sectors and their respective responsibilities provides for a stable and sustainable society. There has been a tendency, especially during the past two decades, for an increasing influence of the business sector in government policy decisions, sometimes resulting in decisions that do not necessarily represent the wishes or benefit the majority of the population.[84]

Governments as sectors of society have an important and distinct role in providing for policies and programs that are focused on the "common good." Therefore it is a role distinct from the private sector, which provides a special role distinct from government. The role of government as an institution providing for the common good of the population includes basic services such as education, health and general public services required in a community or country for the equitable benefit of all the population, as well as establishing democratic institutions that serve the citizens fairly and maintain checks and balances for all sectors.

The private, primarily business sector is distinct in that its activities have a basic requirement to make a profit. A business that does not make a profit cannot of course survive, but the question sometimes arises as to how much profit is reasonable and positive, and when does it become greed. This sector also plays an important role of employment creation in society, aside from the human benefits gained from their products and services, as well as their community and ecological benefits.

Civil society has a vital role that is often forgotten or not taken seriously, as much of the work performed by this sector is unpaid. It is what the economist Hazel Henderson[85] refers to as the "love economy," and so does not show up on any GDP figures, even though it includes a large sector, if all this work were "priced" according to the vital services it fulfills. In this love economy are included charitable organizations and their huge group of volunteers, families contributing to community projects, raising and caring for children in place of sending them to day care, and people looking after elderly parents or disabled family members. This sector includes many of the services that provide stability to a community, and often fills a social role when governments have cut back on social services, health care and education of different types, as well as focus-needed environmental issues.[86] [87]

6. The concept of progress is measured in quality of life and activities, and respect for nature—as opposed to quantity of economic gain:[88]

Heretofore all progress has been measured in terms of purely economic-based indicators, resulting in a distorted picture of what is really happening in a country. These distortions for example include measuring national income on the average of all citizens in a country, which could have a very small very wealthy elite, but the rest of the population is very poor. Other examples include as positive economic activity the revenue gained from activities that are considered negative, such as cleaning up environmental damage, or even from health issues that are the result of neglect in health services. Now we are beginning to see new methods of measurement that also take into account social and ecological indicators in addition to economic-based ones, such as the United Nations Human Development Index (HDI)[89] among a number of others.

7. Trade is important between communities, regions and countries (with a small sector of international trade):[90] [91] [92] [93]

Trade should be under the control of nation states as an important part of the stability and sustainability of each country or region. Local and regional trade should be emphasized, while the role of international trade takes a minor role. As Herman Daly has pointed out in much of his work in relation to the focus of the WTO, the direction we are going will eventually "lift" all trade into the international "free" arena, leaving countries without a base for national economic, social or ecological development. Local and regional trade provides income and stability for countries, respects diversity in local development to satisfy local needs, as well as reducing transportation and ecological damage.

International organizations fulfill a role related to global resources such as marine life and climate change, among others, where international agreements between countries are essential for the benefits to be equitable and fair for all nations. All international organizations must be closely controlled and monitored to provide reliable service to all nation states. This is in sharp contrast to the present situation, where trade is global and nation states are losing control over their own trade and productive sector in general, which serves as their main source of national income and security, and the basis for social stability and economic security.

8. Money is important as a vehicle of exchange in trade, not as a commodity to be traded:[94] [95] [96]

Money basically lost its stabilizing role when it was taken off the gold standard in 1973 and was free to roam as a commodity to be bought and sold, instead of having its value stabilized by being related to a precious metal. Over the past decade particularly we have seen an explosion in the use of money as a commodity. We are now at the stage where the trade in money is the dominant one. Based on recent studies, if one takes into account all the financial activity that takes place around the world each day, only 10 percent is involved in trade in products, and 90 percent is involved in trade in money. This is clearly not a sustainable situation.

9. Economic activity is controlled by nature's ability to regenerate its resources and natural systems:[97]

Earth's natural systems and their limitations control the man-made subsystem of economic activity in order to ensure a sustainable way of life for all present and future generations.

This principle brings out the essence of a controversy related to the relationships between major systems and subsystems. The average person today perceives, through the media and daily working life, that our whole economic system is the dominant one in the world, and ecological system is a subsystem of the economic one. This principle is now being turned on its head, as indicated in Daly's work. Our planetary ecological world is in fact our major overarching system on which everything and everyone depends for life on Earth. The economic system is a subsystem of the ecological system and is totally dependent on it for its existence. Therefore there is little confusion as to where the rethinking needs to take place.

10. All economic activity must ensure equitable wealth distribution for all its participants:[98] [99] [100]

Distortions in wealth distribution is presently a major dilemma that is directly related to the unsustainability of our development focus, which encourages the concentration of wealth in very few hands through the promotion of gigantism and weakening of country control over all productive development and trade.

11. Nonviolence, cooperation and participation are all essential elements of a sustainable long-term society (for all economic and political activities):[101] [102]

This is reflected in attitudes and behaviors as well as activities that are essential in communities, regionally and globally. Violence and aggression are incompatible with sustainability. Examples such as fierce competition between powerful and weak organizations or nations create win/lose outcomes, which are considered unsustainable. The alternative is a win/win relationship that promotes cooperation, quality, and equity in benefits for all in the longer term, as well as the preservation of nature for the future.

This represents a huge challenge in our present distorted wealth distribution reality. However, once most of the other principles are in place, these will evolve as natural tendencies and controls that favor equitable wealth distribution and cooperation.

Some Conclusions

To conclude this section, the reader will note that all of the emerging principles flow out of the emerging values discussed in the previous chapter. It is also recognized that many of these principles are in direct contrast to the present-day conventional principles, and therefore represent a challenge to both individuals and organizations.

It appears clearer than ever that in order to make this transition we will need to utilize both our highly developed intellectual capacities for objective knowledge and our capacity for higher consciousness in order to fully comprehend what is really needed, and for the transformation to have depth, meaning and long-term benefits for all humanity and the natural world.

However, it is also apparent that we are seeing some changes already beginning to take place, where communities, regions and even some countries are beginning to actually measure their genuine progress in social and ecological areas. The work of Mathis Wackernagel[105] is highly respected in this field related to his work on our "ecological footprint." Thus new paths are being formed that lead directly to sustainability. That is good news, and one on which we can build.

Summary Chart: Emerging Principles

Social	Ecological	Economic/Political
1. Human Inherent Goodness	1. Harmony and Balance - Sociocultural and Ecological	1. Quality of Life - Human well being
2. Right to equitable use of resources	2. Long-term Planning - Affects all ecological outcomes	2. Development - Long-term, Equitable, Sustainable
3. Diversity: cultures, ideas, tastes	3. Earth - A Living System	3. Institutions - Democratic, Accountable, Transparent
4. Equality of Opportunity	4. Commitment – Protection,Conservation, Restoration.	4. Integration/Balance - Economic, Social, Ecological
5. Tolerance, Non-violence	5. Precautionary Principle	5. Distinct Societal Groups and Responsibilities- Roles for Government, Private Sector, Education and Social Sector
6. Social/Economic Justice	6. Renewable Resources - Balance, Regeneration and new Substitutes	6. Progress-Measured by Quality of Life
7. Work- Intrinsic Value	7. Biodiversity- natural state, responsibility to conserve	7. Trade Balanced - Local, National and International
8. Education – Lifelong	8. Integrated Thinking	8. Money - Exchange Tool, not a Commodity
	9. Research – Share Knowledge	9. Economic Sector- Subsystem of Whole Earth Ecological System
	10. Polluter Pays	10. Human Scale Development
		11. Equitable Wealth Distribution
		12. Cooperation, Non Violence

Figure 3

Organizations:
Transformation to Sustainability
Linear view

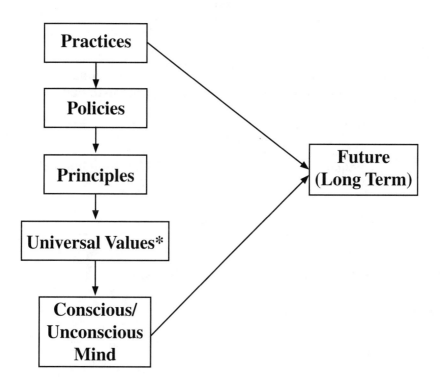

*Universal values: Foundation for Sustainability

Figure 4

Organizations:
Transformation to Sustainability
Interconnected Systems View

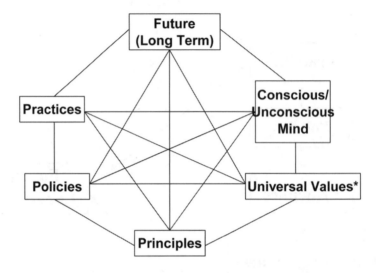

*Universal values: Foundation for Sustainability

Figure 5

Chapter VI

DIALOGUES: TWO CONTRASTING VIEWS

The following "conversation" or exchange of views is a summary of e-mail conversations between two middle-level executives that have taken place over a period of ten years.

John, one of the participants, has worked exclusively with a large international multinational company in a highly industrialized country. His friend Tony has worked with medium-sized companies in a number of international locations, in both highly industrialized as well as developing countries. John and Tony have been friends since their university days, but they have taken rather different career paths in the business world. During their working careers, their views on the role of business in society have developed differently. These e-mail conversations reflect many of the conflicting views present today in relation to business and its role and behavior in society. Readers will naturally find themselves in agreement with some aspects and not with others.

While the characters in the dialogue are fictional, the content itself comes from real case studies that have been drawn from different regions of the Americas.

The readers will discern many different values and principles that underpin the views on the topics touched on in the dialogue. Many have been examined in the course of this study. These dialogues are meant to provide the reader with a basis for reflection on the diversity of views that exist, and an opportunity to reflect on the values that underpin them, as well as examine which values and principles could result in long-term viable organizations and societies.

Dear Tony,

I just came back from a short holiday, and wanted to share with you an interesting thought I had. I brought my computer with me on my holiday of course, and believe it or not, started to look back on our e-mail conversations during the past years, showing all the changes, and the ups and downs we have had. I found it fascinating to see how the two of us have developed such different perspectives on many things over this period of about ten years. I think these e-mails could almost make an interesting book sometime that our kids could appreciate because it certainly gives a real life view of the incredible speed with which things are happening, and also how you and I—old friends—have developed such different perspectives on many realities of the bigger picture of business.

Anyway, I have tried to summarize some of these e-mails, and together they make quite and interesting perspective of where I come from, with my many years of experience with a large multinational company.

Why don't you do the same on your side when you have an afternoon free? I remember your mentioning not long ago that you also saved our e-mail conversations. It would be interesting to compare views between old friends.

To begin the process from my side, I will send you what I have summarized from our interchange from my perspective, and you can do the same from yours. We will of course end up with two different perspectives, but finally this may be helpful to both of us . . . and maybe even one day for other young graduates who will have to deal with some of these contradictions and clashes of perspectives in the future. We certainly live in an interesting world of constant change!

From the outset, the multinational business sector has enjoyed many advantages during these years vis-a-vis government support for business. One of the things that has developed to protect the interests of business is the lobby system, especially in Washington. This makes a big difference when it comes to government trying to pass legislation that may be disadvantageous to us. It seems, over time, these lobby groups have become very professional and powerful, and I must say, in many cases have a bigger influence on what legislation gets passed than the influence of elected political representatives. It certainly has been a big help to the business sector in protecting our interests. This is, of course, also positive for the CEO and shareholder interests, which of course come down the line to protect our market position and finally our own jobs.

As you know, to remain competitive many companies have promoted mergers and takeovers, and companies have become ever larger. Today, as you know so well, the economic size of our company is bigger than most of the countries we deal with. That of course is an advantage in negotiations, and in developing countries we can get the best deals in terms of concessions and tax breaks. It also helps in terms of protecting our interests, in case there are any longer-term, unintended negative affects from our business. These are naturally countries that badly need investment (due to high debts), so they have little choice if they want our business. Also, these countries have to provide a good control on legal guarantees and social stability. These are things we cannot do. From where I stand, what else happens in these countries is not really our concern or responsibility, as long as things work well for our company and guarantees are respected. We have a huge responsibility to our shareholders in terms of profit commitments, so we need to do everything possible to achieve that. . . . Later I will also comment on the maquiladoras, which are special kinds of investments that took off several years ago.

One of the issues we are dealing with in the US is the tremendous explosion in technology, and its effect on the structure of business and jobs that go with it. In spite of the bubble bursting in the dot.com companies, in the past ten years especially we have seen a dramatic transformation in our company. Those of us who have been longer in the field have had to continue to study and work hard to update ourselves constantly, and remain on top of the latest technologies and their applications. As a result we have seen whole sections of especially middle-management-level jobs disappear as computerization has taken over more and more. True, some new jobs have been created for the high-tech specialists, but the general tendency has been toward reduction in the number of jobs as modern technology takes over. Where this will lead no one knows, but for now the CEO is happy, as most of these major downsizings have also increased earnings on the stock market. There is no doubt that the next generations are the ones who will have to deal with these issues, as we move toward ever more sophisticated technologies, and fewer jobs. Thank goodness for developing countries, where we can cut costs at the basic manufacturing level, and keep our competitive edge.

How does the media handle all this? Do they help or hinder us? On that vein, it seems the media (TV mainly, as few people seem to read anymore), gives one a certain comfort level. The main thing we hear every day is that things are basically good as long as we keep buying and spending money. So when consumption is up we can be assured of economic progress, and that means everyone must be making money. So the focus naturally is on promoting new ways of making money. It is amazing how "money talks" in everything that happens around us. I guess that is what has made the US what it is today.

But that does not mean that we are without difficult problems and challenges to maintain our dominant position in the world marketplace. For example, one area you and I have talked about at some length is the constant need for new research in order to remain on the cutting edge of new ideas, technologies and applications. To move that along our company has managed to make agreements with a couple of big universities, where we provide funding for research in specific areas of interest to us. I see it is working well, as the universities are mostly happy to have much-needed funding for research, and for us, we have the advantage of top-notch researchers who can provide the research results we need for profitable applications. But of course we have to maintain control over the focus of the research so it remains a practical applied approach. Some friends of ours in another company have had some difficulties. They had similar agree-

ments with a university in the region but had some problems with the research results, which did not come out very positive in relation to their company objectives, so they moved to another university and that apparently is working better. It is understandable that some researchers find this difficult as they have little or no experience working with profit-oriented business operations. They are not used to working with profits in mind, and the need for results that can be translated into producing profitable products or technologies as quickly as possible.

A few particularly aggressive environmental groups have recently caused us some negative press. I am sure most of them are well intentioned, but some are certainly bad for our business image. Over time we have been trying to control this negative publicity. After all, we try to respect the basic environmental regulations as much as possible, provided they do not damage our business, so we should not be bothered by anyone in this area. But I think we have found a way that may be beneficial to us, and seems to work quite well.

As environmental groups are mostly short of funding, we have found that there are a few that are happy to have some funding from a company such as ours. So in exchange for helping with funding, they will help to protect our interests when environmental issues come up. But not many will do this, so we have found it better to form a completely new "environmental" organization separately, which can support our needs. This system has worked quite well even though there have been some complaints from the more conservative ecological groups. We feel that if we comply to the best of our ability with basic environmental regulations, the government should also respect our need to have conditions for a profitable business.

We are now of course very globally oriented, and so much of our business is run in different countries. I remember your asking me about how we view the new developments in a couple of key international organizations that are closely associated with the global business picture. One of these organizations is the World Trade Organization and the controversies over its role. I gather it is viewed differently depending on where you are located, and hence how you are affected. Basically, those of us who have our livelihoods dependent on the MNC of course view the WTO as our friend. It pushes for opening up countries to free trade, and makes it easier for us to operate wherever we wish without problems in taking our profits out. Also, it gives us good security of investment in developing countries, as according to WTO rules they have to abide by strict open door requirements in the free flow of capital. It really erases all the walls of country-based restrictions in trade, and that also places us at a tremendous advantage in terms of economies of scale, so our competitive edge is well secured. Smaller companies in these countries cannot compete with us.

But not everyone agrees with us and sometimes we have to deal with what some developing countries feel are unfair trade practices, due to the differences in size. As well, we now have to deal with a backlash from a broad spectrum of mainly non-governmental organizations (NGOs), and some trade unions. They apparently created the main disturbances in the Seattle confrontation. It is understandable that some of these people may have been affected by downsizing or salary limitations. But on the other hand, business is business and our job is to make profits in the best way we can. These other problems should be handled by governments as social issues, and they will have to find viable solutions without affecting our freedom to do business.

Fortunately, governments now seem to be much more sensitive to business interests than they used to be. I guess they realize that they wouldn't get into power without the support of the big business sector, so they have to take our interests seriously. Also, it seems there are more people now moving from business to government related positions (and vice versa), as advisors or even filling political posts. That is good for us.

Regarding international organizations, of course we have had close association with the work of the International Monetary Fund (IMF) for many years. They have naturally been working with developing countries for their restructuring programs related to debt relief. This process has always been of interest to us, because part of this restructuring always has a requirement for privatization of many of their companies. This has produced some interesting opportunities for investment at a good price, as well as ready made market potential. Naturally most of these poor, highly indebted countries have not much choice in these privatizations and other structural requirements as the IMF has made them a condition for providing much-needed loans so they can pay the interest on their foreign debt. Another benefit we often get in these situations is that invariably these countries have to devaluate their currency, which reduces markedly the salaries we need to pay the local people. This also makes local costs and other financial investments more attractive.

Another large international organization that we basically have little relationship with is the United Nations (UN). The main area of the UN that has created some difficulties for us though is the United Nations Environmental Protection Program (UNEP). They have sponsored some high-profile international conferences related to environmental issues involving the business sector. The multinational corporations have had real challenges in defending our interests, but we finally fared very well in Rio de Janeiro as well as the conference in Kyoto. True, there are regions where there are some environmental problems, but with new technologies these should certainly be controllable by governments. We have to be careful that we don't begin to pass laws that could restrict free trade, because that could really affect our growth objectives. At any rate, most highly industrialized countries have environmental regulations that we respect as much as possible. Now the UN should also put pressure on the developing countries to do the same. We should be cautious not to take too seriously all the doom and gloom stories about the environment. After all, very little of this has yet to be proven scientifically, and there is every indication that business has good potential worldwide.

Still on the international scene, one topic about which we have had a lot of discussion back and forth is the maquiladora sector (offshore manufacturing companies). The biggest of these of course is the US/Mexican border region, and it certainly has been a booming business for over twenty years, especially the past ten years, with a massive influx of US companies. It has really been a tremendous cost reduction mechanism for our manufacturing sector, and now operates even quite sophisticated types of operations. Of course the main objective of our companies is to maintain the special tax concessions that we had from the beginning. This we hope will continue even though under NAFTA regulations, as you may recall, the long-standing companies are supposed to revert to a "permanent" category, and hence would have to respect national tax requirements. This would increase our costs considerably, so it seems they have managed to get an extension on the time limit. This is positive for our business interests and also for Mexicans who don't want to lose business either, especially with China on the scene with attractive cost-saving offers. For our part also, if wages and other costs begin to increase significantly in Mexico, we would move without hesitation to another low-cost country. It is the only way we can be assured of a good profit picture.

As we have discussed back and forth many times, there have been a lot of challenges setting up operations in Mexico, due to both poor infrastructure and also the workforce having a very different mindset at work. Fortunately, most employees now seem to accept the fact that if they want to work with us they will have to learn our ways of working, and for the most part our plants on the border seem to work like US plants. This is a real advantage for us as our costs have remained reasonable in terms of percentage of US-based costs for similar production. Let us hope this will continue for some time, as it is certainly advantageous to have low-cost plants so conveniently located.

Coming closer to home, in terms of how we live, and what we have often commented on as "quality of life," this may be the area where you and I have one of the biggest differences in perspective. On our side, we have mostly considered that our level of happiness or satisfaction in life is closely associated with our level of income, so most everyone works hard to earn as much as possible. With our earnings, we acquire our many valuable possessions and a feeling of satisfaction and success—these are things like our nice house, a new car (if possible), good clothes, holidays, etc. And combined with that is always present the great motivator—competition. That seems to keep most people constantly working hard to move up the income ladder, get new opportunities, and have a better lifestyle. Of course we need it too, as our cost of living is high. For example, health care services are expensive (which not everyone can afford), as well as transportation, and you need a car to go almost everywhere. It is a country made for cars. Also, university education is expensive and many families have special savings funds for their children from the time they are very young. I do not know how the minimum or general low-wage sector manages. That is a challenge for our government, as most of these people need some kind of welfare assistance, but it seems they have not found a system that really works. Certainly most people also worry about the level of violence and drug use in the country as a whole. And now there is the added concern about terrorism, which is difficult to understand. But what can we do? Our company responsibilities are outside these fields. We basically provide jobs for qualified people, plus downsize as a necessary part of running a profitable business. The government will have to help find alternatives for the people who lose their jobs. Unfortunately most of the people in the lower income sectors lack advanced education and many skills, so there is little opportunity for them except low-wage jobs. We certainly hope the government can do its part in solving these problems because it tends, as we know, to create dissatisfaction and insecure environments in some regions, and that is not good for business.

I agree with you that some people are beginning to ask a number of difficult questions related to the new role of business in general in our society, especially now that we are becoming so linked internationally and really more dependent on a workforce in developing countries. This globalized world with the new influence and power of the business sector internationally in many respects is really outside my experience, as I view these issues from our own company perspective. We deal with the challenges of a multinational company and what we have to do to ensure its success. We believe very much that the "business of business is business," and other issues that may be affected by our business will need the support of governments. After all, it is within their interests to have successful global businesses in their countries.

In general I see things working reasonably well for us on the global scene. It seems to me that the biggest challenge is for the developing countries to put "their house in order" if they want our business. This means getting rid of corruption and putting laws into practice that are compatible with our laws. From our vantage point it is a matter of them accepting our international rules of the game in order to attract more of our business. At the same time we can remain in an advantageous position as a large corporation. That is good business!!

That's all for now, Tony, and I look forward to receiving your part of this interesting two-sided dialogue.

All the best to you,
John

Dear John,

It was good to hear from you again, and especially to see the interesting idea you have of putting our e-mail dialogues into a "two-perspective" story. I think it could prove most useful, not only for ourselves, but also in helping young graduates try to make some sense of the dramatic transformations taking place.

From my perspective, I seem to create more questions than answers, but we may begin to get to the root of where the different perspectives come from. As you so well know, I have gone through many years of gradually changing my perspective. It is amazing what happens when one begins to look "from the outside" so to speak. With my different experiences, especially in developing countries, one begins to gain some new insight into the different approaches to business and how they affect the population in general. This is especially revealing with the rapid changes in the past ten years or so.

I want to mention to you, John, at the outset, that it may sound like I am bashing multinational companies (MNC), but that is not the intention. I have seen a few exceptional companies whose management is very thoughtful and responsible, that show genuine concern about their role in foreign (especially poor) countries, but they are very much the exception in my experience.

To begin, there seems to be something fundamental that is motivating this massive move of MNCs to developing countries. It seems that for the first time the MNC now really needs the countries of the South (developing countries) for their mainly manufacturing functions to considerably reduce costs without losing productivity, and thus

146

maintain a competitive edge. However, this constant need to reduce costs will not be a short-term need. What happens in these countries as a result of massive influx of MNCs is important, as the continued investment and profit picture of these companies are closely linked to the basic stability of these developing countries, and most especially their social stability so needed for successful business operations.

This brings us to the whole question of progress. What is progress? What we are learning is that most of these developing countries do not see progress only in monetary terms (with some notable exceptions). Most have a deeply rooted cultural side that is human oriented. That means their values are often very different from the MNCs, which of course are basically profit oriented. So social stability in these countries does not just depend on providing a few jobs (which, of course, they need too), but a whole social framework into which their work fits.

What we have seen over the past fifteen years in the developing countries is an increasing development of "dual economies." Governments, together with a handful of large national companies (usually closely allied with government), have been very happy to welcome investment from MNCs and have been offering them attractive conditions to locate in their country. The income helps to pay the interest on their usually high debts, and for that they need hard currency, plus the new contacts help them locate export market opportunities for the handful of large national companies. An example of this was when Mexico entered NAFTA, only 2% of Mexican businesses were in a position to participate in the NAFTA trade agreement. The "first economy" has grown out of this combination, where the country begins to be plugged into the global marketplace, with only a very few companies and strong government support. This "first economy" sector is of course also the one that controls development decisions for the rest of the country. The percentage of population that actually benefits from the first economy directly and indirectly is somewhere between 15% and 25%, depending on the country. The MNCs naturally work well with this sector, which generally supports opening up the country to foreign investment and privatizing government-owned companies. On the other hand, for governments this has meant heavy cuts in social programs for the poor (which is the largest percent-

age of the population), cuts in assistance to small businesses (the majority of businesses and employment), the subsistence agriculture sector (the biggest agricultural sector), as well as cuts in health and education services. Through adherence to these rules (outlined by the International Monetary Fund) many developing countries have been successful in meeting IMF requirements for new loans and debt repayment schemes. But sad to say this arrangement clearly carries a heavy social cost.

What happens to the population that is not in the "first economy?" They belong to the "second economy," which includes 75% to 85% of the population. In this sector we find the micro, small and medium-sized businesses, small-sized agricultural sector, and all indigenous groups. During these past years, as governments have withdrawn much of their assistance to these sectors, the populations have experienced increasing stagnation of their economy, increased poverty, increased unemployment (giving rise to a huge underground economy), and deteriorating health and education conditions. Governments have also been increasingly restricted in their budget planning and priorities, due to the need to give priority to the requirements related to the first economy if they want to maintain an attractive economic environment for foreign investment, and satisfy IMF guidelines. This whole second economy represents the majority of the population, and it is here where we are beginning to see real signs of social problems. Many analysts consider that this second economy population has managed to somehow cope for many years of a downhill slide (including a dramatic shrinkage of what was a middle class), and many have now simply come to the end of their capacity. In the growing poor regions this includes children dying of malnutrition, and no real hope for the future. At the same time they see a few in the small first economy becoming very wealthy. This situation is not positive for business stability anywhere.

All of these uncertainties have brought up a number of thought-provoking questions:

-- Since when did the priorities of money (profits) take precedence over human-based needs and rights? How did we allow this to happen?

-- Where is the government responsibility in all this? Or is the

government somehow compromised by the power of big businesses, which helped to put them in power and on whom the government depends to stay in power?

-- Does business really have any social responsibility in all this, whether at home or in other countries? It is now generally accepted that the large business sector is the one that has the most influence on how a country will or can develop. Then, does it not mean that the large business sector will have to begin to take responsibility for the longer-term consequences of its actions no matter where they are located?

-- Isn't it to their long-term benefit to take this responsibility seriously if they want to maintain social stability in the countries where they have low cost operations?

Coming back to the question: What actually happens in most cases in a developing country or region when large MNCs move in? What are the positive and negative effects? If we can identify those, perhaps we can begin to understand more clearly the root of the problems.

Firstly, I should repeat that there are a few corporations (mine included) that have gone through this painful exercise of reflection during these years, and have adopted a new philosophy that takes seriously the social and ecological implications of their operation, and their real responsibility in the healthy development of the community where they operate. But, sad to say we are very few. This whole subject, as you know, has covered many of our e-mail dialogues. As you may recall, a small group of us here locally from different backgrounds meets once a month to take part in very soul-searching discussions about these issues, such as the problems of debt, the main economic-based focus, social aspects and the deteriorating ecological conditions.

Returning to some of the topics you highlighted, I will try to follow your format somewhat so we can more easily make comparisons in perspectives.

The concept of lobbies, as you mentioned in your perspective, work rather differently in most of the developing countries. But the tendency certainly is the small elite group at the top of government, and a small core of businesses have the most influence on the develop-

ment direction of the country, and their decisions in turn are controlled to a great extent by the rules of unrestricted (free) trade. Lately we are seeing some examples where the broader population is protesting some of these decisions, but in most cases without very much effect. It seems that the whole opening up of these countries to unrestricted trade has happened so quickly that the international organizations and the MNCs have not agreed upon any specific guidelines or regulations for checks and balances. Hence it has become a "free for all casino," where the bigger you are the more advantage you have. Even money has become a commodity for trade. The process has in fact become a vicious circle, where the IMF comes in to "save" these countries with more loans, under conditions of "restructuring," which trans- lates into more privatizations, more opening up of markets, even for strategic goods needed for feeding the population, production cost reductions that show up in lower wages, reduced and more costly services and social programs, plus increased local taxes. True, many of these countries also tend to have a high level of corruption, so that complicates the situation, but in general they are in a box (in terms of development) over which they have little control.

In this picture lobbying is generally restricted within the circle of the small elite first economy, often with the assistance of interna- tional advisors who are specialists in globalization. Any opposition (and that certainly exists) from the second economy to the govern- ment policies imposed under IMF guidelines comes out in the form of public protests over specific issues, which governments try to calm with lower-level dialogues, with promises of better times to come, or even in cases by force. The problem is that the major part of the population of developing countries has been living this downward slide for almost two decades, so a time comes when they cannot survive on more of the same, and in many cases no longer believe in government promises.

In this whole process it is interesting to hear what people are really looking for. As we all mostly do, they look at their daily lives and possibilities in their own communities or regions. They are not interested in or concerned with what happens on the other side of the world, nor the financial markets. They want to have control over their lives again—with local job opportunities so they don't have to leave

150

their communities, good and affordable schools, secure health care and freedom to make decisions related to their communities. This of course is sometimes culture-related and means also renewed support of the "local," as related to micro, small and medium sized businesses rooted in the community, participation of the people in community activities, and local control of their lives in general. With the arrival of "modernization," and the inability to make a living in rural areas, villages or towns, there has been extensive migration to large cities, and the corresponding problems of slums. Modernization has also brought with it large international companies, and government policies and priorities have disrupted the viability of community and village economies. Not only do local businesses go bankrupt, as they cannot compete or are simply displaced, but there exists a general feeling of losing control of their lives and instability in their communities, which are fast disappearing. They feel subject to some foreign forces that seem to have more rights and privileges than the locals. Of course, some are pleased with a few new job opportunities—but at what price? These new companies seem to have strange working cultures and ways of thinking, and these companies mostly expect adaptation to their way of doing things, with little concern, interest or respect for the culture of the community in which they operate.

Technology is certainly one of the items at the top of the list of concerns, and most countries are very aware of its importance, not only in production, but also communications. For many thoughtful local leaders with whom we have had contact, there is real concern for where all this will lead, as there doesn't seem to be a longer-term international plan or criteria established that can direct technology in positive and ethical directions. Many see it as a free for all, with everyone running to keep up with the latest "toy." This lack of development direction is viewed as dangerous for the future.

At the local level, the small business sector needs "appropriate technologies" especially designed for their needs so they can become effective and capable of filling the local and regional niche markets that exist. After all, this smaller business sector is where the majority of the population is employed in the North and the South, so if we do not take their needs seriously, we have more ingredients for discontent, and social unrest in many regions.

In terms of the media, many people view the media organizations as another large MNC, and hence their interests are obvious, so what we find in mainline TV programs supports the main interests of the world of the MNC. Some even go to the point of saying the media is in fact constantly in the process of "self-censorship" in order to eradicate anything that could be interpreted as contrary to MNC interests. After all, the MNC are their big clients, and the media corporations depend on them for their existence.

The developing countries are of course inundated with TV programming from rich countries. Many thoughtful people worry that this broad coverage is one of the most powerful influences on values, and is proving destructive to the deeply held positive cultural values in these countries, affecting the very fabric of society. On the other hand, it is also viewed often as a source of social discontent, as the poor see wealthy livelihoods on TV, while their own lives are worsening. The "message" is that economic prosperity and a "happy life" are supposed to already be happening.

Based on your mention of some major international trade related organizations, I certainly have a different perspective from where I stand. For example, the World Trade Organization (WTO) is probably one of the most controversial. Many see it as the "last straw," so to speak, in terms of the control of all economic activity being taken out of the control of countries and regions, and placed under the control of one organization, the WTO. The benefits seem only a very few, mainly huge MNCs. Many analysts now think that the WTO as such will need to be totally rethought if it is to survive, as it was planned without the real input from a broad spectrum of developing countries in terms of the affects it would have on them. And now that they are becoming more aware and informed, these countries are reconsidering their position, and some now believe that the WTO will need their full backing and involvement to survive as a viable internationally representative organization. Perhaps we are beginning to see this happening, based on the meeting in Mexico where a number of poorer countries formed a strong common front.

Regarding the International Monetary Fund (IMF), as you say it is viewed as a friend of the MNCs and the WTO. Certainly indebtedness and restructuring packages have provided many benefits for the

MNCs and international financial institutions. Also these developing countries are now of special interest to the globalized organizations as sources of cost reduction, as well as new sources of natural resources and trade in monetary exchanges. Unfortunately, many also view this whole form of development as a key factor in these countries developing dual economies. This whole unhealthy wealth distribution situation is viewed as worrisome, and many believe a recipe for potential social unrest. It appears that some deep rethinking of the development model is essential for future survival of these countries, as well as for the long-term interests of the MNC.

The United Nations we view as having played an important role over the past fifty years, but presently needs major revision for it to continue to play that role. It is still seen as an international organization that has a genuine interest in the problems of the less powerful countries, and still has credibility as an international stabilizer for most rich countries. The UN has lost considerable funding, especially from an important member such as the United States, which has a major UN debt.

On the environmental side, the UN has found an area where it has gained much respect and support, but also discord, because it has been touching on environmental issues that question some the policies and actions of some of the MNCs and the WTO.

This is certainly true, especially because many, especially poor countries, view the policies and actions of these global organizations as responsible for much of the destruction they experience in their countries related to uncontrolled growth and the desire of MNCs to continue "business as usual." These environmental issues are now considered to be serious by a large part of the UN membership, but no one is completely clear about what to do next, or what time frame we have to mend our ways before irreparable damage occurs. It seems clear that short-term financial considerations are taking precedence over long-term environmental and human viability, even in many developing countries. As you so well know, people in dire poverty are in a survival mode, and cannot be expected to have much ecological concern. On the other hand, these countries desperately need consideration in implementing long-term global trade and debt-related regulations in order to allow social issues and ecological issues to be seriously considered as priorities. Something clearly needs to be done to help, as social unrest and worse ecological problems are undoubtedly coming, and this is negative for everyone—both the country as well as international companies.

Finally we arrive at the subject you so rightly pointed out as the one that creates a big gap between our two perspectives—in what we refer to as "quality of life."

I referred to the concept at the beginning, so shall mention only some key areas that are so different from your perspective.

Firstly, people in general see happiness and fulfillment in life in human terms. Therefore, in most of these countries the family (meaning also extended family) is the glue that keeps societies together and gives meaning and purpose to life in general. It is also viewed by many as one thing that has given people strength and courage to withstand the upheavals they have had to face over many years.

Together with the family comes spirituality. This does not necessarily mean structured religion (even though the majority are Roman Catholic in Latin America), but is seems most have inherited an innate spirituality that comes out in many ways, such as their capacity to withstand loss, disappointment and destruction of their livelihood. Somehow they have tremendous courage and inner strength to begin again and work hard to move ahead. These factors of course have their limits too, as poverty and frustration over long periods have shown.

Another factor in quality of life involves the importance attached to human relationships. Even in work situations these relationships are vital and must be solid in order for work to be performed to the best of their abilities—at all levels. Even though some have tried to "modernize" their administration by using "first world" methods, it does not really work very well. The human side of society is so deeply engrained that it must be respected in all aspects of life. On the other side, a few genuinely successful local companies have managed to do both—conserve their important cultural values and still run efficient, successful companies.

Today, of course, in order to even provide the most fundamental aspects, such as food and shelter, the economic side is vital. Hence we see painful migrations to city slum areas, or often illegal entry *into another country. However, even with these moves, most still feel a strong attachment to their home communities and regions. As we see these ties slowly weakened, due to survival needs, young people especially are exposed to a wilderness that offers only short-term instant gratification, as seen on TV. There is a real concern in these countries due to what they see as values-destructive television programs, and the negative influence and power these have on the cultural values of the young especially.*

We are also seeing, even in the North, much soul searching going on as people are looking for new inner meaning in their lives, which money has not provided. We see this also among many of our colleagues in the MNCs. So there must be something that has gone "off track" at the highest level of these and other organizations that make up the countries. Many feel that the speed with which the uncontrolled globalization has taken place has been part of the problem. Within a very few years everything became deregulated, plus the explosion of the financial "casino," where money is now treated like a commodity. This has all happened, it seems, without any ground rules to direct or control it. This situation any organization knows cannot work. So the worst of human attributes have taken over—such as greed. It is like creating a monster, letting it loose, and no one dares to control it for fear of being destroyed. Instead we keep feeding it.

As far as I can tell, we are now seeing a whole movement toward humanization of work and development in its broadest sense, and needing to move the concept of control more toward the local level, where I think it ought to be. This of course does not combine with the basic motivation behind globalization, so we certainly have the ingredients for a collision course. But I am optimistic, as I see the basic positive aspects of human nature prevailing for the common good. I hope I (and many of my colleagues) am right.

Hopefully this more or less summarizes my perspective. I really look forward to having these ideas discussed more widely, especially as you say among university students. They are the ones who will likely find new paths that we have not seen yet.

Best Regards,
Tony

CHAPTER VII

I. Organizational Transformation

A. INTRODUCTION[1]

Organizational transformation is a complex phenomena that is closely related to our personal views of our own reality. Following are some insights from visionaries in the field.

1. Ervin Laszlo (related to the "macroshift" or major transformation we are presently experiencing): "A macroshift is a transformation of civilization (including organizations) in which technology is the driver and the values and consciousness of a critical mass of people, the decider)."[2]

2. Paul Hawkins, Amory Lovins, L. Hunter Lovins: "Natural capitalism and the possibility of a new industrial system are based on a very different mind-set and set of values than conventional capitalism . . . there are growing numbers of business owners and managers who are changing their enterprises to become more environmentally responsible because of deeply rooted beliefs and values."[3]

3. Willis Harman: "The latter third of this century (twentieth century) is a period of fundamental transformation of the modern world, the extent and meaning of which we are only beginning to grasp. . . . The role of business in that transformation

is absolutely critical."[4]

For us to be motivated to rethink our values usually requires a catalyst of some kind. There is considerable controversy over what type of catalyst ignites particularly management people to rethink their personal values. Some researchers believe that the motivation usually comes from dissatisfaction at work, while others believe it most often comes from a very personal feeling of need to find new meaning and purpose in life and work. Finally, only individual readers can know their own motivation. In this particular section on organizational transformation we are focusing on personal transformation first, but it could well be that work itself has been your initial catalyst.

This next step, dealing with the process of implementation of these values into life and work, is often more complex. It requires each of us to actually commit ourselves to something new and strange in many ways—to a fundamental personally felt conviction to "live" our own values in life and work in order to find genuine inner tranquility and new meaning and purpose.[5][6] In one way, it appears an impossible task, as everything around us (with a few notable exceptions) still operates on conventional thinking and values. However, an increasing number of people are going through this process of questioning and rethinking every day. Some are doing this consciously, and others unconsciously; that is, sometimes we are only really aware of our changing way of thinking when we begin to read about emerging values and realize that some of these values are ones that we already hold. In this case we will have a much easier transition in terms of implementation of these values into our everyday lives, and work.

This chapter is mainly directed to readers who are convinced that we need and want to find a better path in life and work, and are prepared to make a sincere effort to achieve it.[6][7] This process is not easy. One cannot compare it to learning a new skill or a new computer program, which are understood and captured using basically intellectual capacities and our objective mind. On the other hand, the transformation to a new set of values requires, in addition to our intellectual capacities, the use of our higher consciousness capacities. In our higher consciousness are found our intuition, our sense of purpose and meaning in life, our creativity, our deep feelings about right and wrong, and in its broad sense our spirituality.[8] All of these aspects are essential to fully comprehend our new emerging values, and especially our inherent connection with our natural environment and the whole web of life on Earth. Therefore, we need to find ways of tapping into our higher consciousness (which we all have the capacity to do) and benefit from its incredible storehouse of wisdom and knowledge. In this way we will have the capability to balance our thinking between these two capacities to finally develop a fulfilled, whole person. This is a giant step in finding new meaning to life and work—a new path.

For many of us, the concept of transformation in thinking seems a very dramatic reaction to needed changes in ways of thinking and working. We have usually made changes in the past that have been achieved reasonably well by making perhaps some modifications in our attitudes, or introducing new work techniques. Why are we talking about such a complete and deep transformation at the very depths of our personal belief system? This is a very valid question, and one that we can realistically ask. The difficulty lies in the magnitude of the dilemmas we face. The intractable and life-threatening problems that exist have not responded to our conventional way of thinking about how to solve them, and in fact many are worsening rather than improving. Therefore, over the past two decades especially, the situation has deteriorated to the point where many people are questioning the "system" itself.

As indicated by Madron and Jopling, "The main barrier to adopting a (new) systems approach is not the difficulty with the concepts, but our own habits of mind."[9]

Once we question the system we question the philosophy or truths on which the system is seated, and ultimately the values at its root. This is where we are now. In the previous chapters we discussed these emerging values and the principles that follow. Now we need to consider how to put the rethought values into practice in life and work.

The purpose of this chapter is to assist the reader in this process by providing some guidelines to help redirect our emerging values toward a new, fulfilling path in life and work.

A key aspect in this process involves the use of our higher consciousness in addition to our already highly developed intellectual, objective thinking. As has been explained previously, we all have this capacity for higher consciousness thinking, but it has been, for most of us, very little developed. It also appears clearer every day that we absolutely have to begin to develop our higher consciousness in order to gain full understanding of our deeply held human values, including the very nature of humans, how we view and value the natural environment around us, and in total terms, how we as humans fit into this larger web of all life on Earth. Experience has shown that once we begin to develop our higher consciousness, a whole new series of valuable insights occur and a new depth of inner meaning begins to form within each of us. Therefore, the guidelines that follow can begin to further develop this incredible human capacity—our higher consciousness.

B. TRANSFORMATION PROCESS: PERSONAL LEVEL

The central core of this transformation process is focused on *the roots of our thinking*—our deeply held personal values. This new thinking is described by Marilyn Ferguson:[10]

"The great shuddering, irrevocable shift overtaking us is not a new political, religious or philosophical system. It is a new mind—the ascendance of a startling worldview that gathers into its framework breakthrough science and insights from earliest recorded thought."

Speaking of these new thinkers as "aquarian thinkers," Ferguson states:

"Once a personal change began in earnest, they found themselves rethinking everything, examining old assumptions, looking anew at their work and relationships, health, political power and "experts" goals and values."

These rethought values form the foundation for all our thinking, attitudes and behaviors. Therefore it is to this root level that we need to penetrate in order to initiate genuine transformation.[11]

Firstly, we need to identify our values that have produced positive outcomes. These we need to protect and conserve as valuable for our life. Secondly, we need to identify the ones that have produced negative outcomes—the source of our problems. Next we need to take the painful step of rethinking and modifying the negative values, or discarding those that cannot be altered or readapted, as they usually appear as the deep source of negative outcomes and our worries or unhappiness.

This examination process can be painful because many of these values have been a part of us for many years, and perhaps even most our lifes, as a solid groundwork of beliefs, and still exist in most of mainstream society. But it is becoming clear that once we begin to develop our higher consciousness we also find new strength and clarity that makes it possible for us to feel the opening of a new direction based on positive values—the ones that give us inner peace and purpose in life. Once these values begin to bubble to the surface, a whole series of things begin to happen in our lives, such as the new way we view ourselves as a person, how we relate to family, friends, colleagues and even strangers, how we view our work, and how we view nature and our interconnectedness with our natural environment as a part of all living beings.

We should remind ourselves, as mentioned earlier in this study, that we are fortunate enough to live in a period that many visionaries tell us involves the most important transformation in thinking in 300 years—a major phenomena in human history.

1. No Magic Bullet

The transformation process itself can take many different forms depending on the person. There is no "magic bullet," so all of us will have to find the process that suits us best. Much work has been done in this area by psychologists, spiritual leaders and development specialists.[12] [13] [14] This section therefore is meant to provide some overall guidelines for personal preparation. This process of personal transformation comes first, before organizational transformation can be fully successful.

It should be remembered that this is not an easy process. It delves into deeply held personal values and beliefs, so it can be painful and unsettling at times. However, this period of "unsettlement" is not negative, but a natural reaction whenever we have a major transformation in our life and work. On the contrary, most specialists in the field, as well as participants, tell us that they come out of this process as much stronger people, more self-confident, more convinced of what they believe, and a deeper feeling of who they are, thus enhancing both their personal and working lives.

2. Commitment[15]

Most readers initially drawn to the topic of this study probably already have a number of questions or worries about the direction that their own work and lives are taking, and would like to gain more insight into the roots of some of their dilemmas. However, it is one thing to read interesting information related to this subject, but it is something very different to commit to participating in a journey of change of one's own. This usually takes time, and should not be taken lightly, as the anticipated results can form a new foundation for all our thinking, our goals in life and all our relationships—with ourselves, with family and friends, with work colleagues, and with our community at large.

For most it is a very important commitment and a new chapter in our lives for which we are very thankful. It is a step that requires genuine commitment for the process to work positively. Without this commitment, the efforts and insights at each stage will likely be superficial, perhaps purely intellectual and disappointing. Therefore, a full commitment from the beginning is essential. It goes without saying that together with commitment goes a sincere openness to change. This naturally should provide new hope and promise, rather than fear and worry about change itself. Fundamental change in thinking such as this transformation depicts, involves a period of feeling uncertainty, vulnerability and uneasiness—and even emotional pain at times, as the old values are questioned or discarded and the new or readapted ones appear to replace them. Our whole human system has to process and readapt to this whole transformation in thinking. It affects everything we think and do, so we can expect the transition period to be unsettling. The length of time involved in this period varies greatly with the individual. It can vary all the way from a very rapid sensation of "opening of the mind" (or higher consciousness) and new way of viewing oneself and the world—all the way to a gradual longer-term process of study, and reflection and experiencing new situations and impressions that ignite new ways of interpreting them.

Once we begin to feel the inner sensation of quietness of the mind, we may also find ourselves questioning many things. We need to allow time for this necessary and natural transition period to develop little by little. As the "pieces begin to fall into place," with new or altered values gradually emerging, one begins to feel a new inner peace and new positive energy.

3. Patience[16]

This whole process takes time and patience. It cannot be accomplished in terms of deciding a certain number of weeks or months, as judged through our objective mind, but through how we feel in our inner self, and the degree to which it begins to have a significant effect on our thinking about daily life. We are all different individuals, and the way this continuous process manifests itself for each of us is different. One thing however is certain, that to continue to benefit from this new development of the unconscious subjective mind and its new balance with the conscious objective mind (both are needed and important) will require regular quiet times each day where we can totally let go of all our preoccupations to allow our mind to be quiet. This is essential in our daily lives in order to find inner peace and real meaning in life and work.

The concept of patience is not an easy one to deal with in our present world of priorities on speed and efficiency. But it must be borne in mind that when we deal with our deep inner self and the values we hold there, another concept of time exists that has no relationship with our objective mind's concept of time. The deeply felt value we can gain from this whole process will be greatly dependent upon our capacity to respect the indications of our own human system—how we personally respond and feel. Some days will be very positive and new thinking seems to feel right and comprehensible. Other days will seem negative as we are bombarded with the merits of the comfortableness of conventional thinking. So patience is essential, as we must have faith in the wisdom of and pace of our inner self—this deep wisdom is finally the one that tells us when (at what time) we are ready for the next step along the new path.

4. Some Suggested Steps in Personal Transformation

Personal transformation lies at the foundation of both personal life and organizational transformation. In other words, organizations that plan to go through a transformation will need to take into account the deeply held personal values of the organization's decision makers. These values will need to be carefully examined and adjusted in order that this foundation is completely sound and sustainable. Consequently, these suggested steps in personal transformation could apply to everyone, for personal as well as professional life.

i) Study:[17]

The motivation for participating in a transformation process usually begins either through study based on existing questions and deep concerns about what is happening, or through some unusual experience that has had a profound affect on a person's thinking. Whatever the case, there needs to be some deeply felt motivating reason to actually embark on this process of transformation. We must feel a deep desire to improve our lives—to change direction. That said, most feel uncertain of exactly how and where to begin the process. Hopefully these suggestions, based on experience of other participants, will assist the reader in this search.

In addition to what we learn through different studies, it also reassures us that there are many other people with similar worries and dissatisfactions as oneself. Also, we soon realize that many highly respected researchers and visionaries are now providing much relevant and valuable information and wisdom that provides new insight into the reasons for many of our problems and questions. The very fact that others, including highly respected economists and scientists, are showing concern gives us confidence in realizing what we are feeling is part of quite a widespread genuine concern about our human state and how we as humans are contributing directly to the problems we are experiencing.

There is no doubt that for most of us this transformation in our thinking process requires a considerable amount of study. We have to satisfy our intellectual curiosity and knowledge about what is happening in the world at present in order to feel how we fit into the whole picture. A wide range of published material exists. Undoubtedly some studies will be directed toward our human capacity for higher consciousness, as this is one area that has only in recent years become important and of interest to many in the scientific and business communities. Some of the publications referenced in this section may prove of interest as well as some of the publications mentioned in the bibliography. But this is only a small number, and an extensive supply is also available for a wide variety of areas in this field. Studying is important for most, and motivation to do so is natural as our curiosity is sparked with the new ideas that are brought out once we begin delving into our own thinking and that of our working world.

ii) Meditation/Contemplation:[18] [19]

We all need some way of reducing stress, relaxing and bringing quietness to the mind. Through the experience of many thousands of people and throughout human history, some form of daily meditation or contemplation has proven extremely helpful. This requires about fifteen to twenty minutes a day, a short rest period for the mind. This functions best for most when guided by a professional and it has some structure. This means locating a professional in the field in order to provide maximum benefit from this short period of relaxation. There exists a wide variety of techniques, and each of us needs to find the one most suitable for our own personality. Using these techniques makes it possible to achieve quietness of the mind in a relatively short period of time, and it can take place in our own homes or even workplace. With the quietening of the mind we begin the first steps in accessing our higher consciousness.

There are of course other ways to find this quietness and relaxation of the mind, and some of these could be more effective for some of us, depending on our own circumstances, personal sensibilities and time available.

Earlier in the book it is noted that Roger Walsh[20] has worked in this area, and has studied many of the spiritual traditions where the higher consciousness is highly developed. Walsh states that the great spiritual traditions suggest that wisdom that involves peace of mind and purpose in life (coming from our higher consciousness) can be found in a number of places.

These are:

a. In nature: Many people find genuine release and quietness of the mind from being in nature. This can take many forms, such as: viewing a beautiful sunset; looking at a quiet lake or sea; walking in the mountains; the serenity of a forest. All of these we note require a period of quiet time to allow the mind to relax and disconnect from the concerns of our busy life, and enter a period of calm, as the individual feels totally absorbed into a different "space," so to speak, when surrounded by nature.

b. Silence and solitude: This can take place in many different circumstances, but nature provides an atmosphere and surroundings sought out by many. Whatever the selected special place, it is the place where the mind can become quiet. We can, if we have the desire, find a way to participate in this period of quietness as part of our everyday life.

c. From the wise: Indeed, if we are fortunate enough to have contact with a genuinely wise person who is highly evolved in his/her higher consciousness, we can benefit a great deal. The wisdom such a person displays in everyday attitudes and actions can be an important inspiration and can often help us access our own higher consciousness. This usually requires frequent contact over a period of time to give our minds time to quieten sufficiently to comprehend the wisdom of such a special person.

d. Yourself: We are sometimes surprised at the depth of thought that we ourselves are capable of once we allow our minds to become quiet. Oftentimes this leads to feelings of clarity related to our thinking, lives and work, and can spark us to alter our lives as a result. The important part of this capacity usually means the need for quiet periods, plus listening closely to the small feelings or thoughts that we perceive, which begin to guide us in a certain direction of thinking. These are usually subtle feelings or thoughts—and we must have the courage and patience to listen to them, and have the confidence to let them guide us little by little to our deeper examination of our beliefs and aspirations.

e. The nature of life and death: Human attitudes and feelings related to death especially are often most notable through the personal experience of the death of a loved one. One begins to realize that our time here on Earth is a short interlude considering the timelessness of our universe. This realization also helps us to put life and death in context, and the importance of living as full a life as possible every day. It awakens the concept of quality in life in terms of our spirituality, our interpersonal relationships, as well as the simple un-importance of acquiring "things." Life is essentially related to qual-ity, not quantity. These thoughts often help us to recognize our deep consciousness capacity and our relationship with the universality of the spiritual world in its overall sense. Thus some people have found a deep transformative experience as a result of experiencing death in one's own family. As well, these same feelings of awe and spirituality often produce immense joy accompanying new life in one's family.

In conclusion, in addition to reading about our present problems, transformation usually requires some form of quiet exercise in the form of some type of meditation or contemplation. This can become the window to developing a deeper understanding of our personal feelings, beliefs and values. This will provide us with the first indi-cations of access to our higher consciousness, which is essential to understand the whole person that we are, our connection with nature, and the true values that are deeply imbedded in our inner minds. Each reader will need to choose the form most suitable for him/herself individually. This may also require, to initiate the process, contacting a professional in the field for assistance. The use of these techniques for quietening the mind and "listening to" our mind is thousands of years old. But it is very helpful even today as most working people search for relief from the stresses in work and daily life, and want to feel an inner peace and relaxation.

iii) Support Person(s)[21]

As we proceed through these complex and uncertain times in our lives, we can often benefit from the support of others to provide extra strength and courage. These support persons can come from a wide variety of sources, depending very much on individual needs and circumstances. Naturally a family member or a close friend is an ideal person who can be very supportive and helpful. Others have found a professional person in the field as being the most suitable, and still others have found a spiritual leader as the one whom they can best relate to, due to the often spiritually related experiences that may occur as we begin to access our higher consciousness. Whomever seems most helpful to the individual is a very personal decision, but experience shows that in most cases it is very beneficial to have a support person(s), especially during the early stages of the transformation when one feels especially vulnerable and uncertain.

iv) Small Changes[22]

As we move along the path of rethinking our deeply felt values, most find that without realizing it, we begin to be conscious of some of our daily attitudes and behaviors changing. In this way we begin to see small signals of change in our thinking. They can often motivate us to make very small changes in our daily routines. For example, we perhaps feel we want to spend more time in the garden; maybe call on someone who is ill or lonely; maybe spend more time with our children or spouse; maybe even think twice when we buy an item that now does not seem that important. These are all very small changes, but they are important and valuable to notice. As time goes on other things will gradually change. Then one day, when we feel more secure within ourselves, we may begin to think about our work. Many questions can come to mind, some of which have never come to mind before. Examples of questions may be:

-- Does my work have meaning for me?

-- Does work cause me anxiety?

-- Is there anything I can do to change that?

-- Is it a type of work I would like to continue to do for a long time?

-- Does my work allow me time for my family, friends and community?

-- Do I feel good about the product (or service) my organization produces?

These are only a few of many questions that may come to mind as we develop in our transformation and begin to see our world through a different lens—through a different way of thinking based on different values—a new consciousness.

C. ORGANIZATIONAL LEVEL TRANSFORMATION [23] [24] [25] [26] [27] [28]

1. Introduction

Within many organizations that decide to initiate a major transformation, few people will have gone through a complete process of reflection and personal transformation, as described in the previous section. As well, an organization's motivation for change usually comes from other sources, which are viewed through the conventional organizational lens. Some typical examples of problems that motivate organizations to change may include:

a. The organization is not profitable and the future looks complex and uncertain.

b. The organization has just had a major change in ownership and wishes to start anew.

c. The organization is wanting to plan longer term, views their product or service as valuable and profitable, and wants to redirect the organization toward long-term, viable goals as opposed to conventional, shorter-term goals.

d. The organization has a viable product or service, but has been plagued with "people problems" in management, employees and unions, which is affecting the whole operation.

Whatever the problems or motivation, the desire for in-depth change or transformation is usually very genuine. However, management is often unaware of what is really involved at the human level, and how this affects other areas of the organization and wider community. This is an area that is considered the soft side of management and often thought to be one of the easiest to change. With the advent of ever more sophisticated technologies, many top managers have become convinced that technology combined with more sophisticated organizational development and management techniques will for the most part solve their "people problems." Nevertheless, there needs to be a realization that in total terms, the economic success of an organization depends very heavily on the human element, which basically controls all technologies and organizational management, and finally involves the decision makers and how they think, resulting in how the organization functions. If we are not successful in genuinely involving the human element in the total development of the organization, it will suffer.

Madron and Jopling provide a very positive view of this process of change: "the shift in thinking that precedes fundamental change is already happening in every sphere (outside the closed mind sets)."[28]

Much has been published in recent years regarding the need for addressing the human side of all kinds of organizations, and especially the new role that private sector organizations play in society.[29] We have arrived at the point of recognizing that the business sector is the one that in fact presently has the most influence in how a country or region develops, and business and governments are now very closely interconnected. This is a relatively new phenomena in society. It also follows that this situation places new and different responsibilities on the business sector related to its responsibilities for the longer-term consequences of its behaviors and actions. This new world of business is one often difficult for this sector to accept—being accustomed to only having to worry about making profits. Fortunately we are slowly beginning to see a few examples of businesses (mainly in the smaller sector) recognizing this new responsibility.[30] Here is where the importance of the human side of business becomes paramount, and how it is also linked to responsibilities in the local community, to the natural environment, and the planet as a whole.

The following section approaches these challenges for fundamental change from a case study perspective. It is hoped that readers will be able to find some ingredients that can assist in their own organizational search for transformation in thinking and practice.

2. Organizational Transformation: Some Views[31 32 33 34 35 36 37]

i) Views of some visionary thinkers

The concept of transformation to "sustainable thinking" is different from most publications on "change" in organizations.

Two important reasons for these differences are:

-- this change, or transformation, involves the fundamental rethinking of the deep-rooted values on which the organization is seated, including the rethinking of the personal values of the decision makers.[38]

-- this transformation involves a new balance between intellectual analytical thinking and higher-consciousness "thinking."

Gary Zukav[39] addresses this concept in a more direct "inner self" sense, when he states:

"As individuals within the business community come to recognize themselves as immortal souls, and experience within themselves the shift from pursuit of external power—the ability to manipulate and control—to the pursuit of authentic power—alignment of the personality with the soul (higher consciousness)—their understanding of the dynamic that lies beneath the concept of ownership will cause them to question the utility of this concept."

Madron and Jopling,[40] in referring to the essentials of successful change, indicate:

"Put very simply, we have to change the way we think. Fundamental change (as distinct from operational improvements) in any purposeful human system starts to happen when a significant number of people within that system begin to think differently."

Warren Bennis, in relation to transformation in organizations, has published widely on the need for competent leaders, and the distinct role of leaders in transformation in organizations.

Bennis emphasizes the importance of quality in leadership, when he states:

"Modern society has been oriented to quantity . . . quantity is measured in money. . . . Quality often is not measured at all but is appreciated intuitively. Our response to quality is a feeling. Feelings of quality are connected intimately with our experience of meaning, beauty, and value in our lives."

He also defines four competencies in examples of good leaders as: "management of attention; management of meaning; management of trust; management of self. . . . Leaders manage attention through a compelling vision that brings others to a place they have not been before."

These insights are meant as food for thought. Some of them may come to mind during the impressions gained from the following case study.

D. ORGANIZATIONAL CHANGE: A CASE STUDY [41] [42] [43] [44] [45] [46]

1. Introduction

This case study in which the author has participated takes place in different phases. It focuses initially on the emerging changes in ways of thinking by business managers from principally two culturally different countries (Mexico and US), and the values that underpin management thinking. The results of these changes in thinking for managers has had an effect on everyday management decisions, attitudes and behaviors inside and outside the companies. This phase is followed by phases focused on Mexican management transformation, and finally brings together an overview of the realities of overall sustainability that exists in Mexican and Latin American businesses.

The entire case study spans a period of twenty years, and the first phase includes mainly a number of company managers from private-sector US and Mexican organizations. The majority of these companies have been offshore "maquiladoras" manufacturing companies operating in Mexico, as well as other phases of the case involving 100% Mexican companies.

The transformation in thinking in general appears to draw largely from managers discovering commonality in some basic values (as well as diversity in others) across cultures that are housed in particular business issues. Throughout the different phases of the case study these become apparent in a variety of cross-cultural management experiences.

2. Types of Companies

A large section of this case study has involved the management of a significant number of private-sector transculturally managed business organizations, mainly from the US and Mexico.

It demonstrates examples of the management challenges these companies have been facing for many years, and the central role of cultural differences and how these differences fundamentally affect the overall management approach and interpretation of each group.

The first phase of this case study has involved the offshore maquiladora operations that have been operating largely along the US-Mexico border for many years. This phase is followed by one involving 100 percent Mexican companies that have decided to enter the process of transformation from a traditional authoritative management approach to a "modernized" participative one, considered essential for Mexican companies to work most effectively, both nationally and internationally. The final phase of the case study involves an assessment of the overall sustainability of the business sector in Mexico and Latin America. The central core running through all these phases is a group of emerging underlying values on which company policies and management practices are seated.

3. Management Style

The management style that the participating managers from US and Mexico had been accustomed to were quite different. Mexican managers who have been hired to work in US companies have mostly been accustomed to a traditional hierarchal structure with an authoritative management style. On the other hand, the US managers have been mostly accustomed to a corporate controlled directed management style where responsibilities for results are delegated to the local operation, which are individually held responsible for the performance of their particular area. In addition, a third type of management style has been attempted. This involves managers of mixed US-Mexican heritage who have been brought up (and mostly born) and educated in the US, but have maintained a large part of their Mexican heritage. This group, the US corporations have felt, could be the solution for the Mexican operations, because they could work the US way and also speak Spanish and understand the Mexican culture. This arrangement unfortunately has rarely been successful, as they are not well accepted by the Mexican managers for many reasons, and in most cases changes have had to be made.

4. Mexican-US Working Environment: Economic/Social/ Environmental

a) The companies in the first phase of the case study have involved US and Mexican management, and largely US manufacturing companies operating as maquiladoras in Mexico, producing a wide variety of products for direct export to the US.

Most of these have been located along the US-Mexico border region, but also includes several operations in the interior, in cities such as Guadalajara and Chihuahua.

b) The main objective of the foreign companies setting up operations in Mexico is monetary. This involves reduction in costs, largely through wages paid, special tax arrangements, and more relaxed environmental regulations. As a result, profit margins are considerably increased.

c) Socially related factors in Mexico have not generally been a priority concern for most maquiladora operations (with a few notable exceptions). Instead, reduction of monetary costs has been a priority. Wages paid have largely been low, following the Mexican peso scale, with a very few exceptions for some highly specialized jobs that also involve high stress and long working hours. There have also been significant cost reductions during Mexican currency devaluations. On the other hand, these new manufacturing operations have provided the potential for employment for certain sectors of the Mexican society where none existed before.

In the border region however, especially at the worker level, important challenges exist in the social area. Some of these include separation of families (with extensive employment requirements for young women), almost non-existent housing, and general lack of communities that have served as the stabilizer for behaviors, values and family support.

The Mexican management group in general has had more favorable conditions due to their level of education, skills and considerably higher income than the worker group.

d) "Flexibility" in ecological requirements has proven a strong attraction for foreign companies. Ecological aspects have in many areas been "negotiated" with Mexican government authorities and laws often "bent" due to the Mexican government's perceived need to encourage foreign investment as a priority.

5. Identifying the Initial Challenge

With the large number of foreign companies setting up operations in Mexico, it soon became clear to some that the companies would not able to operate exactly as they had been accustomed to in the US. They were in a very different working environment with a very different culture and management experience. Many companies seemed to "solve the problem" by deciding to impose fully the US management style, and hire Mexican managers who were sufficiently flexible to accept the US way of working. It was then the manager's job to train the workers accordingly. For some companies this has worked reasonably well in the shorter term, as there has been an ample workforce from which to select, but this supply has gradually decreased through the years. A smaller number of companies, however, have become aware of the cultural differences fundamentally affecting the management level, and considered it essential to make some adjustments in their management style, mainly for longer-term productive and economic reasons, as well as their image and acceptability in Mexico.

Here are found the beginnings of cross-cultural management concerns, which began around the early 1990s. Management in some companies were searching for ways of improving communications and management performance in their operations. It was to satisfy this recognized need that the first phase of transcultural management work became essential, and led to a major research study by the author and publication of the book, *Management in Two Cultures*. During the past two decades many companies have sought information and further assistance related to transcultural management, in both English and Spanish.

6. Phases in Organizational Change

Each of the following phases form, in many ways, a continuous process, with each one growing out of the previous phase. In an attempt to try to share a few priority points related to these experiences, a simple format has been followed that can perhaps put each phase more easily into a context of the whole.

This format, in general terms includes:
-- objective or purpose of each phase
-- special study projects related to each phase
-- results and lessons learned from each phase.

This whole "case study" has come together through many different experiences, leading to an ever deeper search for fundamental values that underpin culturally diverse organizations and countries (mainly Mexico, other Latin American countries, US and Canada), while at the same time respecting and valuing the richness of diversity in cultures, languages and tastes. The whole journey has been an incredible learning experience, especially because it has involved real situations and working with and learning first hand from people with widely diverse ways of thinking and values. One feels humbled by these experiences because there is a realization that with each step we are only just "scratching the surface" in terms of understanding the vast capacities of human nature, and how different cultures enrich us as human beings.

This "case study" has evolved through different phases. It began with transcultural management and moved through different phases in the overall search for positive values and sustainability in general. It takes place over a period of several years and can be viewed as separated into three main phases. These phases are:

a. Phase I: Transcultural Management (Mexico-US): Part I and Part II.
b. Phase II: Mexican Management in Transition
c. Phase III: Sustainable Development and Business in Mexico and Latin America.

a. Phase I: Transcultural Management: Part I

This phase was motivated initially by a strong indication of need to find some way of alleviating the challenges that have grown out of differences in culture and values between US and Mexican managers working side by side in transcultural organizations. These challenges, related to cross-cultural communication, cultural interpretations and different ways of thinking, were (and still are in many organizations) creating a host of challenges to their overall company success.

Some important questions or concerns that have surfaced in relation to the cross-cultural difficulties include:

-- What does "culture" mean to US and Mexican managers?

-- How does culture affect day-to-day business, or does it? Is business culturally neutral?

-- When US and Mexican managers work together, whose culture should take priority? Which is better?

-- If everyone can speak English as a common language, does that solve the problem?

-- Can we "homogenize" management style?

-- How can we find a common working "code of conduct" if we have two different cultures and two ways of thinking?

These questions have required basically primary research in order to gain insight into the cultural aspects that have most affected both the US and Mexican managers in their everyday work. Thus began the first of a number of research projects needed to assist the decision makers at all levels with their management challenges.

Research Study Project: Management in Two Cultures:

This research project proved to be much more complex than anticipated. One of the challenges involved the lack of publications dealing with this subject, except for some philosophical and sociological studies on the Mexican side, and a large number of US-based business management books reflecting US business style. It seemed that working cross culturally in a way that respected and valued both cultures was relatively new in those early years of the maquiladora operations.

Another aspect that needed to be taken into account was the particular style of management that was most used on each side. It soon became clear that most Mexican managers had been accustomed to a traditional autocratic hierarchal management style. On the US side the most common style that was being "exported" was a corporate-controlled, highly structured style, which meant a high level of decision making was taking place at the corporate level.

The main question of the study was: What are the key cultural aspects that most affect how managers think, behave and practice their different functions in management?

Research Challenges:
a. It soon became clear that primary research was essential as the main source of reliable information. This meant finding suitable company executives to learn from, and gaining access to them to have in-depth interviews.
b. Interviews: Needed to ensure that the interviewees would disclose what they really believed was true, and not what they thought the interviewer wanted to hear, or slanted toward one culture or the other. This meant, especially for the Mexican side, a complex process of finding someone in each case to provide a special introduction and recommendation to the owner of a business selected.
c. Needed to avoid having affiliations with any US, Canadian or Mexican institution or organization. This was perceived as possibly jeopardizing neutrality, and also possibly slanting company executive answers, as well as interpretations. This meant contributing time and efforts gratis as a service to the project. This is what happened and it made a huge difference in perception. The interviews all took place in the offices of the selected interviewee, in Spanish or English, depending on the person's native tongue.
d. Needed to develop a special series of questions from which it was possible to discern the cultural values that underpin them. These questions were provided in advance for each interviewee so they knew what to expect. This proved very valuable.
e. The interview format as well as the assessment of the results proved complex, as there was no recording of the interview, and the qualitative aspects often became of key importance.

This whole research project lasted about five years, and resulted in a book, *Management in Two Cultures*,[47] which has proven widely used in both cultures, as well as very helpful in the cross-cultural seminars that followed. The book had to be rewritten for each culture, as it was essential that the interpretations of its content provided a common understanding of its content.

Following the publication of the book, a whole series of events took place, including cross-cultural seminars in business, university teaching and numerous presentations in different countries involving both private-sector businesses and educational institutions (mainly universities).

Cross-cultural Seminars

The cross-cultural management seminars proved particularly valuable as they involved working directly with US and Mexican managers. In this process a number of issues became apparent. A few of the most important seemed to be:

    a) In a company, who would take the initial step in recognizing the need for cross-cultural considerations? What motivated this interest?

    b) What were the outcome expectations of managers on each cultural side, including of course the CEO?

    c) What follow-up and commitment could be expected?

In response to the above questions, we have learned some valuable lessons about how to best reach the managers in terms of helping them think about their own values and accepting that cultures cannot be judged as good or bad, superior or inferior—but just different. This has proven a huge step forward, as most managers had been accustomed to working in one culture, often assuming everyone else generally thinks and responds in the same way in the management function of a business. This step has been especially difficult for the US managers to accept, considering their long history of "exporting" management as a largely neutral "science."

On the other hand, in countries like Mexico, the deeply held cultural values have a profound effect on how managers think and behave. This has had a significant influence on management style. Combining these factors, many companies have come to the conclusion that some forms of adaptation are essential in order to provide an environment for positive longer-term operational success in their Mexican operations.

The initial questions indicated previously became key in initiating the process of taking concrete steps to "solve" the problems associated with transcultural adaptations. In this process it soon became apparent that the CEO or general manager needed to be fully convinced, personally involved, and initate, support, and lead this kind of intervention to come to grips with cross-cultural issues. Many companies have tried other administrative avenues first to "solve" their problems, but finally have in these cases come to accept that perhaps there were cultural issues that were creating constant misunderstandings and misinterpretations among the managers. Because most US management has been very much focused on the technological and administrative side, it has been difficult to bring into consideration the concept of values that underpin most issues as a real influence in management. This was (and still is) mostly considered personal and not something that usually belongs in a logical, analytical, value-neutral business. On the other hand, Mexican managers have been accustomed to bringing "the whole person to work," and mostly believe that deeply held cultural values are an important part of all life, including daily work and management.

As a result of this thinking, expected outcomes have differed. US management in many cases (not all) have felt that learning about Mexican culture was not much different from learning a new system or computer application—once learned it could be implemented without delay. However this idea has usually changed once the US managers have become involved in the cross-cultural seminars, and most have responded very positively as they begin to recognize the roots of many of the blockages and communications problems they have been experiencing.

The Mexican managers, in contrast, have been relieved to have their cultural values discussed, respected and understood, and have felt that this would lead to a much better understanding, trust and working harmony among cross-cultural managers.

On the other hand, they have also learned that they have to change many work habits and customs that are counter-productive in management, but these changes continue to respect the deeply held Mexican cultural values.

Seminar Format:
Cross-cultural management seminars have been used as the

most helpful vehicle to understand the cultural issues affecting management.

These seminars have been divided into two parts. One seminar has been dedicated to Mexican managers, in Spanish, discussing US cultural values that affect different aspects of management. Another similar seminar has been dedicated to US managers, in English, to discuss the Mexican cultural values that affect management. These seminars (or workshops) have been highly participative and provided a common ground to unload their frustrations and personal interpretations.

Outcomes of Cross-cultural Management Seminars

a) One of the most valuable outcomes has been providing a place for participants to freely speak out, and at the same time learn about the sources of their frustrations—in other words, begin to understand where a particular US or Mexican manager finds himself in the transition to cross-cultural sensitivity. The main outcome of the seminars has been positive in the sense that once we begin to understand and can externalize our own values, we can begin to understand how and why our counterparts think and act as they do, and this renews mutual respect.

b) The seminars have been a process through which managers on both sides have begun to broaden their way of thinking, especially related to identifying what values underpin their own beliefs about management, and to begin to realize that there is more than one way to look at an issue.

c) Most managers have developed new ways of communicating and listening to their counterparts, and thus have themselves usually come up with suggestions for adaptations on both sides.

d) Most companies have experienced much-improved communications and resulting productivity. The longer-term level of success has depended on the ongoing particular management style of a specific company and the previous transcultural experience of the new managers and CEOs involved.

e) A few examples of companies that have participated in cross-cultural seminars and workshops include: Baxter Corporation, Bendix Corporation, Grupo Cementos Chihuahua, Ford Motor

Corporation, General Motors Corporation, General Electric Corporation, Hewlett Packard Corporation, Jabil Circuit Corporation, Unisys Corporation, Grupo Vitro, Whirlpool Corporation.

Lessons Learned: Cross-cultural Management Seminars

a) Managers from different cultures working together require management style adaptations that respect both cultures.

b) For company operational purposes, the cultural values of the country where a company is physically located usually needs to take precedence over the cultural values of the "guest" company related to adaptations in management style. On the other hand, new technologies and administration techniques of the guest company remain a top priority, but the process of implementation and working culture needs to adapt to the culture of the country where the company is located.

c) Traditional Mexican (and other Latin American) management style, to which most Mexican managers have become accustomed, needs to be rethought and transformed to a more participative, "world-class" style for long-term success in Mexico and internationally. Managers who have been exposed to this transformation in management style have also made their adaptations to other management cultures easier and more effective.

d) Cross-cultural management sensitivity in US companies is still limited. Many researchers relate this to a number of different influences that, broadly speaking, are associated with "conventional" management thinking. There appears also to be a deeply seated feeling of superiority within US management and culture when exposed to other cultural values.

Cross-cultural Management: Part II

Following a period of time conducting cross-cultural seminars it became clear that the individual sessions for groups from each culture was not sufficient to make concrete, deeply rooted modifications and adaptations to satisfy specific issues that existed. Therefore a second session or workshop was added where the two different cultural groups of managers (US and Mexican) are combined into one group. This has brought in a whole new set of dynamics and resulting outcomes.

Rationale

The rationale for the combined cross-cultural group included:

a) Participants in culturally separate group seminars had learned a great deal about ways of thinking of their counterparts but most were still unsure of how to use this new knowledge to deal with specific issues, and the most effective implementation process.

b) Language and culture are complex issues. Very few US managers speak Spanish and most Mexican managers are expected to speak English in order to be hired in US companies operating in Mexico. Many Mexicans are very fluent in English, and many others have a limited command of the language. However, fluency in English does not mean that Mexican cultural values have been replaced with US values. In Mexico deeply held cultural values remain intact, but a series of more superficial customs and habits have changed to become more "international," but not necessarily US. This fact has often created confusion, as many US managers have assumed that learning to speak English, and becoming more international in thinking, generally means learning to think and work the US way.

It should be borne in mind that there are now more people in the world who speak English as a second language than there are native speakers. This also means that English has become a type of "Esperanto," and thus learned for communications purposes, but "delinked" from culture.

c) It has been very important that the participants (managers), when combining both cultures, are the ones who *decide* how to approach an issue. Following their new insights into each other's cultures, the combined participative decision-making process has proven a huge positive step for them to find consensus and commitment for all.

d) A comfortable "safe" environment has been needed where managers could sit together in a nonconfrontational atmosphere and discuss openly their differences. This has been especially important for Mexican managers, who often feel overwhelmed by superior US knowledge in company technologies and systems, and their more direct approach. As a result they have tended to be reluctant to express their genuine views on work-related issues.

e) A follow-up mechanism has been essential to facilitate and review ongoing cross-cultural issues and make adjustments where essential.

Combined Sessions

These combined, "Day 2" sessions have been added to the initial cross-cultural seminars with significant success. The sessions utilize a process of identification of *issues*, followed by small group workshop sessions. Participants are carefully selected to match issues and cross-cultural participants. These sessions are followed by careful tabulation of agreed upon "solutions" to which all participants become committed through consensus agreement.

It should be noted that these sessions have added dimensions of "breakthrough" in levels of confidence, trust, tolerance and enthusiasm on both sides. A new type of mutual respect and almost friendship seems to evolve. Both groups feel involved and have control over how they operate—as they themselves have decided jointly on how to handle each issue in their area, and their new "rules of conduct" evolve. This transformation in cross-cultural agreements has been quite surprising. A new sort of spark has seemed to motivate the different groups, which manifests itself in new enthusiasm related to their own decisions on a new way forward. This reaction seems to repeat itself time after time.

The "rules of conduct" that have resulted from these sessions are interesting to study. What has in fact been happening is that we are finding that the results do not seem to be trade offs between one culture or another, but in most cases a "new way"—one that has the influence of each culture, but is different from both. With the evolution of this process, it was realized that it is possible to work across cultures in business, while still respecting the cultures of each country.

The role of the facilitator is complex in all these types of sessions (both parts I and II). Firstly one has to be certain that everyone participating has attended an initial cross-cultural seminar in order to have a certain level of confidence in understanding how the other person is thinking. These sessions, in my experience, have required that I was accepted as "one of us" in each group—both in way of thinking, understanding and appreciation of their cultures, and of course language. In this way I have been perceived as being sufficiently unbiased. The combined sessions that follow have proven stressful as the facilitator needs to jump from one culture to another, and in the process try to find ways of expressing issues that reflect exactly what the participant wishes—in both languages and cultures. Nevertheless these combined session have also been wonderfully satisfying as one sees people from two cultures moving from a position of frustration and lack of communication to one of sitting together and openly discussing solutions to their issues.

At the end of the combined sessions, a small follow-up committee (with cross-cultural participants) is then selected to take responsibility for "publishing" (within the company) and distributing agreed-upon solutions to issues, which form a new "code of conduct" or new working culture. The committee also serves as facilitator for future cross-cultural issues that arise, as well as making any needed adjustments to the code of conduct.

Lessons Learned

1) We have learned that diversity in cultural values underlying business management are "real" and affect significantly transcultural management operations and long-term success.

2) Utilizing cross-cultural extended two-day sessions, managers (and companies) have successfully instituted concrete changes in behaviors and attitudes on both sides.

3) The follow-up committee has proven an important factor in providing ongoing support and avoiding major cross-cultural issues negatively affecting company operations.

4) The role of corporate headquarters of a company has been extremely important, and has sometimes had a negative effect on the positive cross-cultural adaptations achieved in the local operations. This has been largely due to the lack of cross-cultural knowledge or sensitivity of many corporate specialists who interrelate with the local operations.

b. Phase II: Mexican Management in Transition

The main catalyst for Phase II grew out of the lessons learned from Phase I in the Mexican management context. The major challenge involved a need to transform the traditional autocratic and paternalistic style of management to a participative style, in order for Mexican companies to be successful in the long term, locally and internationally, while still respecting the deep cultural values of Mexico

Research Study Overview

The challenge related to the transformation of Mexican management to a participative "world class" approach required a whole new research project to learn from the very few Mexican organizations that already existed and were operating successfully on a participative basis, while respecting the deeply seated values of the country.

As in the case of Phase I research, it required another intense four-year period of primary research.

Some of the challenges involved in this phase were:

a) Locating possible candidates (companies that had gone through the major part of the transformation process), bearing in mind the need to have various sizes, types of organizations and different regions represented. This proved more difficult than phase I in many ways, as many companies liked to feel they were "modern," but could not qualify, based on the guidelines that were established for selection. My network of knowledgeable and trusted colleagues filled an important role in helping me gain access to valuable candidates for the study, and introductions to their owners or senior management. In Mexico, there are basically three kinds of companies: state owned, privately owned and foreign companies. The ones I focused on were basically privately owned, representing the major sector of Mexican businesses.

b) The next challenge within this project involved in-depth interviews in the different companies. This involved assessing not only what was revealed in terms of how the company interviewees thought, and the expressed values on which they seated their transformation, it also meant being able to "read" a number of qualitative aspects.

Examples of these include body language, eye contact, hesitancy in expression of some views, and general atmosphere experienced in the company when talking to other employees and groups in the company. All of these aspects combined provided a window into how the organization was focused, organized, and the attitudes that existed within management and how these affected the practices.

Gradually it was learned that these organizations had mostly learned through trial and error, taking ideas from different practices in different countries, such as some ideas from the US, some from Europe and a few from Asia. These ideas were combined and finally adapted to the deep cultural values of Mexico. Therefore, it appears that we can have a transformed company, which is participative and efficient, while still preserving the basic cultural values of the country

c) Following the interviews, the next step involved searching out some commonalities in management principles and practices that would begin to form a "modern Mexican style" of management suitable especially to the small and medium sized companies—which includes about 80% of Mexican companies. This resulted in a book[48] related to Mexican mangement in transition, which provided sufficient ingredients for smaller companies to begin their own process of assessment and begin to transform their management style. Larger companies, however, have also benefited from the fundamental values thinking and related management approach involved.

Learning Experiences from the Study

The study provided some very valuable learning experiences. Some of the insights included:

a) Level I and Level II cultural values: This study revealed the existence of two levels of cultural values that existed side by side.

The Level I values include the very deeply rooted values that form the essence of Mexico and has provided people with the strength and courage to survive many devastating experiences. These values seem to be deeply instilled for their lifetime, and show a strong need to be preserved in all transformed businesses. They generally correspond to what are considered universal values.

This insight into the identification of these deeply rooted values has provided a valuable basis for understanding the evolution of values in the country and how some values seem to change while others remain deeply held and able to withstand a large part of the external pressures over a period of many years. It has also led to new insights concerning the possibilities for future sustainability in the evolution of the country.

Level II cultural values, on the other hand, include cultural customs and habits that have changed somewhat over time. Many of these Level II values are the ones companies realize have to change when Mexican companies "modernize" and become participative, if they hope to survive and have longer-term success.

b) The concept of participative management is recognized as essential, but a very difficult concept to accept for a business owner or senior manager. The reason for this appears to be closely related to the hierarchal society. The owner is highly respected, and he is considered the only one with the knowledge and right to make decisions in the business. His whole status in the company, in the community, among family and friends is influenced by the respect and status he has gained as the owner of a business. Therefore, the concept of delegation of any authority to combine with delegation of tasks is a huge hurdle. For him to delegate any decision-making authority could make him look weak, and often could lead to fear of loss of control.

However, in Mexico today this situation is changing, especially in the larger cities, as well as the arrival of a new generation of managers (and potential owners) who are much more open to the participative approach.

c) Sensitivity: The Mexican continues to bring the "whole person" to work, as a deeply felt need, even in transformed companies. This means that personal sensitivity is a factor that has to be taken into account, especially related to criticism, control systems and performance reviews of all kinds. However, in the participative approach these sensitivities are greatly diminished as people feel a surge of self confidence, trust and motivation as they become participants in solutions to problems, in place of just following instructions. Their much closer working relationships across the different levels also provide an environment where they dare to try out new ideas without fear of failure or losing their job.

d) The transformation process has been successful when it basically begins from the top down, initiated by, and led by the company owner. Experience has shown that the top-down approach to transformation has been essential in Mexico. Some explain this as related to the hierarchal society. When new ideas (like the transformation to a participative approach) come from other levels the owner needs to "digest" them first and convert them to his own before any actions can normally be taken. Therefore, attempts at transformation have shown significant progress once the owner is convinced (and totally involved), that this is something he can personally identify with and feels is positive for the company.

Implementation of the Study

In general terms, the implementation of the results of this study (book) have been slow, but evidence of the importance of its message is seen in a number of places.

In the business sector, this has been mostly seen in smaller or medium sized business operations where the owner (especially the younger generation) has been convinced that a fundamental change in management approach is essential, but at the same time has wanted to preserve the deeply held values of Mexico. A few large companies have also been encouraged by the possibility of maintaining the values base of the country while still being able to work as a world class organization. However, these examples are few to date, and many still view the US conventional model as the road to success.

Universities have shown significant interest, especially in business programs. The results are slowly being experienced as the next generation is working and some taking charge of companies. However, the dominance of business textbooks that promote conventional thinking is the norm, and graduates have been trained with the focus that in order to succeed one needs to embrace the conventional way of thinking about business.

Lessons Learned

a) Cultural values need to be considered at different levels, separating out the deeply rooted universal values from the more changeable customs and habits.

b) In most hierarchal societies, like we see in Mexico and Latin America, organizations can adopt participative management styles and run efficient operations while still maintaining their deeply rooted cultural values. They form the essence of the country and its people.

c) "Modernized" participative companies in Mexico possess some significant "sustainable" ingredients, especially related to the importance of human-related values in organizations.

d) US companies mostly find this transformation in Mexico confusing, as most US companies view "modernization" as related to how closely it resembles a conventional US-oriented approach. This confusion continues to be a challenge in transcultural companies.

e) Ecological-related aspects and their integration with the whole operation in transformed Mexican companies are still little understood and few seriously considered as a top priority. Ecological aspects need much research and integration for companies to accept that they are essential for viable long-term business operations.

c. Phase III: Sustainable Development and Business in Mexico and Latin America

The lessons learned in Phase I and II have led to new encouraging insights related to possibilities for organizational transformation toward sustainability in Mexico and other Latin American countries. The optimism involves what appears to be some deeply held "sustainable" values on which Mexican and all Latin Americans have built their societies for many generations. These have penetrated the business world in the region as part of the overall culture, and seem to be, for the most part, about to withstand much of the turmoil of especially the past two to three decades.

On the other hand, since the advent of the rapid and uncontrolled economic developments associated with globalization, these deep (Level 1) values have come under great pressures, and businesses have needed to survive in a world that often clashes with these deeply felt values. This stress has been evident for many years now as businesses recognize that they have little choice but to embrace the conventional globalized business "values" to survive. This acceptance of the values that underpin the global marketplace is also the only way, it is often believed, to be fully accepted as equal "players," and not to be labeled as a third-world business person.

Throughout this process, a large proportion of businesses in the smaller sector (mostly local family businesses) have disappeared or are barely surviving, usually in small niche markets. The agricultural sector has been particularly hard hit. In addition, the focus of businesses has become increasingly economic focused, which has seriously compromised many local communities and families, and eroded the strength of their deeply held values. This is especially evident among the large younger generation, who mostly see their future and employment depending to a large extent on embracing the conventional global values and economic marketplace.

This situation has created much worry among business leaders and society as a whole. However, among business leaders there continues to exist a small group that has somehow managed to "modernize" their management, while still maintaining their deeply rooted values, as discussed in Phase II. As a result, much soul searching is taking place among business leaders in Mexico and Latin America, especially as it relates to events of recent years, where some of the worrisome consequences of globalization are becoming clearer. Many visionaries in these countries are beginning to rethink and rediscover the importance of their deep cultural values as a fundamental foundation for all organizations, and their importance for human meaning and purpose.

This whole dilemma has sparked an interest in trying to provide some initial insights into how business organizations in the region generally are respecting what we can interpret as sustainable development in business. This study project has meant extending the search beyond everyday management specifically, and moving into the realities of their beliefs and actions related also to nature. Up to this point, as noted, the areas where this case study has been mainly focused are in the areas of management related to economic and social development.

Thus began a new, broader study with a purpose of examining where Mexico and other Latin American countries in general presently stand related to overall sustainable development principles and practices.

Overview of the Study[49]

The purpose of this study was to provide a broad panorama related to the realities of business and sustainable development in the region. This covers a number of sections related to overall sustainable development and how the business sector is performing.

These sections include:

a) Sustainable development in a global context

b) Sustainable development in Mexico, which included Mexico in the context of Latin America; Mexico in its present situation; positive and negative indicators for sustainable development; and sustainable development and universities.

c) New sustainable business management potential in Mexico, which includes some positive aspects (values); sustainable business manager profile in Mexico; and a sustainable Mexican company profile.

Overall, the conclusions have shown some encouraging aspects for building a strong foundation for sustainability, as well as negative aspects that present huge challenges.

The positive aspects include:

-- very importantly, some deeply rooted cultural values, and a strong cultural heritage that provides stability for the country.

-- strength and courage of the people for withstanding repeated turmoil.

-- a wealth of natural resources, which are rapidly being depleted by both international global interests and national interests.

--a young, dynamic population, which is intelligent, creative and flexible, given an opportunity.

The negative aspects include:

-- severe ecological damage due to rapid, uncontrolled industrialization, accompanied by government's uneven application of
ecological laws.

-- lack of ecological "consciousness" is widespread.

-- problems of poverty, which involves about 50 percent of the
population. The changes in agriculture related to globalization have
had a significant social impact.

-- unemployment and underemployment with large sectors of
the population working in the "informal" economy.

This study concludes with a summary of findings based on hy-
potheses set out at the beginning of the study. These point clearly to
the positive aspects of deeply rooted cultural values (Level I values)
in organizations, and the positive outcomes where transformation to
a participatory management style has taken place. On the negative
side, aspects related to lack of ecological awareness and conservation are very important and worrisome, as well as the growing need
to transform organizations to a participative management focus to
provide opportunities for all to contribute.

Lessons Learned from the Study

The study, which resulted in the publication of *Sustainable Development and Business in Mexico and Latin America*, has produced
some mixed lessons related to sustainability, such as:

a) Mexico, as well as a number of other Latin American
countries, has some very positive policies and regulations related
to ecological aspects. However, governments continue to be under
pressures to "bend" or apply "unevenly" many ecological laws due
to their need for foreign investment. On the other hand, the majority
of smaller local businesses are living "on the edge" of survival, and
any additional expense could be fatal. In general, there still seems
to be a very limited awareness in business operations of the direct
linkage between successful long-term business operations and the
environment.

b) The social aspects of sustainability related to deeply rooted
cultural values is one where Mexico and other Latin American countries have strength. Most wish to conserve these deeply held cultural

values within their business sector and the broader society. These values have been under significant stress over the past twenty years, as their economic survival has often depended on moving toward conventional globally based business values.

c) Universities and other educational institutions are showing signs of concern related to both preservation of deeply rooted values as well as ecological factors. Nevertheless, for many professors it remains a challenge, as most use textbooks that are based on conventional principles, and priorities are placed on economic factors as the key to business success. In addition, few textbooks are focused on small and medium sized family businesses that are by far the majority in these countries, and the ones that are key to long-term job creation and stable communities.

d) On the economic side, most small and medium sized business are struggling, especially since the passage of NAFTA and other globally based agreements. A large sector of these businesses have disappeared, and the ones that exist live a precarious existence, unable to compete with globalized businesses. Thus has evolved the unsustainable condition of an underground economy that is outside the formal economy, not only economically, but is also not supervised for ecological or social aspects. In most countries in Latin America this "informal economy" can range from 50% to 80% of the working population.

Sustainable development in general in Latin America is fragmented, but one encouraging aspect involves the deeply engrained cultural values that still exist, though damaged. For the future, this is considered extremely important, as it forms a valuable foundation for sustainability in the overall sense.

Case Study—Some Final Conclusions and Questions

The different phases of this long case study have provided a number of insights into the challenges that exist in transcultural organizations, plus the differences in values and ways of thinking that exist in both national and international organizations.

There appears to be little doubt that a number of commonly held and deeply seated values (universal values) can form an important part of a solid foundation for successful cross-cultural operations, as well as long-term, sustainable national organizations.

At the same time it appears important to recognize the importance of respecting the differences in local, regional and country cultural values, language and tastes that enrich different regions and countries. It appears that these two groups of cultural values (universal ones and local cultural ones) can exist amicably side by side.

Throughout the different phases of this study another aspect related to deeply held values seems to be emerging. There appears to be a growing recognition of something rather difficult to describe—an underlying new "consciousness or spirituality" in its broadest sense. For the Latin American managers this seems more of a natural cultural phenomena, but for the US managers this concept has usually been delinked from the business world, and considered a personal matter. However, this new "consciousness" seems to be slowly emerging as the importance of values and the realities of ecological breakdown become more evident.

The whole ecological side of business is an aspect that has been recognized as a huge challenge in this case study. The "delinkage" between business and ecological realities experienced in much of the US-Latin American business operations is a serious concern, and ecological systems continue to be exploited by principally globalized actors, but also at the local and national levels in Latin America. The unsustainable thinking and actions that result have created short-term unsustainable economic approaches to business operations and living in general.

This case study has also brought to light the importance of trying to understand more about the realities that exist beyond our borders. There appears a need for international knowledge, ways of thinking, and insights in order to make longer-term wise or sustainable decisions in our own communities. This appears especially important in the rich countries, as our capacity to maintain our present lifestyle, many studies stress, depends heavily on depletion of ecological (and social) conditions in poorer countries.

Presently the poor countries of Latin America are faced with a dilemma, which involves a struggle with two worlds, so to speak. On one side they have their local businesses that are culturally integrated, but are "on the edge" in terms of their existence due to their inability to compete with the huge multinational corporations. The values that underpin most of these large organizations have created difficult pressures on the deep cultural values of the countries in which they operate (for youth especially). For many it seems a choice between being viewed as a person with "old fashioned" values, or a person who is modern and can absorb the modern world values. Fortunately, this trend is now showing signs of changing, as we have seen in this case study, and the resurgence of regional and country values are slowly becoming more important, as well as a small number of international businesses that have shown cultural sensitivity. This emerging sensitivity to cultural value differences has proven beneficial to both national and international organizational success.

Overall, this case study has followed through a period of transition for Latin American and mostly US globalized organizations. Some are now questioning the values that underpin the globalized approach on the one hand, while on the other hand are rediscovering some valuable deeply seated values that both Latin American and US company managers have in common. During this transition period the challenges are huge on both sides, but it appears that a solid new foundation of values is slowly emerging.

In addition to these conclusions, many new questions have emerged related to this case study. A small number of key questions can be summarized as:

1. Is it possible to develop an international "working culture" in organizations where a common foundation of sustainable universal values exist, while still respecting local cultures, and languages?

2. Can forward-thinking universities and other educational institutions become an essential catalyst for change, especially in their role of developing youth for a sustainable working world? Do universities need to rethink their own fundamental principles and values to consistently fulfill this role across all disciplines?

3. How can we today live in two worlds at the same time? One is the "real" world where we presently live and work in a conventional system with a conventional way of thinking; on the

other hand there is the other world to which we aspire and is emerging slowly, based on a number of universal values, ways of working and thinking that are very different—a new sustainable world?

Thus we evolve into another phase in our ongoing studies toward a new reality. In so doing we progress in new understandings related to our daily working world. Business leaders appear to be slowly moving in this positive direction. What can we do to help move our conventional "system" into this new world?

Chapter VIII

SOME FINAL COMMENTS AND CONCLUSIONS

When I began this "values" book project I thought I had quite a good grasp on how to approach and develop the main theme, and felt reasonably confident of how it would evolve.

How differently it turned out! It has been a good lesson in humility to realize that one is only really "scratching the surface" of a broad field of study that appears more and more essential to us all in our transformation to sustainable thinking. This involves the whole transdisciplinary world related to all the facets needed in order to build a solid foundation of sustainable values—values that have both commonality in some basic ones, but at the same time involve the recognition of very rich and diverse culturally related ones.

As a result, this whole study has been, and continues to be an incredible learning experience. It is my hope that this short book contains ingredients that spark your own thinking and eventual new fulfilling experiences.

Some conclusions:

In this field, in which we are learning so much about our own thinking, conclusions may perhaps be presumptuous, but I will briefly outline some of the most significant points I have learned in this long (and ongoing) process.

a. It appears clear that we need to understand our own thinking and values before we can thoughtfully hope to advise others about what sustainability really is and what it consists of in organizations. Then we need to be prepared to "walk the talk" in personal and work life.

b. A number of visionaries in various aspects of this field are an invaluable source of wisdom in our search for new ways of thinking.

c. The transition from sustainable "sounding" policies to actual sustainable practices in many organizations appears to be blocked by the "mindset" (values) of the decision makers. It seems they have not, for the most part, made the transition to sustainable thinking.

d. There exists a rich groundswell of community-level individuals and organizations that have adopted many aspects of sustainable thinking. Many of these are involved in mostly small-scale sustainable projects, a few businesses and new networking efforts. This is encouraging, as these individuals and groups are gradually influencing the political agenda at the local level—the first step to moving into higher political levels.

e. We have a wealth of virtually untapped or little-understood sustainable wisdom and experience in developing countries, especially in the large indigenous communities. Even many "mestizo" communities have managed to maintain many deeply held human and spiritual values that they have passed on through the generations. For example, in Mexico and Latin America this group is now struggling with outside pressures from the rich consumer world to replace these values with consumer, economic-based ones. In the process, a few organizations have found ways of preserving their deep values and still maintaining economically successful businesses.

f. Modern marketing of "sustainability" is mostly being used as a tool to promote increased consumerism, and preserving conventional unsustainable thinking and accompanying values. A total transformation in thinking is essential for marketers to begin to promote genuinely sustainable policies and practices.

g. We need to move from policy-level thinking down to principles and values level if we hope to make a viable long-term transformation to sustainability in organizations.

In summary, this study probably provokes more questions than it answers related to our lives and work in organizations. This can be viewed as positive, as it can form a viable first step toward a motivation to examine our own workplace and its principles and practices. We have much to learn in this process.

WELCOME TO THE NEW WORLD, WHERE WE BEGIN TO RECOGNIZE THE IMPORTANCE OF OUR INCREDIBLE HUMAN NATURE, WHERE OUR CONSCIOUS AND UNCONSCIOUS MINDS COMBINED CAN BRING OUT OUR CAPACITY FOR WISDOM AND GENUINE SUSTAINABILITY.

FOOTNOTES

CHAPTER I

[1]Wackernagel, Mathis, 1998, "The Ecological Footprint: An Indicator of Progress toward Regional Sustainability," Environmental Monitoring and Assessment 51.
[2]Meadows, D.H., Meadows, D.L.and Randers, J., 1992, *Beyond the Limits: Global Collapse or a Sustainable Future*, Earthscan.
[3]Harman, Willis, 1998, *Global Mind Change*, Barrett-Koehler.
[4]Korten, David, 1999, *The Post Corporate World*, Barrett-Koehler.
[5]Henderson, Hazel, 1996, *Building A Win-Win World*, Barrett-Koehler.
[6]Clark, Mary, 2002, *In Search of Human Nature*, Brunner-Routledge.
[7]Schumacher, E.F., 1997, *This I Believe*, Green Books.
[8]Laszlo, Ervin, 2001, *Macroshift*, Barrett-Koehler.
[9]Einstein, Albert, 2000, *The Expanded Quotable Einstein*, Alice Caprise, Ed., Princeton University Press.
[10]Kras, Eva, *Management in Two Cultures*, 1995, Intercultural Press, Yarmouth, Maine, USA

Kras, Eva, *Modernizing Mexican Management*, 1994, Editts Publishing (Two Eagles Press), Las Cruces, NM, USA.

Kras, Eva, *Sustainable Development and Business in Mexico and Latin America*, 1995, Grupo Editorial Iberoamerica, Mexico City.

CHAPTER II

[1]Ervin Laszlo, president of the Club of Budapest, is one of the early modern visionaries in the area of systems philosophy and general theory of evolution. He has published over seventy books in eighteen languages and is one of the most highly respected visionaries in his field worldwide. Laszlo publishes a jounal, "World Futures," and is program director for the United Nations Institute for Training and Research. He has received many awards throughout his long career

in systems research and evolutionary thinking. His recent and highly acclaimed book is *Macroshift*, 2001. Barrett-Koehler.

[2]Harman, Willis. 1998, *Global Mind Change*, Barrett-Koehler. Also refer to *New Metaphysical Foundation of Modern Science*, 1994, Institute of Noetic Sciences.

[3]J Harman, Willis, 1998, *Global Mind Change*, Barrett-Koehler. Also refer to *The Scientific Exploration of Consciousness: Toward Adequate Epistemology*, 1994, Institute of Noetic Sciences.

[4]Harman, Willis, 1998, *Global Mind Change*, Barrett-Koehler.

[5]Laszlo, Irvin, 2001, *Macroshift*, Barrett-Koehler.

[6]Harman, Willis, 1998, *Global Mind Change*, Barrett-Koehler.

[7]Ferguson, Marilyn, 1993, "The Transformation of Values and Vocation," article in book, *The New Paradigm in Business*, Eds. Michael Ray and Alan Rinzler, Jeremy P. Tarcher/Perigee Books.

[8]Korten, David, 1996, "The Mythic Victory of Market Capitalism," article in book, *The Case Against the Global Economy*, Sierra Club Books.

[9]Smith, Adam. Many new insights and interpretations, related to the genuine philosophy and beliefs of Adam Smith are now appearing in diverse publications. The following brief summary has been drawn from a number of sources over many years, but the recent principle insights have come mostly from the work of David Korten, *The Post Corporate World*, and Hazel Henderson, *Building a Win-Win World*, as well as Adam Smith's own book, *An Inquiry into the Nature and Causes of the Wealth of Nations*. In addition, insights come from E. F. Schumacher, *This I Believe*, Ervin Laszlo, *Marcoshift*, and Willis Harman, *Global Mind Change*, as well as some dates of some events from the Encyclopedia Britannica.

[10]The following discussion of the philosophy and thinking of Teilhard de Chardin draws on the work of: Ursula King, *The Spirit on one Earth: Reflections on Teilhard de Chardin and Global Spirituality*; Charles P. Henderson, in his book, *God and Science*, as well as Teilhard de Chardin's most noted work, *The Phenomenon of Man*. Also, some insights came from Ervin Laszlo, *Macroshift*, and Willis Harman, *Global Mind Change*.

[11]Albert Einstein. This brief summary is focused on the human side of Albert Einstein. A large number of publications exist related to various aspects of his philosophy. One of the most well know of these is *Einstein: The Human Side*, by Helen Dufas and Banesh Hoffman, Eds., Princeton University Press, 1979. Several direct quotes from this publication appear in the text. In addition, reflections from Willis Harman, *Global Mind Change*, and Ervin Laszlo, *Macroshift*, have also added to the interpretations. Most of the quotes are found in extensive publications of Einstein quotes, such as *Quotable Einstein* by Alice Calaprice, Ed.

[12]The work of Mahatma Gandhi is particularly important to the theme of this study. The points that follow stress his well-known philosophy related to Swadeshi, Sarvodaya, and Satyagraha. These insights draw on the work of his granddaughter, Ela Gandhi, in *Gandhi and Development*; Thomas Weber,

2004, *Gandhi as Disciple and Mentor*, Cambridge University Press; Thomas Weber, 2001, "Gandhian Philosophy: Conflict Revolution Theory and Practical Approaches to Negotiation," Journal of Peace Research. Vol. 38, No.4. As well, Gandhi's work is referred to by E. F. Schumacher in *This I Believe* and Ervin Laszlo in *Macroshift*.

[13]E. F. Schumacher. He had a very extensive and varied career. A broad base of publications exist which provide insights into his profound contributions. The sources used in much of this discussion come from the following: The Schumacher Society, UK.; Schumacher publications: *Small is Beautiful* and *This I Believe*; Hazel Henderson in *Building a Win-Win World*; Willis Harman in *Global Mind Change*; Ervin Laszlo in *Macroshift*; Leopold Kohr in *Tribute to E. F. Schumacher*, 1980.

[14]Willis Harman. Willis Harman became an important mentor to me as I moved through the transition to sustainable thinking. His wisdom and knowledge were profound and his writings related to science and spirituality became widely respected internationally in the 1980s and 1990s. The discussion that follows reflects his most important work, *Global Mind Change*. In addition, these insights have been influenced by a number of other works by Harman, including: *New Metaphysical Foundations of Modern Science, Higher Creativity: Liberating the Unconscious for Breakthrough Benefits, Intuition in Work: Pathways to unlimited Possibilities, The New Business of Business: Sharing Responsibility for a Positive Global Future, New Paradigms in Business*. Added details and other Harman publications are found in the Institute of Noetic Sciences, of which Harman was cofounder and president for twenty years.

[15]Ervin Laszlo. The following insights draw on some major works of Ervin Laszlo. These include: *Macroshift, The Consciousness Revolution: A Transatlantic Dialogue: Two Days with Stanislav Grof*, Ervin Laszlo and Peter Russell, *Whispering Pond: A Personal Guide to the Emerging Vision of Science, The Choice: Evolution or Extinction? A Thinking Person's Guide to Global Issues, Vision 2020: Reordering Chaos for Global Survival, Inner Limits of Mankind: Heretical Reflections on Today's Values, Culture and Politics*.

[16]Herman Daly's work has become particularly respected over the past two decades in international economics circles, and has been instrumental in exposing new insights into economic philosophy related to Ecological Economics. He provides new ways of applying economics principles based on the principles of sustainability. The brief summary that follows draws on some of his most important books and writings. These include: *For the Common Good*, co-authored with John Cobb, Jr., *Economics, Ecology and Ethics: Essays, Globalization vs Internationalization, Steady State Economics, Ecological Economics and Sustainable Development: The Economics of Sustainable Development*.

[17]David Korten, 1999, *The Post Corporate World*, Barrett-Koehler.

[18]Richard Tarnas, 1991, *The Passion of the Western Mind*, Ballantine.

[19]Boulding, Kenneth, 2003, from address delivered to the "Dancing with

Machines" panel of the World Futures Conference, San Francisco.

[20]Kras, Eva, 1995, *Management in Two Cultures*, Intercultural Press, Yarmouth, Maine.

Kras, Eva, 1994, *Modernizing Mexican Management*, Editts Publishing (Two Eagles Press) Las Cruces, NM.

Kras, Eva, 1995, *Sustainable Development and Business in Mexico and Latin America*, Grupo Editorial Iberoamcrica. Mexico City.

[21]Ray, Paul, 2002, *Cultural Creatives*, Harmony Books. Also included is a special research report, "The New Political Compass," 2002, Values and Technology, Inc.

CHAPTER III

[1]Various key sources have supported the overall contents of this section. In addition, various references are indicated where specific studies are involved. The key references include:

Ervin Laszlo, 1997, *Third Millenium: The Challenge and the Vision*, First Report of the Club of Budapest, Gaia Books. (Laszlo is the president of the Club of Budapest.) Other Laszlo publications included are: *The Choice: Evolution vs Extinction? A Thinking Person's Guide to Global Issues*, 1994, Jeremy P. Tarcher/Putnam; *The Consciousness Revolution: A Transatlantic Dialogue*, 1999, with Stanislav Grof and Peter Russell, Element Books; *Macroshift*, 2001, Barrett-Koehler.

Eva Kras, 1995, *Sustainable Development and Business in Mexico and Latin America*, Grupo Editorial Iberoamerica, Mexico City, and 1994, *Modernizing Mexican Management*, Editts Publishing (Two Eagles Press), Las Cruces, NM.

Hazel Henderson, 1999, *Beyond Globalization: Shaping a Sustainable Global Economy*, Kumarian Press. Also refer to: *Paradigms in Progress: Life Beyond Economics*, 1993, Kumarian Press, *Creating Alternative Futures: The End of Economics*, 1996, Putnam, Hartford, Conn.

Edward Goldsmith , 1993, *The Way: An Ecological World-view*, Shambhala Publishers, Boston.

Willis Harman, 1998, *Global Mind Change*, Barrett-Koehler. Other Harman publications include, "The Transpersonal Challenge to the Scientific Paradigm: The Need for a Restructuring of Science," 1988, *Revision*, Vol.11, No.2; "A System in Decline or Transformation?" 1994, *WBA Perspectives*, Vol.8. No.2. ; Noetic Sciences Review, Willis Harman, president for twenty-five years, where he wrote numerous articles dealing with these same transformative thinking issues.

Roy Madron and John Jopling, 2003, *Gaian Democracies*, Green Books

[2]The Earth Charter is an authoritative synthesis of values, principles and aspirations that are widely shared by growing numbers of men and women in all regions of the world. The origin of the concept was sponsored by the United Nations Commission on Environment and Development, 1987, followed by the Earth Charter Commission, 1997. The International Earth Charter Secretariat is located in San Jose, Costa Rica.

The sources of the material published in the Earth Charter indicate extensive and comprehensive research, as indicated in the document as follows: "Together with the Earth Charter consultation process, the most important influences shaping the ideas and values in the Earth Charter are contemporary science, international law, the wisdom of the world's great religions and philosophical traditions, the declarations and reports of the seven UN summit conferences held during the 1990's, the global ethics movement, numerous nongovernmental declarations and people's treaties issued over the past thirty years, and best practices for building sustainable communities."

This Charter provides a strong source of support for the insights expressed related to values and sustainability in this study.

[3]Roger Walsh, 2001, "The Seven Practices of Essential Spirituality," *Noetic Sciences Review*, Dec.2001-Feb. 2002, taken from *Essential Spirituality*, 2000, John Wiley and Sons.

[4]Earth Charter—please refer to reference no. 2 above.

[5]Willis Harman, 1998, *Global Mind Change*, Barrett-Koehler.

[6]Earth Charter—please refer to reference no. 2 above.

[7]David Korten, 1999, *The Post Corporate World*, Barrett-Koehler.

[8]Roger Walsh, 2001, "The Seven Practices of Essential Spirituality," *Noetic Sciences Review*, Dec. 2001-Feb. 2002.

[9](a) Helen Norberg-Hodge and Peter Goering, 1992, *The Future of Progress*, Green Books,

(b) Hazel Henderson, 1996, *Building a Win-Win World*, Barrett-Koehler.

(c) Victor Toledo, 2001, *Biodiversity and Indigenous Peoples*, Academic Press, and *Ecologia, Espiritualidad, y Conocimieto*, 2003, Univ. Iberoamericana y PNUMA.

[10]Ervin Laszlo, 1997, *3rd Millenium: the Challenge and the Vision*, First report of the Club of Rome, Gaia Books.

[11]Teilhard de Chardin, 1961, *The Phenomenon of Man*, Harper Torchbooks, and Ursula King, *The Spirit of One Earth: Reflection on Teilhard de Chardin and Global Spirituality*, 1989, Paragon House. Also note Willis Harman, 1998, *Global Mind Change*, Barrett-Koehler.

[12]Dalai Lama, 1995, *Awakening the Mind, Lightening the Heart*, Harper, and Ursula King, 1989, *The Spirit of one Earth* (see reference no. 11 above).

[13]Willis Harman, 1998, *Global Mind Change*, Barrett-Koehler.

[14]Thomas Berry, 1988, *The Dream of the Earth*, Sierra Club Books, and Peter Russell, *The Global Mind Awakens: Our Evolutionary Leap*, 1995, Global Mind, Palo Alto, CA.

[15]Vandana Shiva, 1991, *The Violence of the Green Revolution*, Third World Network, Penang, Malaysia. Also refer to Victor Toledo, *Ecologia, Espiritualidad y Conocimiento*, 2003, Univ. Iberoamericana y PNUMA.

[16]Club of Budapest, founded in 1993 by Ervin Laszlo, consists of a number of internationally respected and highly creative members, including the Dali Lama, Sir Peter Ustinov (now deceased) and Vaclav Havel. The founder believes that "only by changing ourselves can we change the world." The mission of the club

is to be a catalyst for the transformation to a sustainable world through promoting the emergence of planetary consciousness, interconnecting generations and cultures, integrating spirituality, science, and the arts and fostering learning communities worldwide.

[17]Victor Toledo—please refer to references in No. 9 above.

[18]Club of Budapest—please refer to reference No. 16 above.

[19]Earth Charter—please refer to reference No. 2 above. Also refer to the following:

Roger Walsh, 2001, "The Seven Practices of Essential Spirituality," *Noetic Sciences Review*, Dec. 2001-Feb. 2002.

Ervin Laszlo, 2001, *Macroshift*, Barrett-Koehler

Tom Bentley and Ian Hargreaves, 2001, "Introduction: The New Ideology," article in book, *The Moral Universe*, Demos Collection, Issue 16.

[20]Ursula King, 1989, *The Spirit of One Earth: Reflections on Teilhard de Chardin and Global Spirituality*, Paragon House.

[21]Ervin Laszlo, 2001, *Macroshift*, Barrett-Koehler

[21a]Kras, Eva, 1994, *Modernizing Mexican Management*, Editts Publishing (Two Eagles Press) LasCruces. NM.

[22]Henry W. Lane, Joseph J. DiStefano and Martha L. Maznevski, 1997, *International Management Behavior*, 3rd edition, Blackwell Publishers.

[23]Stephen Covey, 1992, *Principle Centered Leadership*, Simon and Schuster, Fireside edition.

[24]Hazel Henderson, 1996, *Building a Win-Win World*, Barrett-Koehler.

[25]David Korten, 1999, *The Post Corporate World*, Barrett-Koehler.

[26]Peter Brown, 2001, *The Commonwealth of Life*, Black Rose Books

[27]Willis Harman, 1998, *Global Mind Change*, Barrett-Koehler.

[28]Parliament of World's Religions, 1993, "Declaration of a Global Ethic," Chicago, Editorial Committee of the Council of the World's Religions.

[29]Aldous Huxley, 1945, *The Perennial Philosophy*, Harper Brothers. Also refer to Eva Kras, 1995, *Sustainable Development and Business in Mexico and Latin America*, Grupo Editorial Iberamerica, Mexico.

[30]E. F. Schumacher, 1997, *This I Believe*, Green Books.

[31]Willis Harman, 1998, *Global Mind Change*, Barrett Koehler.

[32]Roger Walsh, 2001, "The Seven Practices of Essential Spirituality," *Noetic Sciences Review*, Dec. 2001-Feb. 2002. Also refer to complete book *Essential Spiritualiy*, 2000, John Wiley and Sons.

[33]Roger Walsh—please refer to reference No. 32 above.

[34]E. F. Schumacher was a renowned, innovative economist, known for his work related to "human scale" development and "Buddhist economics," as well as being a pioneer in the concept of "appropriate technology." He is most well-known for his book, *Small is Beautiful*, 1973, Hartley and Marks (now reprinted and available through Green Spirit Books). This note refers to his book, *This I Believe*, 1997, Green Books.

[35]Roger Walsh, *Paths Beyond Ego: The Transpersonal Vision*, (with Frances Vaughan and John Mack) 1993, J.P. Tardier.

[36]Sigmund Freud was a world-renowned (and controversial) psychotherapist who influenced much of modern western thinking related to human development and the human role in society. Refer to *The Ego and the Id*, James Strachey, Ed., W.W. Norton Publications. (description source—internet)

[37]Erich Fromm was a highly respected psychoanalyst whose theories were influenced by both Sigmund Freud and Karl Marx. Fromm added another dimension, that of the idea of freedom of choice. His most valuable and original legacy is understanding human character in relationship to society. Two of his most well known books are *The Sane Society*, 1955, and *The Anatomy of Human Destructiveness*, 1973. (description source—internet)

[38]Karl Marx was the most influential socialist thinker to emerge in the nineteenth century. Marx saw people as determined by society, and most especially by their economic system. He believed the foundation of reality lay in the material base of economics. Together with Frederick Engels, Marx wrote *The Communist Manifesto* in 1849. (description source—internet)

[39]Albert Einstein quote. Alice Calaprice, Ed., 2000, *The Expanded Quotable Einstein*, Princeton University Press.

[40]Ervin Laszlo, 2001, *Macroshift*, Barrett-Koehler. Also refer to *The Consciousness Revolution*, 1999, with Stanislav Grof, Ervin Laszlo and Peter Russell.

[41]Vaclav Havel, Feb. 1991, Address to US Joint Session of Congress, Washington, DC.

[42]Victor Toledo, 2003, *Ecologia, Espiritualidad y Conocimiento*, Univ. Iberoamericana y PNUMA.

CHAPTER IV

[1]The Earth Charter, 1997, United Nations Earth Council, San Jose, Costa Rica. For further details on the Earth Charter, please refer to Chapter III, note no.2.

[2]Paul Ray and Sherry Anderson, 2000, *Cultural Creatives*, Harmony Books. Also refer to a special research survey project, "The Political Compass," 2002, Values Technology Inc.

[3]The Institute of Sathya Sai Education, New Zealand.

[4]World Values Survey, Ronald Inglehart Survey, 1997, "Modernization and Post Modernization: Cultural, Economic and Political Change," (included forty-three countries, representing 70% of world population), Princeton University.

[5]Transparency International, 2001, National Survey on Corruption and Good Governance, Mexico.

[6]Parliament of the World's Religions, 1993, "Declaration Towards a Global Ethic," Chicago (included representation of the world's fourteen most important religions), Editorial Committee of the Council to the Parliament of the World's Religions.

[7]United Nations Education, Scientific and Cultural Organization (UNESCO), 1997, "The Universal Ethics Project," Division of Philosophy and Ethics (refers to associated studies related to ethics, biodiversity and cultures).

[7a]Kras, Eva, 1994, *Modernizing Mexican Management*, Editts Publishing (Two Eagles Press) Las Cruces, NM; 1995, *Sustainable Development and Business in*

Mexico and Latin America, Grupo Editorial Iberoamerica, Mexico City.

[8]The Earth Charter. Please see reference no. 1.

[9]This section has benefited from the wisdom of many visionaries and researchers. Following are included the resources that have had the most influence on the contents of this section.

(a) Ervin Laszlo, 1997, *3rd Millenium: The Challenge and the Vision*, Report of the Club of Budapest. Gaia Books. Also refer to *Macroshift*, 2001, Barrett-Koehler.

(b) Ursula King, 1989, *The Spirit of the Earth: Reflections on Teilhard de Chardin and Global Spirituality*, Paragon Books.

(c) Willis Harman, 1998, *Global Mind Change*, Barrett-Koehler.

(d) Ela Gandhi, 2002, "Gandhi and Development," *Resurgence*, no. 214 . Additional references for Gandhi's philosophy are included in the work of Thomas Weber, referenced in no. 14.

(e) Hazel Henderson, 1996, *Building a Win-Win World*, Barrett-Koehler.

(f) David Korten, 1996, *The Post Corporate World*, Barrett-Koehler.

(g) Thomas Berry, 1988, *Dream of the Earth*, Sierra Club Books.

(h) Abraham Maslow, 1968, *Towards a Psychology of Being*, Van Nostrand Reinhold. Also refer to *Religions, Values and Peak Experiences*, 1964, Penguin Books, and "A Theory of Human Motivation," 1943, *Psychological Review*, 50.

(i) Dalai Lama, 1995, *Awakening the Mind, Lightening the Heart*, Harper.

(j) Mary Midgley, 2005, "Visions and Values," *Resurgence*, no. 228.

[10]Ursula King, 1989, *The Spirit of the Earth: Reflections on Teilhard de Chardin and Global Spirituality*, Paragon Books.

[11]Satish Kumar, 2002, *You Are Therefore I Am*, Green Books.

[12]Bishop Desmond Tutu, 1999, *No Future without Forgiveness*, Rider Publishing, UK.

[13]Zygmunt Bauman, 2001, "Whatever Happened to Compassion?" article in book, *The Moral Universe, Demos*.

[14]Thomas Weber, 2004, *Gandhi as Disciple and Mentor*, Cambridge University Press. Also please refer to Mandhu Dandavate, *Gandhi's Human Touch*, 1996, Gandhi Foundation, India.

[15]Teilhard de Chardin, 1961, *The Phenomenon of Man*, Harper Torchbooks.

[16]Charles Darwin, 1968 (reprint 1985), *The Origin of Species by Means of natural Selection*, Penguin Books. The work of Darwin in recent years has been developing an additional controversial dimension based on the work of David Loye, described below in reference no. 18.

[17]Robert L. Heilbroner, 1992, *The Worldly Philosophers*, Touchstone Books.

[18]David Loye, 2004, *The Great Adventure: Toward a Fully Human Theory of Evolution*, SUNY Press. Loye is founder and developer of the Darwin Project. Refer to www. Darwinproject.com. Loye expressed his concerns in a presentation to the *Tikkun Community Magazine* in 2004, titled "George Bush and the Darwin Wars Debate." In the presentation, Loye stated, "For a decade bottled up in the obscurity of scientific journals and academic books of limited circulation has been the discovery of 'the rest of Darwin,' the Darwin who tells us in *The*

Descent of Man that natural selection drops away at the level of human evolution and 'higher agencies take over.'"

[19]Ervin Laszlo, 2001, *Macroshift*, Barrett-Koehler.

[20]Joseph Campbell, 1988, *The Power of Myth*, Doubleday.

[21]Roger Walsh, 2001, "The Seven Practices of Essential Spirituality," *Noetic Sciences Review*, Dec. 2001-Feb. 2002. Also refer to *Paths Beyond Ego: The Transpersonal Vision* (with Frances Vaughan and John Mack), 1993, J. P. Tarcher.

[22](a) Desmond Tutu, 2002, "Path to Forgiveness," Interview with Desmond Tutu (with Mark Swilling, Eve Anneke, Wilhelm Verwoerd, of *Insurgence* No. 214.

(b) Dalai Lama, 1999, "The Dalai Lama's Book of Wisdom," extract from *Power of Compassion*, 1993, Thorsons Publishers, London.

(c) Gary Snyder, 1995, *A Village Council of all Beings: Ecology, Place and the Awakening of Compassion*, Green Books.

[23]Satish Kumar, 2002, *You Are Therefore I Am*, Green Books. Kumar describes Gandhi's philosophy related to "service."

[24]Thomas Berry, 1988, *The Dream of the Earth*, Sierra Club Books.

[25]Abraham Maslow, 1968, *Towards a Psychology of Being*, Van Nostrand Reinhold. Also refer to *Religions, Values and Peak Experiences*, 1970, Penquin Books.

[26]Thomas Weber, 1991, *Conflict Resolution and Gandhian Ethics*, Gandhi Peace Foundation.

[27](a) Abraham Maslow, 1968, *Towards a Psychology of Being*, Van Nostrand Reinhold.

[28](b) Jerry Mander, 1996, "The Rules of Corporate Behavior," article in *The Case Against the Global Economy*, 1996, Sierra Club Books.

(c) Hazel Henderson, 1996, *Building a Win-Win World*, Barrett-Koehler.

(d) Paul Hawkin, Amory B. Lovins, L. Hunter Lovins, 1999, *Natural Capitalism: The Next Industrial Revolution*, Earthscan.

(e) David Korten, 1999, *The Post-Corporate World*, Barrett-Koehler.

(f) Henry W. Lane, Joseph J. DiStefano, Martha L. Maznevski, 1997, *International Management Behaviour*, Blackwell Books.

(g) Eva Kras, 1995, *Management in Two Cultures*, Intercultural Press. Also refer to *Modernizing Mexican Management Style*, 1994, Editts Publishing (Two Eagles Press), and *Sustainable Development and Business in Mexico and Latin America*, 1995, Grupo Editorial Iberoamerica, Mexico.

[29](a) Willis Harman, 1998, *Global Mind Change*, Barrett-Koehler.

(b) Bishop Desmond Tutu, 2002, "Path of Forgiveness." Interview: Please refer to reference No. 22 for details.

(c) Satish Kumar, 1992, *Path Without Destination*, Green Books.

(d) Dalai Lama, 1993, "The Dalai Lama's Book of Wisdom," extract from *Powers of Compassion*, London, Thorsons.

(e) Henry Lane et al, 1997, *International Management Behavior*, Blackwell Books. Please refer to reference no. 27 (f) for full details of all authors.

(f) Kras, Eva, please refer to no. 27/28 (g).

[30]Thomas Weber, 1991, *Conflict Resolution and Gandhian Ethics*, Gandhi Peace Foundation.

[31]T. Weber, 2001, "Gandhian Philosophy, Conflict Resolution Theory and Practical Approaches to Negotiation," *Journal of Peace Research*, vol. 38, no. 4. Also refer to "Nonviolence is Who?" Gene Sharp and Gandhi, Peace and Change, vol. 28, no. 2.;"Gandhi , Deep Ecology, Peace Research and Buddhist Economics," 1999, *Journal of Peace Research*.

[32]Ela Gandhi, 2002, "Gandhi and Development," *Resurgence* no. 214.

[33](a) Thomas Weber, 1999, "Gandhi, Deep Ecology, Peace Research and Buddhist Economics," *Journal of Peace Research*.

(b) Matthew Fox, 1983, *Original Blessing*, Bear and Company Inc.

[34]Satish Kumar, 2002, *You Are Therefore I Am*, Green Books.

[35](a) The Earth Charter, please refer to reference no. 1 above.

(b) Edward Goldsmith, 1995, "Biospheric Ethics," article in *The Future of Progress*, 1995, Green Books.

(c) Edward Goldsmith, 1993, *The Way: An Ecological World-view*, Shambhala Publishers.

[36](a) David Korten, 1999, *The Post Corporate World*, Barrett-Koehler.

(b) Hazel Henderson, 1996, *Building a Win-Win World*, Barrett-Koehler.

[37](a) Thomas Berry, 1988, *Dream of the Earth*, Sierra Club Books.

(b) Matthew Fox, 1983, *Original Blessing*, Bear and Company Inc.

(c) Teilhard de Chardin, 1961, *The Phenomenon of Man*, Harper Torchbooks.

[38](a) Thomas Berry , please see reference no. 37.

(b) Willis Harman, please see reference no. 29.

(c) Joseph Campbell, 1988, *The Power of Myth*, Doubleday.

(d) Ervin Laszlo, 2001, *Macroshift*, Barrett-Koehler.

(e) C. G. Jung, 1965, *Memories, Dreams, Reflections*, Random House.

[39]Roger Walsh, 2001, "The Seven Practices of Essential Spirituality," *Noetic Sciences Review*, Dec. 2001-Feb. 2002. Also refer to *Paths Beyond Ego: The Transpersonal Vision* (with Frances Vaughan and John Mack), J.P. Tarcher.

[40](a) Ervin Laszlo, 1997, "3rd Millenium: The Challenge and the Vision," Report of the Club of Budapest, Gaia Books.

(b) Herman Daly and John Cobb, Jr., 1989, *For the Common Good*, Beacon Press.

[41](a) David Orr, 1992, *Ecological Literacy: Education and the Transformation to a Post Modern World*, SUNY Press.

(b) Satish Kumar, 1996, "Gandhi's Swadeshi: The Economics of Permanence," article in *The Case Against the Global Economy*, 1996, Sierra Club Books.

(c) Helen Norberg-Hodge and Peter Goering, 1992, "Alternative in Education," article in *The Future of Progress*, 1992, Green Books.

[42](a) James Goldsmith, 1993, *The Trap*, Editions Fixot.

(b) Edward Goldsmith, 1996, "The Last Word: Family, Community and Democracy," article in *The Case Against the Global Economy*, Sierra Books.

(c) Marilyn Ferguson, 1993, "The Transformation of Values and Vocation," article in *The New Paradigm in Business*, Jeremy P. Tarcher/Perigee.

[43](a) Hazel Henderson, 1996, *Building a Win-Win World*, Barrett-Koehler.

(b) David Korten, 1999, *The Post Corporate World*, Barrett-Koehler.

(c) Peter Russell, 1995, *The Global Mind Awakens*, Global Mind, Palo Alto, CA.

(d) Kras, Eva, 1995, *Management in Two Cultures*, Intercultural Press, Yarmouth, Maine; 1994, *Modernizing Mexican Management*, Editts Publishing (Two Eagles Press) Las Cruces, NM.

[44](a) Abraham Maslow, 1968, *Towards a Psychology of Being*, Van Rostrand Reinhold. Also refer to "A Theory of Human Motivation," 1943, *Psychological Review*, 50.

(b) Satish Kumar, 2002, *You Are Therefore I Am*, Green Books.

(c) James Goldsmith, 1978, *The Stable Society*, Wadebridge Press.

(d) Kras, Eva, please refer to note 43.

[45](a) E. F. Schumacher, 1997, *This I Believe*, Green Books.

(b) Edward Goldsmith , please see reference no. 42b.

(c) Abraham Maslow, please see reference no. 44a.

[46](a) Satish Kumar, please see reference no. 44b.

(b) C. J. Jung, 1965, *Memories, Dreams, Reflections*, Random House.

(c) Abraham Maslow, please see reference no. 44a.

(d) David Orr, please see reference no. 41a.

[47](a) Satish Kumar, please see reference no. 41b.

(b) David Korten, please see reference no. 43b.

(c) Sigmund Kvaloy, 1995, "Inside Nature," article in *The Future of Progress*, 1995, Green Books.

[48]Satish Kumar, please see reference no. 44b.

[49](a) Satish Kumar, please see reference no. 44b.

(b) Ervin Laszlo, 1997, "3rd Millennium: The Challenge and the Vision," Report of the Club of Budapest, Gaia Books.

(c) Hazel Henderson, 1999, *Beyond Globalization*, Kumarian Press.

(d) Willis Harman, 1998, *Global Mind Change*, Barrett-Koehler. Also refer to *Higher Creativity*, Willis Harman with Howard Reingold, 1984, J. P. Tarcher.

(e) Kras, Eva, 1994, *Modernizing Mexican Management*, Edutts Publishing (Two Eagles Press), Las Cruces, NM; 1995, *Sustainable Development and Business in Mexico and Latin America*, Grupo Editorial Iberoamerica.

[50]E. F. Schumacher, 1997, *This I Believe*, Green Books.

[51](a) E. F. Schumacher, 1974, *Small is Beautiful: Economics as if People Mattered*, Abacus.

(b) David Korten, 2002, "Living Economies," *Resurgence* no. 215. Also refer to *The Post Corporate World*, 1999, Barrett-Koehler.

[52]E. F. Schumacher, 1997, *This I Believe*, Green Books. Also refer to Eva Kras, 1995, *Sustainable Development and Business in Mexico and Latin America*, Grupo Editorial Iberoamerica, Mexico City. Refer to note 49 for other referral.

[53](a) Tom Bentley and Ina Hargreaves, 2001, *Introduction to The Moral Uni-*

verse, Demos.

(b) John Gray, 2001, "Liberalism and Living Together," article in *The Moral Universe*, Demos.

(c) Amitai Etzioni, 2001, "Sustaining the Community of Communities," article in *The Moral Universe*, Demos.

(d) Wendell Berry, 1996, "Conserving Communities," article in *The Case Against the Global Economy*, Sierra Books.

(e) Satish Kumar, 1996, "Gandhi's Swadeshi: The Economics of Permanence," article in *The Case Against the Global Economy*, Sierra Books.

(f) David Morris, 1996, "Communities: Building Authority, Responsibility and Capacity," article in *The Case Against the Global Economy*, Sierra Books.

(g) Edward Goldsmith, 1996, "The Last Word: Family, Community, Democracy," article in *The Case Against the Global Economy*, Sierra Books.

(h) Nicolas Hillyard, 1995, "Liberation Ecology," article in *The Future of Progress*, Green Books. Also refer to "Empowering Communities," *The Ecologist*, Vol. 21, No. l.

(i) E. F. Schumacher, please refer to reference no. 52.

(j) Pooran Desai and Sue Riddlestone, 2002, *Bioregional Solutions: For Living on One Planet*, Green Books.

[54]E. F. Schumacher, please see reference no. 52. Also refer to Eva Kras, no. 49.

[55]Ulrich Beck, 1992, *Risk Society: Towards a New Modernity*, Sage Publications.

[56]David Korten, 1999, *The Post Corporate World*, Barrett-Koehler.

[57]David Morris, please see reference no. 53f. Also refer to Eva Kras, no. 49.

[58](a) Tom Bentley, please see reference no. 53a.

(b) Victor Toledo, 1992, *What is Ethnoecology? Origin, Scope and Implication of a Rising Discipline*, Etnoecologia. Also refer to *Biodiversity and Indigenous Peoples*, 2001, Academic Press.

[59]United Nations Conference on Human Settlements (Habitat II), Istanbul, June, 2004.

[60](a) Abraham Maslow, please see reference no. 44a.

(b) Satish Kumar, please see reference no. 44b.

(c) G. Ramachandrant and T.K. Mahadevan, *Gandhi: His Relevance in our Times*, Gandhi Peace Foundation.

[61]David Orr, please see reference no. 41a.

[62](a) Herman Daly and John Cobb, Jr., 1989, *For the Common Good*, Beacon Press.

(b) Hazel Henderson, 1992, *Paradigms in Progress: Life Beyond Economics*, Kumarian Press.

(c) David Korten, please see reference no. 56.

[63]Thomas Weber, 2001, "Gandhian Philosophy, Conflict Resolution Theory and Practical Approaches to Negotiation," *Journal of Peace Research*, Vol. 38, No. 4.

[64](a) Madhu Dandavate, 1996, *Gandhi's Human Touch*, Gandhi Foundation.

(b) Mahatma Gandhi, 1957, *An Autobiography: The Story of My Experiments with Truth*, Beacon Press. Also refer to *The Essential Gandhi*, 1962, Ed. L

Fischer, Vintage Books.

[65](a) Thomas Berry, 1988, *The Dream of the Earth*, Sierra Club Books.

(b) Edward Goldsmith, 1993, *The Way*, Shambhala Publ.

(c) Teilhard de Chardin, 1961, *The Phenomenon of Man*, Harper Torchbooks.

(d) Ervin Laszlo, Stanislav Grof and Peter Russell, 1999, *The Consciousness Revolution*, Element Books.

(e) United Nations Millenium Manifesto

(f) Ervin Laszlo, 1997, "3rd Millenium," Report of the Club of Budapest, Gaia Books.

(g) Morris Berman, 1981, *The Reenchantment of the World*, Cornel University Press.

[66]Thomas Berry, 1988, *The Dream of the Earth*, Sierra Club Books.

[67]Willis Harman, 1998, *Global Mind Change*, Barrett-Koehler.

[68]Ervin Laszlo, 1997, "3rd Millenium," Report of the Club of Budapest, Gaia Books.

[69]Edgar Mitchell, former astronaut and a founder of the Institute of Noetic Sciences.

[70]Union of Concerned Scientists: This organization, formed in 1969, is an independent, nonprofit alliance of more than 100,000 concerned scientists and citizens. The original group (faculty and students) was formed in the Mass. Institute of Technology, concerned with the misuse of science and technology in society. They believe in rigorous scientific analysis combined with innovative thinking and citizen advocacy to build a cleaner, healthier environment and a safer world.

[71]Ervin Laszlo summarizes the worldview of Union of Concerned Scientists. Also refer to reference no. 68.

[72]Victor Toledo, 2003, *Ecologia, Espiritualidad, y Conocimieto*, Univ. Iberoamericana y PNUMA.

[73]Herman Daly, 1991, *Steady State Economics*, Island Press.

[74]David Korten, 1995, *When Corporations Rule the World*, Barrett-Koehler.

[75]Thomas Berry, 1988, *The Dream of the Earth*, Sierra Club Books.

[76]Mathis Wackernagel and William Rees, 1996, *Our Ecological Footprint: Reducing Human Imprint on the Earth*, New Society Publishers, Gabriola Island, BC, Canada. Wackernagel is also the founder of Ecological Footprint Network, whose mission is to make sustainability specific by transforming Ecological Footprint into a vocal and rigorous measure of human demand on nature (www.footprintnetwork.org).

[77]Precautionary Principle: As defined in Feb. 1998, Rachael's Environment and Health Weekly, No. 586, this is a new principle for guiding human activities to prevent harm to the environment and to human health. It is called the "principle of precautionary action" or "precautionary principle." The principle involves two factors: scientific uncertainty, and suspected harm. These two factors combined form the basis for precautionary actions. "Scientific Uncertainty" includes ignorance, indeterminacy (unknowability of large systems), statistical/model/parameter uncertainties. "Harm" includes serious (covers large areas or extends over long time periods) irreversible or cumulative harm. "Precautionary action" as a

result is preventative and anticipatory. Also refer to work of Tom Oriordan and James Cameron, *Interpreting the Precautionary Principle*, 1994, Island Press.

[78](a) Herman Daly and John Cobb Jr., 1989, *For the Common Good*, Beacon Press.

(b) Hazel Henderson, 1996, *Building a Win-Win World*, Barrett-Koehler.

(c) Karl-Henrik Robert, 2002, *Natural Step Story: Seeding a Quiet Revolution*, New Society Publishers, Gabriola Island, BC, Canada.

(d) James Robertson, 1998, "Transforming Economic Life: A Millenium Challenge," Schumacher Briefing no. 1, Green Books

[79]Mathis Wackernagel, 1998, "The Ecological Footprint: An Indicator of Progress Towards Regional Sustainability," Environmental Monitoring and Assessment 51.

[80](a) Brian Swimme, 1984, *The Universe is a Green Giant*, Bear and Company Inc.

(b) Edward Goldsmith. 1993, *The Way*, Shambhala Publ.

(c) Whilhem Reich, 1973, *Selected Writings: An Introduction to Orgonomy*, Farrar, Straus and Giroux, New York.

[81](a) E. F. Schumacher, 1997, *This I Believe*, Green Books.

(b) Mahu Dandavate, 1996, *Gandi's Human Touch*, Gandhi Peace Foundation.

(c) Satish Kumar, 2002, *You Are Therefore I Am*, Green Books.

(d) Ervin Laszlo, 1997, "3rd Millenium," Gaia Books.

(e) Herman Daly and John Cobb, Jr., please see reference no. 78a.

(f) Hazel Henderson, 1996, *Building a Win-Win World*, Barrett-Koehler.

CHAPTER V

[1]Willis Harman, 1998, *Global Mind Change*, Barrett-Koehler.

[2]E. F. Schumacher, 1997, *This I Believe*, Green Books.

[3]David Loye, 2004, *The Great Adventure: Toward a Fully Human Theory of Evolution*, SUNY Press.

[4]E. F. Schumacher, 1997, *This I Believe*, Green Books.

[5]Ervin Laszlo, 2001, *Macroshift*, Barrett-Koehler.

[6]Peter Russell, 2000, *From Science to God: The Mystery of Consciousness and the Meaning of Light*, Sausalito, Peter Russell.

[7]Willis Harman, please see reference no. 1. Also refer to Eva Kras, 1994, *Modernizing Mexican Management*, Editts Publishing (Two Eagles Press), Las Cruces, NM.

8(a) The Earth Charter is an authoritative synthesis of values, principles and aspirations that are widely shared by growing numbers of men and women in all regions of the world. The origin of the concept was sponsored by the United Nations Commission on Environment and Development, 1987, followed by the Earth Charter Commission 1997. The International Earth Charter Secretariat is located in San Jose, Costa Rica.

(b) Willis Harman, please see reference no.l.

(c) Herman Daly and John Cobb, Jr., 1989, *For the Common Good*, Beacon

Press.

(d) Ervin Laszlo, 1997, "3rd Millenium," Gaia Books.

(e) Eva Kras, 1995, *Sustainable Development and Business in Mexico and Latin America*, Grupo Editorial Iberoamerica, Mexico City. Also refer to no. 7 for Eva Kras reference.

[9]Madhu Dandavate, 1996, *Gandhi's Human Touch*, Gandhi Peace Foundation.

[10]Satish Kumar, 2002, *You Are Therefore I Am*, Green Books.

[11]Ursula King, 1989, *The Spirit of the Earth: Reflection on Teilhard de Chardin and Global Spirituality*, Paragon Books.

[12]Dalai Lama, 1995, *Awakening the Mind, Lightening the Heart*, Harper.

[13]The Earth Charter, please see 8a.

[14]Vandana Shiva, 1991, *The Violence of the Green Revolution*, Third World Network, Penang, Malaysia.

[15]Mathis Wackernagel and William Rees, 1995, *Ecological Footprint*, New Society Publishers, Gabriola Island, BC, Canada.

[16]Ervin Laszlo, please see reference 8d.

[17]Vandana Shiva, 1989, *Staying Alive: Women, Ecology and Development*, Zed Books.

[18]Satish Kumar, 1992, *Path Without Destination*, Green Books.

[19]E. F. Schumacher, 1974, *Small is Beautiful*, Abacus. Also refer to *Intermediate Technology and the Individual*, Appropriate Technology Visions, San Francisco, Boyd and Fraser.

[20]Vandana Shiva, 2002, "Paradigm Shift," *Resurgence* no. 214.

[21]David Korten, 1999, *Post Corporate World*, Barrett-Koehler.

[22](a) Thomas Weber, 2003, "Nonviolence is Who?: Gene Sharp and Gandhi," *Peace and Change*, Vol. 28, No.2.

(b) Vandana Shiva, 2003, " Globalization and Terrorism: Understanding the Roots of Violence," *Resurgence* no. 218.

[23]Desmond Tutu, 1999, *No Future Without Forgiveness*, Doubleday.

[24]Ervin Laszlo, please see reference no. 5.

[25]Hazel Henderson, 1996, *Building a Win-Win World*, Barrett-Koehler.

[26]Victor Toledo, 2003, *Ecologia, Espiritualidad y Conocimiento*, Univ. Iberamericana y PNUMA.

[27]Herman Daly, please see reference 8c.

[28]David Orr, 1992, *Ecological Literacy: Education and the Transition to a Post Modern World*, SUNY Press.

[29]Vandana Shiva, 2002, "Paradigm Shift," *Resurgence* no. 214.

[30]Satish Kumar, please see reference no. 10.

[31]Herman Daly, please see reference no. 8c.

[32]E. F. Shumacher, 1997, *This I Believe*, Green Books.

[33]Hazel Henderson, 1993, *Paradigms in Progress: Life Beyond Economics*, Kumarian Press.

[34]Herman Daly, 1991, *Steady State Economics*, Island Press.

[35]David Korten, 1995, *When Corporations Rule the World*, Kumarian Press and Barrett Koehler

[36]Hazel Henderson, 1993, *Paradigms in Progress: Life Beyond Economics*, Kumarian Press.

[37]Ervin Laszlo, 1997, "3rd Millenium," Gaia Books

[38]Edward Goldsmith, 1996, "The Last Word: Family, Community, Democracy," article in *The Case Against the Global Economy*, Sierra Club Books.

[39]Edward Goldsmith, 1993, *The Way*, Shambhala Publ.

[40]Fritjof Capra, 1996, *The Web of Life*, HarperCollins.

[41]Vandana Shiva, 1991, *The Violence of the Green Revolution*, Third World Network, Penang, Malaysia.

[42]Ervin Laszlo, 2001, *Macroshift*, Barrett-Koehler.

[43]Mathis Wackernagel, 1998, "The Ecological Footprint: An Indicator of Progress Towards Regional Sustainability," *Environmental Monitoring and Assessment* 51.

[44]Herman Daly, 1991, *Steady State Economics*, Island Press.

[45]Hazel Henderson, 1996, *Creating Alternative Futures: The End of Economics*, Putnam 1996.

[46]Ervin Laszlo, 2001, *Macroshift*, Barrett-Koehler.

[47]Meadows, D.H., Meadows, D.L., and Randers, J., 1992, *Beyond the Limits: Global Collapse or a Sustainable Future*, Earthscan.

[48]Peter Soderbaum., 2000, *Ecological Economics: A Political Economics Approach to Environment and Development*, Earthscan.

[49]Vandana Shiva, 2002, "Paradigm Shift," *Resurgence* no. 214.

[50]Hazel Henderson, 1996, B*uilding a Win-Win World*, Barrett-Koehler.

[51]Tom Oriordan and James Cameron, 1994, *Interpreting the Precautionary Principle*, Island Press.

[52]Vandana Shiva, 1991, *The Violence of the Green Revolution*, Third World Network, Penang, Malaysia. Also refer to "Captive Water: Voice from the South," 2003, *Resurgence* no. 219.

[53]David Korten, 1999, *The Post Corporate World*, Barrett-Koehler.

[54]Mathis Wackernagel, please see reference no. 43.

[55]Ervin Laszlo, please see reference no. 37.

[56]Vandana Shiva, 2002, "Paradigm Shift," *Resurgence* no. 214.

[57]Edward Goldsmith, 1993, *The Way*, Shambhala Publ.

[58]James Lovelock, 1979, *Gaia: A New Look at Life on Earth*, Oxford University Press.

[59]Fritjof Capra, 1996, *The Web of Life*, Harper Collins.

[60]Ervin Laszlo, please see reference no. 37.

[61]Ursula King , 1989, *The Spirit of the Earth*, Paragon Books.

[62]Willis Harman, 1998, *Global Mind Change*, Barrett-Koehler.

[63]Mathis Wackernagel and William Rees, please see reference no. 15.

[64]David Korten, please see reference no. 35.

[65]Ervin Laszlo, 1997, "3rd Millenium," Gaia Books.

[66]Herman Daly and John Cobb Jr., 1989, *For the Common Good*, Beacon Press.

[67]Herman Daly, 1991, *Steady State Economics*, Island Press.

[68]Hazel Henderson, please see reference no. 50.

[69]Ervin Laszlo, please see reference no. 65.

[70]David Orr, 1991, 1996, "What is Education For?" *Context Journal*, Context Institute.

[71]Peter Soderbaum, 2004, "Democracy, Markets and Sustainable Development," *European Environment*, Issue 6, Vol. 14.

[72]David Orr, 1992, *Ecological Literacy: Education and the Transition to a Post Modern World*, SUNY Press.

[73]Hazel Henderson, 1999, *Beyond Globalization: Shaping a Sustainable Global Economy*, Kumarian Press.

[74](a) Ervin Laszlo, 1994, *The Choice: Evolution vs Extinction?: A Thinking Person's Guide to Global Issues*, Jeremy P. Tardier/Putnam.

(b) Herman Daly, 1991, *Ecological Economics and Sustainable Development: From Concept to Policy*, World bank Policy and Research Division, Washington. DC.

(c)Willis Harman, 1994, "A System in Decline or Transformation?" *WBA Perspectives*, vol. 8. no. 2.

(d) Hazel Henderson, 1996, *Building a Win-Win World*, Barrett-Koehler.

(e) Eva Kras, 1995, *Sustainable Development and Business in Mexico and Latin America*, Grupo Editorial Iberoamerica, Mexico City.

[75]Willis Harman, 1994, "A System in Decline or Transformation?" *WBA Perspective*, vol. 8, no.2

[76]David Korten, 1999, *The Post Corporate World*, Barrett-Koehler.

[77]Hazel Henderson, please see reference no. 74d.

[78]Herman Daly, 1980, *Economics, Ecology and Ethics: Essays*, W.H. Freeman, San Francisco.

[79]David Korten, 2002, "Living Economies," *Resurgence* no. 215.

[80]E. F. Schumacher, 1974, *Small is Beautiful*, Abacus. Also refer to the work of Hazel Henderson, no. 74(d).

[81]David Korten, 1999, *The Post Corporate World*, Barrett-Koehler.

[82]Hazel Henderson, please see reference no. 74d.

[83]Herman Daly and John Cobb, Jr. 1989, *For the Common Good*, Beacon Press.

[84]Willis Harman, 1993, "Approaching the Millenium: Business as a Vehicle for Global Transformation," article in *The New Paradigm in Business*, Jeremy P. Tarcher/Perigee.

[85]Hazel Henderson, 1996, *Building A Win-Win World*, Barrett-Koehler.

[86]Ervin Laszlo, 2001, *Macroshift*, Barrett-Koehler.

[87]E. F. Schumacher, 1997, *This I Believe*, Green Books.

[88]Mathis Wackernagel, 1998, "The Ecological Footprint: An Indicator of Progress Towards Regional Sustainability," *Environmental Monitoring and Assessment* 51.

[89]United Nations Development Index (HDI), 2000, United Nations Human Development Report. The HDI, included in the report, is considered an alternative to the conventional GDP basis for measuring human development and progress. The HDI report takes into account additional factors not included in GDP mea-

surements, such as life expectancy, educational attainment and basic purchasing power. Additional reports of this kind have also been developed by other economists, such as Herman Daly's Index of Sustainable Economic Welfare and Hazel Henderson's Country Futures Indicators.

[90]David Korten, 1999, *The Post Corporate World*, Barrert-Koehler.

91Herman Daly, 1999, "Globalization vs Internationalization," *Ecological Economics Journal* no. 31.

[92]Roy Madron and John Jopling, 2003, "Gaian Democracies," *Schumacher Briefing* no. 9, Green Books.

[93]Hazel Henderson, 1996, *Building a Win-Win World*, Barrert-Koehler.

[94]Hazel Henderson, please see reference no. 93.

[95]Richard Douthwaite, 1999, "The Ecology of Money," *Schumacher Briefing* no. 4, Green Books.

[96]Herman Daly and John Cobb Jr., please see reference no. 83.

[97]Herman Daly, 1997, *Steady State Economics*, Island Press

[98]Henderson, Hazel, 1996, *Building a Win-Win World*, Barrett-Koehler.

[99]Korten, David, 1999, *The Post Corporate World*, Barrett-Koehler.

[100]Weber, Thomas, 2001, "Gandhian Philosophy, Conflict Resolution Theory and Practical Approaches to Negotiations," *Journal of Peace Reseach*, Vol. 38, No. 4.

[101]David Loye, 2004, *The Great Adventure: Towards a fully Human Theory of Evolution*, SUNY Press.

[102]Mathis Wackernagel, 1998, "The Ecological Footprint: an Indicator of Progress Towards Regional Sustainability," *Environmental Monitoring and Assessment* 51.

CHAPTER VII

[1]This chapter draws from a large number of sources which include a wide spectrum of thinking related to organizational transformation. Following are shown some key references which have influenced most sections of this chapter. Additionally, references are made that pertain to specific topics discussed.

(a) Willis Harman, 1998, *Global Mind Change: The Promise of the 21st Century*, Barrett-Koehler.

(b) Ervin Laszlo, 1997, *3rd Millenium: The Challenge and the Vision*, Gaia Books.

(c) Peter Russell, 1995, *The Global Mind Awakens: Our Evolutionary Leap*, Global Mind, CA.

(d) Herman Daly and John Cobb Jr., 1989, *For the Common Good: Redirecting the Economy Towards Community, the Environment and a Sustainable Future*, Beacon Press.

(e) Hazel Henderson, 1996, *Building a Win-Win World*. Barrett-Koehler; also *Paradigms in Progress: Life Beyond Economics*, 1993, Kumarian Press.

(f) E. F. Schumacher, 1997, *This I Believe*, Green Books; also *Small is Beautiful: Economics as if People Mattered*, Abacus.

(g) Hawkin, Paul, Amory B. Lovins and L. Hunter Lovins, 1999, *Natural Capitalism: The Next Industrial Revolution*, Earthscan.

[2]Ervin Laszlo, 1997, *3rd Millenium*, Gaia Books.

[3]Paul Hawkin, Amory Lovins, and L. Hunter Lovins, 1999, *Natural Capitalism* (page 9, xiii), Earthscan.

[4]Willis Harman, 1993, "Approaching the Millenium: Business as a Vehicle for Business Transformation" (page 14), article in *The New Paradigm in Business*, Eds., Michael Ray and Alan Ringler, Jeremy P. Tarcher/Perigee.

[5]Anita Roddick, 1995, Technology and Values, *Resurgence*, July/August 1995.

[6]Covey, Stephen, R., 1992, *Principle-Centered Leadership*, Simon and Schuster.

(a) Eva Kras, 1995, *Sustainable Development and Business in Mexico and Latin America*, Grupo Editorial Iberoamerica, Mexico City.

(b) Eva Kras, 1994, *Modernizing Mexican Management*, Editts Publishing (Two Eagles Press), Las Cruces, NM.

[7]Ervin Laszlo, 1999, *The Consciousness Revolution: A Transatlantic Dialogue*, Element Books.

[8]Ervin Laszlo, 2001, *Macroshift*, Barrett-Koehler.

[9]Roy Madron and John Jopling, 2003, "Gaian Democracies: Redefining Globalization and People Power", *Schumacher Briefing* no. 9, Green Books.

[10]Marilyn Ferguson, 1980, *The Aquarian Conspiracy: Personal and Social Transformation in the 1980's*, J.P. Tarcher.

[11]Satish Kumar, 2002, *You Are Therefore I Am*, Green Books.

[12](a) Walsh, Roger, 2001, "The Seven Practices of Essential Spirituality," *Noetic Sciences Review*, Dec. 2001-Feb. 2002. Also see *Essential Spirituality*, 2000, John Wiley and Sons.

(b) Abraham Maslow, 1968, *Towards a Psychology of Being*, Van Nostrand Reinhold.

[13]Dalai Lama, 1995, *Awakening the Mind, Lightening the Heart*, Harper.

[14]E. F. Schumacher, 1997, *This I Believe*, Green Books.

[15]Stephen Covey, 1992, *Principle-Centered Leadership*, Simon and Schuster. Also refer to Eva Kras, no. 6.

[16](a)Willis Harman, 1998, *Global Mind Change*, Barrett-Koehler.

(b) Satish Kumar, 2002, *You Are Therfore I Am*, Green Books.

[17](a) Willis Harman, 1998, *Global Mind Change*, Barrett-Koehler.

(b) Jonathan Porritt, 2004, "Seduced by Speed," *Resurgence* no. 222.

(c) Janice Stein, 2001, *The Cult of Efficiency*, House of Anansi Press Ltd.

[18]Michael Murphy and Steven Donovan, 1997, *The Physical and Psychological Effects of Meditation*, Institute of Noetic Sciences.

[19]Larry Dossey, 1993, *Healing Words: The Power of Prayer and the Practice of Meditation*, Harper.

[20]Roger Walsh, 2003, *Paths Beyond Ego: The Transpersonal Vision* (with Frances Vaughan and John Mack), J. P. Tarcher.

[21]E. F. Schumacher, 1974, *Small is Beautiful: Economics as if People Mattered*, Abacus.

[22]Satish Kumar, 2002, *You Are Therefore I Am*, Green Books.

(a) Eva Kras, 1994, *Modernizing Mexican Management*, Editts Publishing (Two Eagles Press), Las Cruces, NM.

[23]The visionaries and researchers who have influenced my thinking over many years in organizational transformation are many. The following references 23-28 are a few of these whose wisdom has helped me in both conceptual thinking as well as practice in national and transnational organizations.

Willis Harman, 1998, *Global Mind Change*, Barrett-Koehler ; also refer to: "Approaching the Millenium: Business as a Vehicle for Global Transformation," 1993, article in *The New Paradigm in Business*, Jeremy P. Tarcher, Perigee.

[24]E. F. Schumacher, 1997, *This I Believe*, Green Books.

[25]Stephen Covey, 1992, *Principle Centered Leadership*, Simon and Schuster.

[26]Matthew Fox, 1983, *Original Blessing*, Bear and Company.

[27]David Korten, 1999, *The Post Corporate World*, Barrett-Koehler.

[28]Hazel Henderson, 1996, *Building a Win-Win World*, Barrett-Koehler. Also refer to *Paradigms in Progress: Life Beyond Economics*, 1993, Kumarian Press. Also refer to Eva Kras, no. 22.

[29]Willis Harman, 1993, "Approaching the Millenium: Business as a Vehicle for Global Transformation," article in *The New Paradigm in Business*, Jeremy P. Tarcher/Perigee.

[30]Rolf Osterberg, 1993, "A New Kind of Company with a new Kind of Thinking," article in *The new Paradigm in Business*, Jeremy P. Tarcher/Perigee.

[31]Please note: References 31-37 have all influenced heavily the thinking related to guidelines for organizational transformation.

Herman Daly, 1996, *Beyond Growth: The Economics of Sustainable Development*, Beacon Press. Also refer to *Steady State Economics*, 1991, Island Press.

[32]Willis Harman, 1998, *Global Mind Change*, Barrett-Koehler.

[33]James Robertson, 1998, "Transforming Economic Life: A Millennial Challenge," *Schumacher Brief* no. l, Green Books.

[34]Stephen Covey, 1992, *Principle Centered Leadership*, Simon and Schuster.

[35]Karl-Henrik Robert, 2002, *Natural Step Story: Seeding a Quiet Revolution*, New Society Publishers.

[36]Roy Madron and John Jopling, 2003, "Gaian Democracies: Redefining Globalization and People Power," *Schumacher Briefing* no. 9, Green Books.

[37]Ervin Laszlo, 2001, *Macroshift*, Barrett-Koehler.

[38]Peter Russell, 1995, *The Global Mind Awakens: A new Evolutionary Leap*, Global Mind, CA.

[39]Gary Zukav, 1993, *Evolution and Business*, Putnam Publ.

[40]Roy Madron and John Jopling, 2003, "Gaian Democracies: Redefining Globalization and People Power" (page 131), *Schumacher Briefing* no. 9, Green Books.

[41]Eva Kras,, 1995, *Management in Two Cultures*, Intercultural Press, Yarmouth, Maine.

Eva Kras, 1994, *Modernizing Mexican Management*, Eddits Press (Two Eagle Press), Las Cruces, NM.

Eva Kras, 1995, *Sustainable Development and Business in Mexico and Latin*

America, Grupo Editorial Iberoamerica, Mexico City.

[42]Willis Harman, 1984, *Higher Creativity: Liberating the Unconscious for Breakthrough Insights*, Tarcher/Putnam.

[43]Herman Daly and John Cobb Jr., 1989, *For the Common Good*, Beacon Press.

[44]E. F. Schumacher, 1974, *Small is Beautiful*, Abacus. Also see *This I Believe*, 1997, Green Books.

[45]Ervin Laszlo, 2001, *Macroshift*, Barrett-Koehler. Also see "3rd Millenium: Challenges and the Vision," Report of the Club of Budapest, Gaia Books.

[46]Marilyn Ferguson, 1980, *The Aquarian Conspiracy*, J.P. Tarcher. Also see "The Transformation of Values and Vocation," 1993, article in *The New Paradigm in Business*, Putnam Publishers.

[47]Eva Kras, 1995, *Management in Two Cultures*, Intercultural Press. Yarmouth, Maine.

[48]Eva Kras, 1994, *Modernizing Mexican Management*, Editts Publishing (Two Eagles Press), Las Cruces, NM.

[49]Eva Kras, 1995, *Sustainable Development and Business in Mexico and Latin America*, Grupo Editorial Iberoamerica, Mexico City.

BIBLIOGRAPHY

Aga Khan, Sadruddin, 2002, "Keeping to Our Word," Resurgence No. 215.

Altieri, Miguel A., 1998, "An Agroecological perspective to guide graduate educational programs in agricultural economics and rural development in Latin America of the XXI Century," Ecological Economics Journal No. 27.

Anderberg, Stefan, 1998, "Industrial Metabolism and the linkages between economics, ethics and the environment," Ecological Economics Journal No.24.

Anderson, Luke, 1999, *Genetic Engineering, Food and Our Environment: A brief Guide*, Green Books.

Ash, Maurice, 2002, *Where Division Ends*, Green Books.

Ariansen, Per, 1998, "Anthropocentrism with a Human Face," Ecological Economics Journal no.24.

Axworthy, Lloyd, 2003, *Navigating a New World*, Vintage Canada, Toronto.

Attenborough, Sir David, 2001, "Strife on Earth," The Ecologist, Vol.31, No.3.

Attfield, Robin, 1998, "Existence Value and Intrinsic Value," Ecological Economics Journal No.24.

Bache, Chris, 2002, "Stepping Into the Fire," Noetic Science Review, March-May, 2002.

Barlow, Maude, 2003, "Water Freedom: Ethics," Resurgence No. 219.

Battle, John, 2003, "Culture of Community," Resurgence No. 218.

Bauman, Zygmunt, 201, "What Happened to Compassion?" article in book, The Moral Universe, Demos.

Beck, Ulrich, 1992, *Risk Society: Toward a New Modernity*, Sage Publ.

Bedi, Kiran, 2003, "Spirituality Behind Bars," Resurgence No. 219.

Bentley, Tom and Daniel Stedman Jones, (Eds.), "The Moral Universe," 2001, Demos.

Bennis, Warren, 1993, "Learning Some Basic Truths about Leadership," article in The New Paradigm in Business, Tarcher/Perigee Books.

Bennis, Warren, 2003, *On Becoming a Leader*, Perseus Publishing.

Bennis, Warren, 1993, *An Invented Life: Reflections on Leadership and Change*, Addison-Wesley.

225

Bentley, Tom and Ian Hargreaves, 2001, "Introduction: The new Ideology," article in book The Moral Universe, Demos.

Berman, Morris, 1981, *The Reenchantment of the World*, Cornell University Press.

Berry, Thomas, 1988, *Dream of the Earth*, Sierra Club Books.

Berry, Thomas and Brian Swimme, 1994, *The Universe Story*, Harper Collins.

Berry, Thomas, 2001, "On the Historical Mission of our Times," comments made as a member of the Club of Budapest, published in Macroshift, Barrett-Koehler.

Berry, Wendell, 1996, *The Unsettling of America: Culture and Agriculture*, Harper Collins Publishers.

Berry, Wendell. 1996, "Conserving Communities," article in The Case Against the Global Economy, Sierra Club Books.

Berry, Wendell, 2003, "A Citizen's Response: Futility of War, Resurgence No. 218.

Boff, Leonardo, 2002, "Liberation Theology," Resurgence No. 215.

Boff, Leonardo, 2001, *Etica Planetaria desde el Gran Sur*, Trotta, Barcelona.

Bond, Michael Shaw, 2002, "Psychology of Conflict," Resurgence No. 215.

Brown, Lester, 2001, *Eco-economy: Building an Economy for the Earth*, W.W. Norton & Co.

Brown, Peter, 2001, *The Commonwealth of Life*, Black Rose Books.

Bunzl, John M., 2001, *The Simultaneous Policy*, New European Publications, London.

Cadman, David, 2003, "A Necessary Simplicity," Resurgence No.217.

Capra, Fritjof, 1982, *The Turning Point: Science, Society and the Rising Culture*, Bantam.

Campbell Joseph, 1988, *The Power of Myth*, Doubleday.

Capra, Fritjof, 1996, *The Web of Life*, Harper Collins.

Carnie, Fiona, 2003, "Alternative Approaches to Education," Resurgence No. 220.

Cashford, Jules, 2002, "Gaia: Myth and Science," Resurgence No. 214.

Cavanagh, John and Jerry Mander (Eds.), 2004, *Alternatives to Economic Globalization*, Battett-Koehler.

Clark, M., 1989, *Ariadne's Thread: The Search for New Ways of Thinking*, McMillan Publishing.

CAUX Round Table, 1997, "The Critical Role of the Corporation in a Global Society: A Position Paper of the CAUX Table," Distributed by the Minnesota Center for corporate Responsibility (MCCR), Minneapolis, Minnesota, USA.

Cleveland, Harlan, 1994, "Ten Keys to World Peace," The Futurist, 28:04, July/August 1994.

Club of Budapest, formed in 1993. Details of the work and philosophy of the Club are found in website: http:/newciv.org/Clubof Budapest. Details are also found in Ervin Laszlo's book, "3rd Millenium: The Challenge and the Vision."

Colero, Larry, 1995, "Common Sense Ethics in Business," WBA Perspectives, Vol.9, No.1.

Council for a Parliament of the World's Religions, 1993, *Toward a Global Ethic*, Chicago.

---Covey, Stephen, 1992, *Principle Centered Leadership*, Simon and Schuster.

Cullinan, Cormac, 2002, "Justice for All," Resurgence No. 214

Dalai Lama, 1995, *Awakening the Mind, Lightening the Heart*, Harper.

Dalai Lama, 1989, "Ethics for a New Millenium," Nobel Peace Prize Speech, Riverhead.

Dalla Costa, John, 1999, "El Imperativo Etico: Porque el Liderazgo Moral es un Buen Negocio," Ed. Paidos.

Daly, Herman E., 1980, *Economics, Ecology and Ethics: Essays*, W. H. Freeman, San Francisco.

Daly, Herman and John Cobb Jr., 1989, *For the Common Good: Redirecting the Economy Toward Community, the Environment and a Sustainable Future*, Beacon Press.

Daly, Herman E., 1999," Globalization versus Internationalization," Ecological Economics Journal #31.

Daly, Herman E., 1991, *Steady-State Economics*, Island Press.

Daly, Herman E., 1991, *Ecological Economics and Sustainable Development: From Concept to Policy*, World Bank Policy and Research Division, Washington.

Daly, Herman E., 1996, *Beyond Growth: The Economics of Sustainable Development*, Beacon Press, Boston.

Daly, Herman, 2004, "Politics with Purpose," Resurgence No. 222.

Dandavate, Mandhu, 1996, *Gandhi's Human Touch*, Gandhi Foundation, India.

Darwin, C., 1968, *The Origin of Species by Means of Natural Selection*, reprinted in 1985 by Penguin Classics, London.

Davis, Erik, 1999, *Techgnosis: Myth, Magic and Mysticism in the Age of Information*, Serpent's Trail, London.

DeBeaupart, Elaine with Aura, Sofia Diaz, 1996, *The Three Faces of Mind: Developing your Mental, Emotional and Behavioural Intelligence*, Quest Books.

Desai, Pooran and Sue Riddlestone, 2002, *Bioregional Solutions For Living on One Planet*, Green Books.

Dossey, Larry, 1993, *Healing Words: The Power of Prayer and the Practice of Meditation*, Harper, San Francisco.

Douthwaite, Richard, 1993, *The Growth Illusion: How Economic Growth has enriched the Few, Impoverished the Many, and Endangered the Planet*, Council Oak Books.

Douthwaite, Richard, 1999, *The Ecology of Money*, Schumancher Briefing No. 9, Green Books.

Dunkley, Graham, 2004, *Free Trade: Myth, Reality and Alternatives*, Zed Books.

Edwards, David, 1995, *Free to be Human*, Green Books.

Einstein, Albert, 2000, Alice Calaprice, Ed., Forward by Freeman Dyson (1996, 2000), *The Expanded Quotable Einstein*, Princeton University Press.

Elgin, Duane, 1997, *Global Consciousness Change: Indicators of an Emerging Paradigm*, Millennium Project, San Anselmo, CA.

Elworthy, Scilla, 2003, "The Potency of Non Violence," Resurgence No. 218.

Estes, Ralph, 1996, "Corporate Accountability: The Tyranny of the Bottom Line," WBA Perspectives, Vol.10, No.1.

Etzioni, Amitai, 1988, *The Moral Dimension: Toward a New Economics*, The Free Press, New York and London.

Etzoni, Amitai, 2001, "Sustaining the Community of Communities" in The Moral Universe, Demos, 107-113.

Fairfield, Roy, 1977, *Person Centered Graduate Learning*, Prometheus Books.

Falk, Richard, 2004, "A New Gandhian Moment?," Resurgence No. 222.

Ferguson, Marilyn, 1980, *The Aquarian Conspiracy: Personal and Social Transformation in the 1980s*, J.P. Tarcher.

Ferguson, Marilyn, 1993, "The Transformation of Values and Vocation," article in book, *The New Paradigm in Business*, Eds. Michael Ray and Alan Rinzler, Jeremy P. Tarcher/Perigee.

Fox, Matthew, 1983, *Original Blessing*, Bear and Company.

Fraser, Matthew, 1998, "The Outlook for Generation X may depend on its Ability to Look Inward," Institute of Noetic Sciences, Feb. 1998.

Freire, P., 1985, *The Politics of Education: Culture, Power, and Liberation*, translated by D. Macedo, Westport CT, Bergin and Garvey Publishers Inc.

Friere, P. 1973, P*edagogy for Critical Consciousness*, Seabury Press.

Freud, Sigmund, 1990, *The Ego and the Id*, James Strachey, Ed., Translator, Joan Riviere, W.W. Norton Publications.

Frolova, Alla, 1998, "Ecological Reasoning: Ethical Alternatives," Ecological Economics Journal No.24.

Fromm, E., 1976, *To Have or to Be*, Jonathan Cape, London.

Fromm, E., 1973, *The Anatomy of Human Destructiveness*.

Galtung, Johan, Carl G. Jacobsen, Kai Frithjof Brand-Jacobson, 2000, *Searching for Peace*, Pluto Press, London.

Gandhi, Mahatma, 2006 (reprint), *An Autobiography or The Story of my Experiments with Truth*, Jitendra T. Desai, Navajivan Mudranalaya, Ahmedabad, India.

Gandhi, Ela, 2002, "Gandhi and Development," Resurgence no. 214

Gangadean, Ashok, 1997, *Between Worlds: The Emergence of Global Reason*, Global Dialogue Institute, Peter Lang, Revisioning Philosophy Series, 1997.

Gangadean, Ashok, 1997, "Dialogue: The Key to Global Ethics," WBA Perspectives, Vol. II, No.4.

Gatschet, Jacob, 1998, "Natural System Agriculture at the Land Institute," Ecological Economics Journal, Vol. 3, No.1.

George, Susan, 1999, *The Lugano Report: On Preserving Capitalism in the Twenty-first Century*, Pluto Press.

Girardet, Herbert, 2003, "Another world is Possible," Resurgence No. 218.

Giscard d'Estaing, Olivier, 1998, *Entreprise Ethique*, Le Cercle d' Ethique des Affaires, Paris.

Glover, Jonathon, 2001, "Never Such Innocence Again," in The Moral Universe, Demos. 35-41.

Goldsmith, Edward, Martin Khor, Helen Norberg -Hodge, Vandana Shiva, et al,

1995, *The Future of Progress*, Green Books and International Society for Ecology and Culture.

Goldsmith, Edward, 1993, *The Way: An Ecological World-view*, Shambhala Publishers, Boston.

Goldsmith, Edward, 2000, "Religion at the Millenium," The Ecologist, Vol. 30, No.1.

Goldsmith, Edward, 1995, "Biospheric Ethics," article in The Future of Progress, Green Books

Goldsmith, James, 1996, "The Last Word: Family, Community and Democracy," article in The Case Against the Global Economy, Sierra Club Books.

Goldsmith, James, 1993, *The Trap*, Editions Fixot.

Goldsmith, James, 1978, *The Stable Society*, Wadebridge Press.

Goodwin, Brian, 2003, "Patterns of Wholeness," Resurgence No. 216.

Gray, John, 1995, *Enlightenment's Wake: Politics and Culture at Close of the Modern Age*, Routledge.

Gray, John, 2001, "Liberalism and Living Together," in The Moral Universe, Demos, 67-74.

Griffiths, Jay, 2000, "Local Time," Resurgence No. 199.

Grof, Stanislav, 1988, *The Adventure of Self Discovery*, State University of New York Press.

Grof, Stanislav, 1998, *The Cosmic Game: Explorations of the Frontiers of Human Consciousness*, State University of New York Press.

Guy, Vincent and John Matlock, 1996, *The New International Manager*, Kogan Page Ltd.

Habermas, Jurgen, 2003, *The Future of Human Nature*, Polity Publishers.

Habermas, Jurgen, 2003, *A Morality for a Genetic Age*, Polity Press.

Hall, Edward and Mildred Reed Hall, 1990, *Understanding Cultural Differences*, Intercultural Press.

Hamilton, Clive, 2002, "Dualism and Sustainability," Ecological Economics Journal No. 42.

Harman, Willis, 1988, "The Transpersonal Challenge to the Scientific Paradigm: The Need for a Restructuring of Science," ReVision, Vol. 11, No. 2.

Harman, Willis, 1984, *Higher Creativity: Liberating the Unconscious for Breakthrough Insights*, Tarcher/Putnam.

Harman, Willis, 1993, "Approaching the Millenium: Business as a Vehicle for Global Transformation," article in The New Paradigm in Business, Jeremy P. Tarcher/Perigee.

Harman, Willis, 1998, "Thinking Allowed: Conversation on the Leading Edge of Knowledge and Discovery" Interview with Dr. Jeffrey Mishlove, Thinking Allowed Productions.

Harman, /Willis, 1988, *Insights into the New Age*, Twenty First Century Publ.

Harman, Willis, 1994, "A System in Decline or Transformation?," WBA Perspectives, Vol.8, No.2.

Harman, Willis, 1998 (new edition), *Global Mind Change: The Promise of the 21st Century*, Barrett - Koehler.

Harman, Willis, and Elizabeth Sahtouris, 1998, *Biology Revisited*, North Atlantic Books.

Harpur, Tom, 2004, *The Pagan Christ*, Thomas Allen Publishers, Toronto.

Heilbroner, 1992, *The Worldly Philosophers*, Touchstone Books.

Havel, Vaclav, 1994, "Post Modernism: The Search for Universal Laws," from The New Measure of Man, New York Times, July 8, 1994, A27.

Havel, Vaclav, 1997, "A Revolution in the Human Mind," WBA Perspectives, Vol. 11, No. 2. (Speech delivered before the Latin American Parliament in Sao Paulo, Brazil, Sept. 1996).

Hawkin, Paul, 2003, "Politics of Sustainability," Resurgence No. 221.

Hawkin, Paul, Amory B. Lovins and L. Hunter Lovins, 1999, *Natural Capitalism: The Next Industrial Revolution*, Earthscan.

Henderson, Hazel, 1996, *Building a Win-Win World*, Barrett-Koehler.

Henderson, Hazel, 1999, *Beyond Globalization: Shaping a Sustainable Global Economy*, Kumarian Press.

Henderson, Hazel, 1993, *Paradigms in Progress: Life Beyond Economics*, Kumarian Press.

Henderson, Hazel, 1978 and 1996, *Creating Alternative Futures: The End of Economics*, Putnam 1996, West Hartford, Conn; Kumarian Press.

Hillyard, Nicolas, 1995, "Liberation Ecology," article in The Future of Progress, Green Books.

Hock, Dee W., 1995, "The Chaordic Organization: Out of Order and Into Order," WBA Perspectives, Vol. 9, No. 1.

Holcombe, Susan, 1995, *Managing to Empower: The Grameen Bank's Experience of Poverty Alleviation*, Green Books.

Holling, C.S., 2001, "Understanding the Complexity of Economic, Ecological and Social Systems," Escosystems 4: 390-405.

Huxley, Aldous, 1945, *The Perennial Philosophy*, Harper Brothers.

International Institute for Sustainable Development (IISD), 1997, *Assessing Principles in Practice*, Winnipeg, Canada.

Jackson, Tim, 2002, "Evolutionary Psychology in Ecological Economics: consilience, consumption and contentment," Ecological Economics Journal #44.

Jai Sen et al (Eds.), 2004, *World Social Forum: Challenging Empires*, The Viveka Foundation.

Jung, C.G., 1933, *Modern Man in Search of a Soul*, Harcourt, Brace & Jovanovich.

Jung, C.G., 1965, *Memories, Dreams, Relections*, Random House.

Kamanetsky, Mario, 1999, *The Invisible Player: Consciousness at the Soul of Economic, Social and Political Life*, Park Street Press, Vt.

Kempfner, John, 2001, "Media Policy and the Crisis in Political Reporting," in The Moral Universe, Demos, 141-147.

Kidder, Rushworth M., 1994, *Shared Values for a Troubled World: Conversations with Men and Women of Conscience*, Jossey - Bass Publishers, San Francisco.

Kilmann, Ralph H., 2001, *Quantum Organizations*, Davies-Black Publishing.

Kimbrell, Andrew, 2002, "Biodemocracy," Resurgence No. 214.

King, Ursula, 1989, *The Spirit of the Earth: Reflections on Teilhard de Chardin and Global Spirituality*, Paragon House.

Kohr, Leopold, 1978, *The Breakdown of Nations*, E.P. Dutton, New York.

Kohr, Leopold, 1980, *Tribute to E.F.Schumacher.*

Korten, David, 2006, *The Great Turning*, Kumarian Press Inc., Barrett-Koehler Publishers Inc.

Korten, David, 1999, *The Post-Corporate World*, Barrett- Koehler.

Korten, David, 2002, "Living Economies," Resurgence No. 215.

Korten, David. 1996, "The Mythic Victory of Market Capitalism," article in book, *The Case Against the Global Economy*, Sierra Club Books.

Korten, David, 1995, *When Corporations Rule the World*, Kumarian Press and Barrett-Koehler.

Kras, Eva, 1994, *Modernizing Mexican Management*, Editts Publishing (now Two Eagles Press), Las Cruces, N.M, USA.

Kras, Eva, 1995, *Management in Two Cultures*, Intercultural Press.

Kras, Eva, 1995, *Sustainable Development and Business in Mexico and Latin America*, Grupo Editorial Iberoamerica, S.A., Mexico City.

Kucinich, Dennis, 2003, Peace as a Civil Right," Resurgence No.218.

Kumar, Satish, 1992, *Path Without Destination*, Green Books, UK, William Morrow, New York.

Kumar, Satish, 2002, *You Are Therefore I Am*, Green Books.

Kumar, Satish, 2003, "Science and Spirituality," Resurgence No. 220.

Kummar, Satish, 1996, "Gandhi's Swadeshi: The Economics of Permanence," article in *The Case Against the Global Economy*, Sierra Club Books.

Kummer, Corby, 2002, *The Pleasure of Slow Food*, Chronicle Books.

Lane, Henry W., Joseph J. DiStefano, Martha L Maznevski, 1997, *International Management Behaviour*, 3rd edition, Blackwell Publ.

Kvaloy, Sigmund, 1995, "Inside Nature," article in *The Future of Progress*, Green Books.

Laszlo, Ervin, 1994, *The Choice: Evolution vs Extinction?: A Thinking Person's Guide to Globlal Issues*, Afterward by Federico Mayor (D.G., UNESCO), Jeremy P. Tarcher/Putnam.

Laszlo, Ervin, Stanislav Grof and Peter Russell, 1999, *The Consciousness Revolution: A Transatlantic Dialogue*, Element Books, Shaftesbury and Boston.

Laszlo, Ervin, 1993, *The Creative Cosmos*, Floris Books, Edinburgh.

Laszlo, Ervin, 1997, *3rd Millenium: The Challenge and the Vision*, Report of the Club of Budapest, Gaia Books, Stroud.

Laszlo, Ervin, 2001, *Macroshift*, Barrett-Koehler.

Lehman, Rob, 1998, "Love and Money: Our Common Work," Noetic Science Review, No. 47.

Linzey, Andrew, 2003, "Church of Love: Christianity and Violence – a case of incompatibility," Resurgence No. 218.

Lovelock, James E., 1979, *Gaia: A New Look at Life on Earth*, Oxford University Press.

Lionel Robbins Memorial Lectures 2003, "Economic Focus: Chasing the Dream—why don't rising incomes make everybody happier?," The Economist, Aug. 9, 2003.

Lovins, Amory, 2002, "Real Security: Prospects for Peace," Whole Earth Magazine, Autumn, 2002.

Lowenthal, Abraham, (Ed.), 1994, *Latin America in the a New World*, Westview Press.

Loye, David, 2002, *A Buddhist History of the West*, State University of New York Press.

Loye, David, 2004, *The Great Adventure: Toward a Fully Human Theory of Evolution*, SUNY Press.

Maaloof, Amin, 2000, *On Identity*, Harvill Press, London.

Mackenzie, Andrew and David Rice, 2001, "Ethics and the Multinational Corporation," in The Moral Universe, Demos, 125-132.

Macy, Joanna, 1998, "The Great Turning," Institute of Noetic Sciences, Feb. 1998.

Madron, Roy and John Jopling, 2003, "Gaian Democracies: Redefining Globalization and People Power," Schumacher Briefing # 9, Green Book.

Mae-wan Ho, 2003, "Dance of Life," Resurgence No. 216.

Mandela, Nelson, 1995, *Long Walk to Freedom*, Back Bay Books, Little Brown and Company, New York.

Mahey, Richard, 2003, "Biophobia," Resurgence No. 220.

Mander, Jerry, 1996, "The Rules of Corporate Behavior," article in *The Case Against the Global Economy*, Sierra Club Books.

Mander, Jerry, 1991, *The Absence of the Sacred*, Schumacher Green Books.

March, David, 2002, "The Soul of Soil," Resurgence No. 211.

Marx, Karl and Frederick Engels, 1999 (reprint), *Das Kapital: A Critique of Political Economy*, Regnery Publishing Inc. (an Eagle Publishing company).

Manoochehri, John, 2002, "How Much is Enough?," Resurgence No. 214.

Maslow, A., 1968, *Toward a Psychology of Being*, (second edition), Van Nostrand Reinhold.

Max Neef, M., 1995, "Economic Growth and Quality of Life - A Threshold Hypothesis," Ecological Economics Journal No. 15.

Max-Neef, M., 1993, *Desarrollo a Escala Huamana*, Icaria, Barcelona.

Max-Neff, Manfred, (1986), "Human Scale Economics: the Challenge Ahead," *The Living Economy*, Ed. Ekins, Routledge and Kegan Paul

Maxwell, Nicholas, 2001, "Can Humanity Learn to Create a Better World?," in The Moral Universe, Demos, 149-156.

Maynard, Herman and Susan Mehrtens, 1993, *The Fourth Wave: Business in the 21st Century*, Barrett-Koehler.

Mayo, Ed, 2003, "Joyless Growth: Myth of Prosperity," Resurgence No. 217.

Mayor, F., 1997, Preface for *Educating for a Sustainable Future*, UNESCO.

McGlade, Jacquie, 2002, "Primacy of Nature," Resurgence No. 214.

McIntosh, Alastair, 2003, "Power of Love," Resurgence, No. 219.

McLean, Polly, 2003, "Worlds of Empathy: Prospects for Peace," Resurgence No. 218.

Meadows, D.H., Meadows, D.L. and Randers, J., 1992, *Beyond the Limits: Global Collapse or a Sustainable Future*, Earthscan.

Mellor, Mary, 2003, "Women and Nature," Resurgence No.216.

Melchett, Peter, 2000, "Public Values," Resurgence No. 219

Meppem, Tony, 1999, "Different Ways of Knowing: a Communicative Turn Toward Sustainability," Ecological Economics Journal #30.

M'Gonigle, Michael, 1998, *Mandating Innovation: A New Frontier*, University of Victoria, Canada, EcoNotes.

Miller, Lynn, 1994, *Global Order Values and Power in International Politics*, Third Edition, Westview Press.

Mitchell, Edgar, 2001, "On the Challenge and the Vision of Science," comments made as a member of the Club of Budapest, published in *Macroshift*, Barrett-Koehler.

Mitchell, Edgar, 1996, *The Way of the Explorer: An Apollo Astronaut's Journey through the material and mystical worlds*, Putnam Books.

Moore, Thomas, 2002, *The Soul's Religion*, Bantam Books.

Morris, David, 1996, "Communities: Building Authority, Responsibility and Capacity," Chapter 37, in book, *The Case Against the Global Economy*, Jerry Mander and Edward Goldsmith (Eds.), Sierra Club Books.

Morrison, R., 1999, *The Spirit of the Gene—Humanity's Proud Illusion and the Power of Nature*, Cornell University Press.

Muller, Robert, 2001, "On Consciousness and the Global Emergency," comments made as a member of the Club of Budapest, published in *Macroshift*, Barrett-Koehler.

Mumford, Lewis, 1956, *The Transformation of Man*, Harper Brothers.

Murphy, Michael, and Steven Donovan, 1997, *The Physical and Psychological Effects of Meditation*, Institute of Noetic Sciences.

Neff, Max, 1999, *Desarrollo d Escala Humana*, Icaria, Barcelona.

Nicholson-Lord, David, 2003, "Ten-Point Plan for Peace," Resurgence No. 218.

Norberg-Hodge, Helen, 1991, *Ancient Futures*,"Green Books.

Norberg-Hodge and Peter Goering, 1992, "Alternative in Education," article in *The Future of Progress*, Green Books.

Norgaard, Richard, 1994, *Development Betrayed: The End of Progress and a Coevolutionary Revisioning of the Future*, Routledge Publishers, London.

O'Hara, Sabine, 1996, "The Challenges of Valuation: Ecological Economics between Matter and Meaning," ISEE Conference paper, Boston, 1996.

Oriordan, Tom and James Cameron, 1994, *Interpreting the Precautionary Principle*, Island Press.

Orr, David, 1992, *Ecological Literacy: Education and the Transition to a Post Modern World*, SUNY Press.

Orr, D., 1994, *Earth in Mind: in Education, Environment and the Human Prospect*, Island Press.

Orr, David, 1996, "What is Education For?" In Context (Context Institute).

Orr, D. 2001, "Foreward" in *Sustainable Education* by Stephen Sterling, Green Books.

Osterberg, Rolf, 1993, "A New kind of Company with a new Kind of Thinking," article in *The New Paradigm in Business*, Jeremy P. Tarcher/Perigee.

O'Sullivan, Edmund, 1999, *Transformative Learning*, Zed Books.

Parikh, Jagdish, Ronnie Lessem and Warren Bennis, 1994, *Beyond Leadership: Balancing Economics, Ethics and Ecology*, Blackwell Publishers.

Parliament of the World's Religions, 1993, "Declaration Toward a Globlal Ethic," Chicago, Editorial Committee of the Council to the Parliament of the World's Religions.

Peat, F. David, 1987, *Synchronicity: The Bridge Between Matter and Mind*, Bantam.

Perez Gongora, 1999, *Valores en la Cultura Empresarial*, McGraw-Hill.

Pettifor, Ann, 2003, "Market society," Resurgence No.219.

Popper, Karl R. and John C. Eccles, 1981, *The Self and Its Brain*, Springer International.

Porritt, Jonathan, and Martin Wright, 2003, "Sustainability and Security: Prospects for Peace," Resurgence No. 218.

Porritt, Jonathan, 2004, "Seduced by Speed," Resurgence No.222.

Quarter, Jack, Laurie Nook and Betty Jane Richmond, 2002, *What Counts: Social Accounting for Nonprofits and Cooperatives*, Prentice Hall, Toronto.

Ramachandrant, and T.K. Mahadevan, *Gandhi: His Relevance in Our Times*, Gandhi Peace Foundation.

Ranjit, Fernando (Ed.), 2000, "The Unanimous Tradition: Essays of the Essential Unity of all Religions," The Sri Lanka Institute of Traditional Studies, The Ecologist, Vol.30, No.1.

Ray, Michael, and Alan Rinzler, (Eds.), 1993, *The New Paradigm in Business*, Putnam Publishing.

Ray, Paul and Sherry Anderson, 2000, *Cultural Creatives: How 50 Million Perople are Changing the World*, Harmony Books.

Ray, Paul, 2002, *The New Political Compass*, Values Technology Inc.

Rees, William E., 1995, "Achieving Sustainability: Reform or Transformation," Journal of Planning Literature, Vol. 9, No. 4, Sage Publications Inc.

Reich, Wilhelm, 1973, *Selected Writings: An Introduction to Orgonomy*, Farrar, Straus and Giroux, New York.

Remen, Rachel Naomi, 1996, *Kitchen Table Wisdom*, Riverhead Publishers.

Rheingold, Howard, 1998, "Thinking about Thinking about Technology," Noetic Science Review, No. 47.

Rifkin, Jeremy, 1995, *The End of Work*, Tarcher/Putnam.

Rifkin, Jeremy, 2002, *The Hydrogen Economy*, Tarcher/Putnam.

Robert, Karl-Henrik, 1991, "Educating the Nation: The Natural Step," In Context, No.28, Spring, 1991.

Robert, Karl-Henrick, 2002, *Natural Step Story: Seeding a Quiet Revolution*, New Society Publishers, USA.

Roberts, Ian, 2003, "Car Wars," Resurgence No. 218.

Robertson, James, 1998, "Transforming Economic Life: A Millenium Change," Schumacher Briefing no. 1, Greeen Books.

Rochem, Peter, 2001, "On What Business 'Could Do,'" comments made as a member of the Club of Budapest, published in *Macroshift*, Barrett-Koehler.

Roddick, Anita, 1995, *Technology and Values*, Resurgence, July/August, 1995.

Roddick, Anita, 2002, *Business as Unusual*, Thorsons.

Roszak, Theodore, 1995, *Ecopsychology: Restoring the Earth; Healing the Mind*, Sierra ClubBooks

Rowell, Andrew, 2003, *Don't Worry (it's safe to eat): the true story of GM food, BSE and foot and mouth*, Earthscan.

Russell, Peter, 1995, *The Global Mind Awakens: Our New Evolutionary Leap*, Global Mind, Palo Alto, CA.

Russell, Peter, 2001, "On the Roots of the Global Crisis," comments made as a member of the Club of Budapest, published in *Macroshift*, Berrett-Koehler.

Russell, Peter, 2000, *From Science to God: The Mystery of Consciousness and the Meaning of Light*, Sausalito, Peter Russell.

Sachs, Wolfgang, 1999, *Planet Dialectics: Explorations in Environment and Development*, Zed Books, London.

Sahtouris, Elisabet, 2002, "The Shifting Worldview of Science," Noetic Science Review Dec. 2001-Feb. 2002.

Sale, Kirkpatrick, 2003, "An Illusion of Progress," The Ecologist, July/Aug. 2003.

Schlosser, Eric, 2004, "Fast Food Nation," The Ecologist, Vol. 34, No.3.

Schumacher, E.F., 1974, *Small is Beautiful: Economics as if People Mattered*, Abacus.

Schumacher, E.F., 1978, "Intermediate Technology and the Individual," *Appropiate Technology Visions*, Ed. Dorf and Hunter, San Francisco, Boyd and Fraser.

Schumacher, E.F., 1997, *This I Believe*, Green Books.

Sekhar, Rukmini, 2003, "Spirituality behind Bars," Resurgence, No. 219.

Sen, Amartya, 2001, "East and West: the Reach for Reason," in The Moral Universe, Demos, 19-33.

Senge, Peter, Nelda Cambron-McCabe, Timothy Lucas, Bryan Smith, Janis Dutton and Art Kliener, *Schools That Learn: A Fifth Discipline Field Book for Educators, Parents and Everyone who Cares about Education*, New York, Doubleday/ Currency.

Senge, Peter, 1990, *The Fifth Discipline*, Doubleday Currency.

Seyyed Hossein Nasr, 2000, "The Spiritual and Religious Dimensions of the Environmental Crisis," The Ecologist, Vol.30, No.1.

Shar, I., 1992, *Empowering Education: Critical Teaching for Social Change*, University of Chicago Press.

Sheldrake, Rupert, and Matthew Fox, 1996, *Natural Grace: Dialogue on Science and Spirituality*, Green Books.

Shipka, Barbara, 1995, "A Sacred Responsibility," WBA Perspectives, Vol.9, No.1.

Shiva, Vandana, 1989, *Staying Alive: Women, Ecology and Development*, Zed Books.

Shiva, Vandana, 1991, *The Violence of the Green Revolution*, Third World Network, Penang, Malaysia.

Shiva, Vandana, 2000, *Water Wars*, South End Press, Cambridge, Mass.

Shiva, Vandana, 2003, "Globalization and Terrorism: Understanding the Roots of Violence," Resurgence No.218.

Shiva, Vandana, 2003, "Captive Water: Voice from the South," Resurgence No. 219.

Shiva, Vandana, 2002, "Paradigm Shift," Resurgence No.214.

Simpson, Alan, 2003,"Who is next? Terrorism cannot be bombed out of exitence," Resurgence No. 218.

Simms, Andrew, 2003, "Causes of Conflict," Resurgence No. 218.

Singh, Karen, 2001, "On the Evolution of the New Consciousness," comments made as a member of the Club of Budapest, published in *Macroshift*, Barrett-Koehler.

Smith, Adam, 1937, *An Inquiry into the Nature and Causes of the Wealth of Nations* (1776), New York, Modern Library.

Snyder, Gary, 1995, *A Village Council of all Beings: Ecology, Place and the Awakening of Compassion*, Green Books

Soderbaum, Peter, 1999, "Values, Ideology and Politics in Ecological Economics," Ecological Economics Journal # 28.

Soderbaum, Peter, 2004, "Democracy, Markets and Sustainable Development," European Environment, Issue 6, Vol. 14.

Soderbaum, Peter, 2000, *Ecological Economics: A Political Economics Approach to Environment and Development*, Earthscan.

Sparkes, Russell, 2002, *Socially Responsible Investment: A Global Revolution*, John Wiley and Sons.

Sperry, Roger, 1987, "Structure and Significance of the Consciousness Revolution," Journal: Mind and Behaviour, Vol.8. No.1.

Spowers, Rory, 2003, "Web of Hope: Ethics," Resurgence No. 219.

Stein, Janice, 2001, *The Cult of Efficiency*, House of Ananse Press.

Sterling, Stephen, 2001, "Sustainable Education: Re-visioning Learning and Change," Schumacher Briefings #6, Green Books.

Stewart, Edward C., 1972, *American Cultural Values: A Cross Cultural Perspective*, Intercultual Press.

Stiglitz, Joseph E., 2002, *Globalization and its Discontents*, Norton Publishing.

Svedin, Uno, 1998, "Implicit and Explicit ethical norms in the environmental policy arena," Ecological Economics Journal No. 24.

Swilling, Mark, 2002, "Flames of Hope," Resurgence No. 214.

Swimme, Brian, 1984, "The Universe is a Green Giant," Bear and Company Inc.

Symynkywicz, Jeffrey, 1991, "Vaclav Havel and the Politics of Hope," Noetic Science Review, Spring/Summer 1991.

Tarnas, Richard, 1991, *The Passion of the Western Mind*, Ballantine.

Tarnas, Richard, 2000, "A New Synthesis," Resurgence No.199.

Teilhard de Chardin, Pierre, 1961, *The Phenomenon of Man*, Harper Torchbooks.

THE EARTH CHARTER, 1997, United Nations World Commission on Environment and Development 1987, followed by Earth Charter Commission 1997 and Earth Council, San Jose, Costa Rica.

The Global Compact, 1999, presented at the World Economic Forum, Davos, Switzerland, by United Nations Secretary General -- challenged world business leaders to "embrace and enact" the Global Compact Principles, including human rights, labour and the environment.

Tolle, Eckhart, 1999, *The Power of Now*, New World Library.

Toffler, Alvin, 1980, *The Third Wave*, William Morrow.

Toledo, Victor, 1992, "What is Ethnoecology?: Origins, Scope and Implications of a Rising Discipline," Etnoecologia 1., 5-21.

Toledo, Victor, 2001, *Biodiversity and Indigenous Peoples*, Academic Press.

Toledo, Victor, 2003, "Ecologia, Espiritualidad y Conocimiento, Universidad IBERO Americana y PNUMA.

Transparency International, 2001, National Survey on Corruption and Good Governance, Mexico.

Tucker, Mary Evelyn, 2002, "Sacred Connections: The emerging Alliance of World Religions and Ecology," Resurgence No. 214.

Tudge, Colin, 2003, "Science and Religion," Resurgence No. 216.

Tutu, Desmond, 2002, "Path of Forgiveness," Interview with Bishop Desmond Tutu (with Mark Swilling, Eve Annecke, Wilhelm Verwoerd of Resurgence), Resurgence No. 214.

Tutu, Desmond, 1999, "No Future Without Forgiveness," Rider Publishing, UK.

Twin Plant News, 2003, "Corporate Ethics, New Approach," Staff report, Twin Plant News Magazine, Jan. 2003.

UNESCO, 1996, "Our Creative Diversity," prepared by the World Commission on Culture and Development, United Nations.

UNESCO. 1997, "The Universal Ethics Project," Division of Philosophy and Ethics, Paris, France.

United Nations Universal Declaration of Human Rights, adopted by the General Assembly of the United Nations, Dec. 10, 1948.

United Nations Conference on Human Settlements, (Habitat II), Istanbul, June, 2004.

United Nations Millenium Manifesto, 2000, United Nations, New York.

United Nations Development Index, 2000, United Nations Human Development Report (HDI).

Union of Concerned Scientists, formed 1969, MIT.

Varela, Francisco, 2001, "Ethical Know-How," in the Moral Universe, Demos, 85-92.

Villoro, Luis, 1982, "Creer, Saber, Conocer," Mexico Siglo XXI, Buenos Aires, Barcelona, Paidos (1998).

Wackernagel, Mathis and William Rees, 1995, *Ecological Footprint: Reducing Human Impact on the Earth*, New Society Publisher, Gabriola Island, B.C., Canada.

Wacknernagel, Mathis, 1998, "The Ecological Footprint: An Indicator of Progress Toward Regional Sustainability," Environmental Monitoring and Assessment 51.

Walsh, Roger, 2001, "The Seven Practices of Essential Spirituality," Noetic Sciences Review, De. 2001-Feb. 2002.

Walsh, Roger, 2003, *Paths Beyond Ego: The Transpersonal Vision* (with Frances Vaughan and John Mack), J.P. Tarcher.

WCED, 1987, "Our Common Future," Bruntland Report, World Commission on Environment and Development, Oxford University Press.

Weber, Thomas, 1991, *Conflict Resolution and Gandhian Ethics*, Gandhi Peace Foundation.

Weber, Thomas, 2001, "Gandhian Philosophy, Conflict Resolution theory and Practical Approaches to Negotiation," Journal of Peace Research, Vol. 38, No.4.

Weber, Thomas, 2004, *Gandhi as Disciple and Mentor*, Cambridge University Press.

Weber, Thomas, 1999, "Gandhi, Deep Ecology, Peace Research and Buddhist Economics," Journal of Peace Research.

Weber, Thomas, 2003, "Nonviolence is Who?: Gene Sharp and Gandhi," Peace and Change, No.28, Vol.2.

Wellwood, John, 2000, *Toward a Psychology of Awakening*, Shambhala.

Wenger. E., 1998, *Communities in Practice: Learning Meaning and Identity*, Cambridge University Press.

Wilber, Ken, 1998, *The History of Everything*, Shambhala Publications.

Wolfer, Barry, 1998, "Societal Transformation: What is our Primary Purpose?" Institute of Noetic Sciences, Feb. 1998. (Wolfer ---a NASA aerospace engineer)

World Commission for Culture and Development, 1995, *Our Creative Diversity*, UNESCO, Island Press.

World Values Survey, Ronald Ingelhart Survey, 1997, *Modernization and Post Modernization: Cultural, Economic and Political Change*, Princeton University.

Zukav, Gary, 1993, *Evolution and Business*, Putnam Publ.

Index

About the Author

Eva Kras, a Canadian citizen, is a transcultural management specialist, author and part-time professor with twenty-five years of experience working and living in Mexico, South America and Europe. Her main areas of work involve transcultural management adaptations and sustainable development in transcultural organizations. She speaks several languages and has published five books in the US and Mexico related to her major areas of interest. One of these is the respected book, *Management in Two Cultures*.

Eva is president of the Canadian Society for Ecological Economics (Canadian chapter of the International Society for Ecological Economies). She is also president of the International Lerma-Chapala Foundation (an international NGO). She currently resides in Canada.